Holding one of those expensive cigars, and clad in turtleneck, Banacek cracks a smile.

"There's An Old Polish Proverb That Says, '*BANACEK*'"

A Behind-the-Scenes History
and Episode Guide
to the 1972-1974
NBC Mystery Movie Series

JONATHAN ETTER

BearManor Media

Albany, Georgia

"There's An Old Polish Proverb That Says, 'BANACEK'":
A Behind-the-Scenes History and Episode Guide to the 1972-1974
NBC Mystery Movie Series
Copyright © 2016 Jonathan Etter. All Rights Reserved.

No part of this book may be reproduced in any form or by any means, electronic, mechanical, digital, photocopying or recording, except for the inclusion in a review, without permission in writing from the the publisher.

All photos in this book, unless otherwise noted, are courtesy of MCA-TV, NBC-TV/Universal Studios.

Published in the USA by
BearManor Media
P.O. Box 71426
Albany, GA 31708
www.BearManorMedia.com

Softcover Edition
ISBN-10: 1593931751
ISBN-13: 978-1-59393-175-9

Front cover: A montage of scenes from *Banacek*
Back cover: A variety of scenes and publicity portraits from *Banacek*;
    photo by Enrique Velazco

Printed in the United States of America

Table of Contents

Acknowledgments — ix

Prologue: A Cleverly Conceived Concept — xi

Chapter 1: Starring George Peppard — 1

Chapter 2: George Peppard as ... *BANACEK* — 21

Chapter 3: Writing *BANACEK* — 31

Decoding *BANACEK*

    Part One: The Games from the Names — 39

    Part Two: The Sign of the Three — 45

Three and a Match: An Episode Guide to *BANACEK* — 49

    The *BANACEK* Pilot — 51

    Season One — 70

    Season Two — 187

    BANACEK Challenges Answers — 283

Epilogue: George Eckstein says goodbye to *BANACEK* — 307

About the Author — 311

For my brother, Dave, who would have welcomed the many brain-teasers presented him in *Banacek*.

Banacek star George Peppard proudly displays a plaque from The Polish American Society honoring the series for its positive presentation of the Polish.

Acknowledgments

As any *Banacek* fan knows, the 1972-1974 *Banacek* series including the pilot film, *Detour to Nowhere,* was a two-year collection of seventeen locked room, impossible mysteries.

As I quickly discovered when I began work on this book, writing a history of *Banacek* was something of a locked room, impossible mystery in itself. A total of three men—a rather appropriate number as the reader will soon learn—provided me with the necessary keys to solve this mystery.

The first of these was *Banacek*'s executive producer, the late George Eckstein. Through certain comments and remarks, he steered me in the right direction. The second of these was Robert Adey, whose meticulous work on the 1979 bibliography, *Locked Room Murders,* helped me realize just what a challenge George Eckstein and his associates faced when they undertook the writing of a locked room, impossible mystery series. Last and not least was the master of the locked room, impossible mystery, John Dickson Carr. Thanks to his novel, *The Three Coffins*, with its "Locked Room Lecture" in Chapter 17, I had the ideal blueprint for just how to construct this book's episode guide.

To the folks at *TV Guide*, Hart Sharp Video, and Arts Alliance America, a big THANK YOU for releasing both seasons of *Banacek* on DVD. Needless to say, without these DVDs, this book couldn't have been. Another "thank you" to the folks at *TV Guide* for their 1972-1974 issues containing publicity, TV Crosswords, and other material pertaining to *Banacek*.

For their time and patience in granting interviews, I am indebted to the late Mr. Eckstein, and the late Harry Carey, Jr., as well as Lou Antonio, Dick Gautier, Don Pedro Colley, Andrew J. Fenady, Michael Forest, and Leslie Martinson. Speaking of patience, a very BIG thank you to my mother Ruthanne and sister Betsy for providing support and encouragement during what was for them, and for me, a very trying time. An even greater THANK YOU to David W. Menefee, BearManor Media Assistant Publisher, for his patience, encouragement, and enthusiasm regarding this project.

My greatest THANKS, however, goes to my publisher Ben Ohmart. Without your patience, tolerance, enthusiasm, support, constructive criticisms, and your love of *Banacek*, this book never could have taken the direction and scope that it did. I hope you and your fellow *Banacek* fans are pleased with the result.

Prologue

A Cleverly Conceived Concept

"Seek and you will find." –Polish proverb

John Dickson Carr's Dr. Gideon Fell says in his "Locked Room Lecture" in *The Three Coffins*, "Now, it seems reasonable to point out that the word improbable is the very last which should ever be used to curse detective fiction in any case. A great part of our liking for detective fiction is based on a liking for improbability. When A is murdered, and B and C are under strong suspicion, it is improbable that the innocent-looking D can be guilty. But he is. If G has a perfect alibi, sworn to at every point by every other letter in the alphabet, it is improbable that G can have committed the crime. But he has. When the detective picks up a fleck of coal dust at the seashore, it is improbable that such an insignificant thing can have any importance. But it will. In short, you come to a point where the word improbable grows meaningless as a jeer. There can be no such thing as any probability until the end of the story."

In *Roget's Thesaurus*, among the synonyms one can find for the word "improbable" are "inconceivable" and "incredible." "Inconceivable" and "incredible" certainly described the thefts committed on the locked room, impossible mystery series, *Banacek*. A racehorse disappearing from under the jockey who was riding the animal, an enormous computer taken from the building that was housing it, such thefts defied belief—they were indeed "inconceivable" and "incredible."

What if the "inconceivable" and the "incredible" went further? During the course of my interviews with *Banacek*'s Executive Producer, the late George Eckstein, he said one thing which really intrigued me. This was that he and his co-writers (first-season story editor Paul Playdon, and second season story editor Robert Van Scoyk) wrote the show "in our own image." *Banacek* was a show about a brilliant amateur detective solving seemingly impossible thefts. How could such a premise reflect Eckstein and his co-writers? Later, I realized that Eckstein's "in our own image" remark was a clue to the very unusual approach he and his collaborators took in writing the show.

Eckstein also directed my attention to one particular Polish proverb of Banacek's, as well as one particular episode. As I soon discovered, there was a connection between that proverb and that episode. Like so much else in *Banacek*, the connection was none too obvious, but just like Eckstein's "in our own image" comment, it proved to be a clue as to how the show was being written.

Paul Playdon provided a lot of such clues with his first-season episode, "Ten Thousand Dollars a Page." Robert Van Scoyk did the same with the second season's "If Max is So Smart, Why Doesn't He Tell Us Where He Is?"

In fact, throughout its two-season run, *Banacek* was constantly giving its audience hints and clues as to the unusual way it was being written, such as Banacek always introducing himself by his last name, or the running gag of others mispronouncing his name and him correcting them. When it came to the character's biography—where he lived, what kind of car he drove, and where he'd been brought up—there were many connections and clues, as well. Episode titles, such as "Project Phoenix," were clues, too. Ditto the repetition of so much dialogue, and the frequent references to the number 3. At the core of this unusual writing was George Peppard, the star.

Chapter 1

Starring George Peppard

"You won't get anything unless you take chances."
–Polish proverb

"I'm a transition human being. I accept it." That was George Peppard talking to *Los Angeles Times* TV critic, Cecil Smith, in 1972 about his first television series, *Banacek*. To many actors of George's stature, moving from big-budget motion-pictures to the more budget-conscious and (in such actors' opinions) less prestigious arena of television was to take a step down artistically. Television wasn't likely to team him with critically-acclaimed leading ladies such as Audrey Hepburn or Sophia Loren. Nor was it likely he'd work with directors comparable to Vincente Minnelli, John Ford, George Marshall, or Henry Hathaway.

Given his background, George seemed perfect for the many big-screen international-cast productions he appeared in on location in such countries as Italy, France, Ireland, Spain, and Germany prior to moving into series television. For starters, there was his father's last name, Peppard. Originally a Norman name, Peppard was one of the principal Irish names in County Meath in 1659, according to Petty's census. There were Townlands of Peppardstown in the Ardee (County Louth) and Kells (County Meath); there was a Peppardstown in County Tipperary (Cashel district); and a Peppard's Castle near Gorey.

The Peppards had a long association with County Wexford, as well as the county north of Dublin. In the sixteenth century, Peppards were mine owners in County Wexford. The family background, and artistic accomplishments of the actor's mother, Vernelle Rohrer, was also impressive. The daughter of Christian Rohrer and Irene D. Newcom, Vernelle was descended from Colonel George Newcom, one of the founders of Dayton, Ohio.* Born February 1, 1889 in Montgomery County in Mad River Township in Dayton, Vernelle went to high school in Dayton, became interested in music, and went on to study at the Cincinnati Conservatory of Music. Graduating from the University of Michigan's School of Music, Vernelle became a protégé of Metropolitan Opera star Ernestine Schumann-Heink. During her career, she enjoyed lead roles in both light and grand opera, performing with such companies as the American Light Opera Company and the San Carlo Opera Company prior to her marriage to building contractor George Peppard in 1927. After that, she began teaching voice at the Detroit Conservatory of Music; Thursdays she taught at home.

She also encouraged her only child, George Peppard, Jr. (born October 1, 1928, in Dearborn, Michigan) to take up music. Studying piano briefly when a child, he gave that up once he discovered football, but he never lost his love for classical music. *Banacek* reflected this. Whenever the series showed the super-sleuth at home and listening to music, the music was always classical.

Brought up during the Depression, throughout his childhood, George and his family moved from one town to another. His father went broke in

1930. To help pay the bills, Peppard, Sr. became a traveling salesman. Each time the family moved, George Jr. was almost always the new kid in town. Time and again he had to prove himself to the other children in the neighborhood. Despite such frustrations, he grew very close to his father. By the time he was nine, he was accompanying his father on most of his jobs. (George's closeness to his dad would become a strong part of the fictional biography created for television series character, Thomas Banacek.)

During his years at Dearborn High School, George played football and ran middle distance for the track team. He began concentrating on math and other subjects appropriate for his planned career in civil engineering.

Upon graduating from high school, he applied to Purdue, the #1 engineering college in the Midwest, and was accepted. Before he could begin, he was drafted into the US Marine Corps. He served with a Marine field artillery unit for eighteen months, first as a Corporal, later as acting Gunnery Sergeant.

After completing his service, George then went back to Purdue to begin studying civil engineering. While there, he developed an interest in the Purdue Playshop, the University's drama group. Soon, he was both writing sketches and acting in the group's productions.

His father's sudden death from cancer in December 1951 brought a temporary halt to his education, however, because his father had fifteen separate houses slated for construction. Since George Jr. had worked with him off and on through the years, he possessed the skills and knowledge to complete the building of these homes. A man who always believed in fulfilling his responsibilities, George dropped out of school to finish the construction.

He sold the entire group within a year. Given this success, George's relatives expected him to continue working in his father's profession, but the acting bug had bitten him. He began looking for a college geared more towards dramatics and found the Carnegie Institute of Technology in Pittsburgh. George earned a Bachelor of Fine Arts degree; then he began looking for work.

One of his earliest jobs was a two-year stint at the Oregon Shakespeare

Festival in Ashland, where he met and became friends with future *Banacek* Executive Producer George Eckstein. Then, George performed at the Pittsburgh Playhouse, where he met and fell in love with actress Helen Davies. The two married in 1954. After the birth of their son, Bradford, in 1955, the young couple moved to New York. Not long after that George became a member of the Actor's Studio.

George mopped offices at night while spending his days looking for acting roles. By November 1956, he played the role of Mickey Argent in Broadways' *The Girls of Summer* (written by *The Rainmaker* author and *Here Come the Brides* creator N. Richard Nash). Produced by Cheryl Crawford (co-founder of the Actors' Studio) and featuring a mostly female cast, *The Girls of Summer* foreshadowed George's early motion picture career situation of often taking a back-seat to his female co-star. Twenty-eight years old at the time he did *Summer* (where he was cast as an eighteen-year-old), George was so unhappy playing a juvenile that he vowed to go hungry before ever playing such a part again. As a result, he worked all kinds of jobs: brick mason, cab driver, janitor, bank clerk, disc jockey, before his screen acting career took off. After some radio and TV guest shots (*The U.S. Steel Hour*, *Alcoa Hour*, *Kraft Theatre*, *Alfred Hitchcock Presents*, *Suspicion*, *Matinee Theatre*), George made his motion-picture debut in *The Strange One* (1957), director Jack Garfein's film adaptation of the Calder Willingham novel and stage play, *End as a Man*. Re-uniting George with his *Girls of Summer* co-stars Arthur Storch and Pat Hingle, and director Garfein, *The Strange One* dealt with the dehumanization and bullying that accompanies the tradition of hazing at a military academy in the South. George, playing Cadet Robert Marquales, and Storch were among the freshman recruits undergoing the hazing. Ben Gazzara played the title character, Cadet Sgt. Jocko DeParis, who is in charge of that hazing.

Quite controversial at the time due to its homoerotic themes and presentation of at least one obviously homosexual character, the movie differed from *End as a Man* because of the character of Peonie, a.k.a. "Rosebud." There had been no female character in either the novel or the play.

Though George had not been in the play with Ben Gazzara, the actor thought he was ideal for the part of Marquales, given that he was an ex-Marine, and, as Gazzara put it, "proper."

In his next feature, *Pork Chop Hill* (1959) based on the book of the same name by military historian S.L.A. Marshall, and directed by Lewis Milestone, George played U.S. Army Corporal Chuck Fedderson. *Pork Chop Hill* told the story of the savage first Battle of Pork Chop Hill between the U.S. Army's 7th Infantry Division and the Chinese and Korean Communist forces towards the end of the Korean War in April 1953.

Remarkable for its depiction of a near constant battle between the Americans and Communists for most of its running time, *Pork Chop Hill* featured many supporting actors who, like George, would go on to greater fame in the years to come. Among them were Harry Guardino, Rip Torn, Robert Blake, Martin Landau, and Gavin MacLeod. While things may have been going well for George on the career front, by the time of *Pork Chop Hill*'s production, his marriage to Helen Davies was crumbling. Though the couple did not divorce until 1964, they were already spending much time apart. She took a job in New Jersey; he lived in a cold-water flat in Greenwich Village. When George moved to Hollywood in the late 1950s, this placed further strain on their marriage.

Praised for his work in *Pork Chop Hill*, up next for George was *Home from the Hill* (1960).

This time he was working with esteemed director Vincente Minnelli (*An American in Paris, The Bad and the Beautiful, Gigi*). Promoted as one of "three young talents destined for stardom,"** George was Rafe Copley, the bastard son of the picture's lead character, Robert Mitchum, an effective showcase for George. Asked by Mitchum to turn legitimate son George Hamilton into a man, Rafe teaches Hamilton how to shoot a rifle, how to talk to women, and so forth. Rafe also serves as Hamilton's back-up during the very tense, excitingly photographed wild boar hunt.

Rafe had memorable dialogue, too. At one point, Rafe characterizes himself as someone "who goes to sleep with his boots on, drinks beer in the morning, and keeps a skunk for a house pet."

George Peppard with Luana Anders in MGM's *Home from the Hill* (1960).

Despite the praise he received for his performance in the movie, George kept things in perspective. "There's a long scene in *Home from the Hill* where the camera stays on me," he stated. "People are always saying what a fine piece of acting it was. Actually, I didn't do anything but walk and stare ahead. All the acting was done by Kaper."[1] [Bronislau Kaper was the movie's Polish-born composer.]

Also in 1960, George played Leo Percepied (the fictional version of author Jack Kerouac) in his second MGM feature, *The Subterraneans*. Based on the Kerouac novel of the same name, the story was a semi-fictional account of Kerouac's romance with a Black woman in New York in the early 1950s. The film version changed the Black woman to a young French girl (the top-billed Leslie Caron) because the studio believed that an interracial romance might be offensive to moviegoers.

In his next feature, *Breakfast at Tiffany's* (1961, the film adaptation of the Truman Capote novel), George again took second-billing to a woman. Once more playing a writer, George's sane and sensible Paul Varjak was the perfect contrast to leading lady Audrey Hepburn's characterization of the eccentric Holly Golightly. Portraying a role originally offered to Steve McQueen, (McQueen had turned the part down as he was still under contract to the TV series, *Wanted: Dead or Alive*), George's method acting style proved something of a problem for Hepburn. Despite this, he and Hepburn remained close friends until her death.

George also had problems with co-star Patricia Neal. Though the actress had known him before *Breakfast at Tiffany's* and the two got along fine in rehearsals, during the actual shooting, Neal found George unbearable!

Thanks to his performance in *Breakfast at Tiffany's*, George was well on his way towards becoming a major motion picture star. Nothing made this clearer than his next feature:, *How the West Was Won* (1962). Produced by MGM on an estimated budget of $15 million***, with production miraculously completed in less than a year, *How The West Was Won* required three directors (John Ford, Henry Hathaway, and George Marshall), four cinematographers (William H. Daniels, Milton Krasner, Charles Lang, Jr., and

Joseph LaShelle) and an all-star cast in order to tell its five-segment story concerning the settling of the American West. Shot on location in such places as the Colorado Rockies, the Black Hills of South Dakota, and Custer State Park, the movie also filmed on the Ohio and Cumberland Rivers in Kentucky, and in Monument Valley on the Arizona/Utah border.

Focusing on four generations of one family, the Prescotts, the movie introduced George's character, Zeb Rawlings, the son of Carroll Baker's Eve Prescott Rawlings in its third segment, "The Civil War." From that point on, George dominated the movie. In the final segment, "The Outlaws," the story of the Prescott family came full circle when Zeb finally meets his still feisty aunt, Lilith Prescott (Debbie Reynolds). Like Lillith, Zeb Rawlings exhibited much character growth during the course of the story. When the audience first sees him, he is a young Ohio lad excited about joining the Union Army and going off to fight the Rebel forces. By the time the picture ended, Zeb has become a sane and sensible middle-aged man, who, though opposed to tangling with outlaws, will fight them if they endanger the safety of his wife and three children.

Along with the physical and dramatic challenge of aging from boy to man, George, like the rest of the cast, coped with the difficulty of working in Cinerama and its three-camera process that resulted in extreme widescreen projected onto three separate panels. For example, in a two-shot (a camera shot of two actors), in order for the scene to appear natural, the actor at the side of the screen had to play behind the actor in screen center; if this wasn't done, the side lens photographed the upstage side of the (side-actor's) face resulting in a false eye-line (with the actor in the center).

Creating another problem for George, he was the only actor in the cast to work with all three directors. Adding further challenges, he worked with two of the film's four cinematographers, Joseph LaShelle and Milton Krasner.

Given the extraordinary production of *How the West Was Won*, it should have come as no surprise that George's next feature, *The Victors* (1963) was another grand undertaking. Written, produced, and directed by Carl Foreman, and detailing in episodic fashion the adventures of a U.S. Army Squad in WWII, *The Victors* story begins in England in 1942 with the Battle of Britain. The movie then follows the Squad through Sicily, France, and D-Day before concluding in postwar Berlin. Anti-war in its presentation, with each segment contradicting the actual newsreel footage that precedes it, the picture was shot on location in England, France, Italy, and Sweden.

Adding further international flavor was the casting of the six European beauties (Senta Berger, Melina Mercouri, Jeanne Moreau, Rosanna Schiaffino, Romy Schneider, and Elke Sommer), who received much publicity in the film's pre-promotion. Despite the casting of these gorgeous women, and the presence of Eli Wallach as the squad's sergeant, George definitely made an impact in the picture as Corporal Frank Chase, the first character to be seen in the movie, along with *Home from the Hill* co-star George Hamilton as Corporal Theodore Trower. Corporal Chase exhibits quite a number of different moods during the course of the story. Conceited, cocky and self-confident when dealing with women, at one point he gives lessons in romance to his shy friend, Corporal Trower. At other times, Chase is grim and disillusioned. Later on, he displays a sense of responsibility and honor.

In his next picture, *The Carpetbaggers* (1964), George improved his career fortunes. He showed that he could handle the part of the leading man. Once again working in a film adaptation of a novel (the best-seller by Harold Robbins****), *The Carpetbaggers* teamed George with Alan Ladd (in his last feature), the Polish-American Carroll Baker (born Karolina Piekarski), plus Bob Cummings, Lew Ayres, Martha Hyer, Martin Balsam, and, George's soon-to-be wife Elizabeth Ashley.

George did so well as the less than ethical Jonas Cord, Jr., producers soon began casting him in similar parts. *The Carpetbaggers* proved so successful that it inspired a prequel, *Nevada Smith* (1966) starring Steve McQueen.

In 1965, after *The Carpetbaggers*, audiences saw George in two movies: *Operation: Crossbow*, a WWII adventure produced by Carlo Ponti, and *The Third Day*, teaming George with future *Banacek* director Jack Smight. In *The Third Day*, George top-starred as Steve Mallory, the general manager of a porcelain company who, upon emerging from a car crash into a river, soon

10   There's an Old Polish Proverb That Says, "Banacek"

George with Carroll Baker in Paramount's *The Carpetbaggers*.

George and Martha Hyer in *The Carpetbaggers*.

realizes he has lost his memory. As a result, he has no clue concerning the identity of the dead woman (Sally Kellerman) who was in the car with him, much less why she was in the car.

Showing traces of George's future TV series character Thomas Banacek through his conversations with co-star Elizabeth Ashley, and through his discovery that pre-amnesia, he was a bit of a lecher, director Jack Smight's beginning of the movie shows George soaked and struggling up a river embankment. The scene was somewhat similar to the pre-credit opening of the Smight-directed *Banacek* pilot, "Detour to Nowhere." Smight would go on to direct the series' first-season premiere, "Let's Hear it for a Living Legend." In another *Banacek* connection, co-starring in *The Third Day* was *Banacek* first season premiere guest Robert Webber. In still another sign of things to come, at one point *The Third Day* featured a sequence with George and Kellerman that takes place in a lodge. Among the furnishings in this lodge are a scull (a light narrow racing boat that is propelled by oars). When the *Banacek* movie introduces its title character, he is rowing a scull across Boston's Charles River. This sequence, which was to remain with the series throughout its two-season run, always signaled the beginning of *Banacek*'s opening credits.

George's other 1965 feature, *Operation: Crossbow*, was a quality piece all the way through. A fictionalized account of the real Operation: Crossbow, (the English/American campaign against all phases of the German long-range weapons program), *Operation: Crossbow* gave top billing to Sophia Loren, the wife of producer Carlo Ponti. Despite that billing, Loren had a very small part; the true lead of the picture was George, who received second billing.

Operation: Crossbow was a perfect example of how cooperative and adaptable George Peppard could be. Playing U.S. Army Air Force Lieutenant John Curtis, the story had Curtis managing to infiltrate the German weapons factory by posing as a German engineer. Making the masquerade all the more credible, Curtis spoke German.

George fared even better with his next German character, Leutnant Bruno Stachel in *The Blue Max* (1966). England's *Star T.V. & Film Annual 1967* was very impressed with George's performance: "George Peppard is acquiring a strong reputation as a player of unsympathetic parts," stated the magazine. "His characterization of the cruelly ambitious Jonas Cord in *The Carpetbaggers* was one of the highlights of his film career. His role of Stachel should establish him even more as one of the screen's most exciting stars."

Like Jonas Cord, George's Bruno Stachel was a very disagreeable character. Eager to win the Blue Max (the highest decoration Germany awarded its aviators during World War I), the obsessed, and glory-dreaming Stachel is willing to run over anyone in his path. If this results in other fighter pilots not receiving credit for kills that are rightfully theirs; if this results in the deaths of other pilots, so be it.

Given the built-in sympathetic qualities Jack Hunter had created for Stachel in the novel on which the movie was based, (the character, who came from the lower classes was "brooding" and "tortured"), George's choosing to portray the man as an obnoxious, "smart-ass, wenching Von Peck's Bad Boy"[2] seemed hardly the kind of thing to win an audience to the character's side, but, just as was the case in *The Carpetbaggers*, George somehow managed to get past all of the character's unappealing qualities to bring out his vulnerability. "Bruno Stachel," noted the actor in the *Star T.V. & Film Annual*, "was the eternal loner, the man fighting desperately to be recognized and accepted. He fights so hard, in fact, that without realizing it he finds himself believing he is superior."

Always striving for honesty and believability in his characters, George also went to the trouble of learning how to fly an airplane (four months of lessons) so he could perform his own aviation sequences in *The Blue Max*. Thus, when the actor went to Ireland to begin shooting, he had 210 flying hours on his pilot's log, and more than 150 of these were solo. In addition to doing many of the movie's flying sequences on his own, at one time, George had to crash-land his plane.

While many reviewers of *The Blue Max* have often cited George's performance as the major defect in what they otherwise consider a very good motion-picture (the adjective most often used is "wooden"), *Blue Max* author

Jack D. Hunter did not agree. "Certainly the casting of George Peppard and James Mason is for me a flash of genius on somebody's part," the author told *Star T.V. & Film Annual*. "They could not have been better chosen if I had written the book with them in mind."

George and Hunter certainly seemed to get along. In addition to Hunter visiting the *Blue Max* set during production, George was one of the special guests when the movie opened at the Sutton Theatre in Hunter's home town of Wilmington, Delaware in late June 1966. Even more significantly, some sixteen years after Hunter published *The Blue Max* sequel, *The Blood Order*, George tried to buy the movie rights to that novel. Unfortunately, because the star and the studio, (presumably 20th Century Fox, the studio that made *The Blue Max*) were on bad terms, nothing came of it.

With *The Blue Max*, another international cast production where he was the only American, George began what was to be a three-picture association with British director John Guillermin. Like *The Blue Max*, the other two movies with Guillermin were action-adventures, as were the two features preceding them: *Rough Night in Jericho* (1967) and *Tobruk* (1967), both from Universal. Described in studio publicity as "the kind of Western they used to make," *Rough Night in Jericho* cast George as former deputy Dolan, a man who figures that any confrontation with former lawman turned ruthless town boss Dean Martin isn't worth the trouble. Thus, much of the movie's tension and suspense came from wondering how much brutality Dolan was willing to allow Martin and his goons to visit on the town of Jericho, and its people, before he finally did something about it. Directed by TV's Arnold Laven, *Rough Night in Jericho* featured some truly graphic violence.

George had an even better part in *Tobruk*. Released during a period when ABC's *The Rat Patrol* was one of television's hottest series, *Tobruk*, like *Rat*, featured an intrepid group of Allies battling the forces of General Erwin Rommel in Northern Africa. Written by tough-guy actor Leo V. Gordon (who also appeared in the movie), and directed by Arthur Hiller, *Tobruk* second-billed George as Captain Kurt Bergman: a Palestinian Jewish officer. A member of the SIG (Special Interrogation Group: a unit of the British Army composed of German-speaking Jewish volunteers who performed commando and sabotage operations against the Axis forces in the North African Western Desert), George's Captain Bergman is one of eighty-three men who set forth on a mission to destroy the fuel bunkers of Rommel's Panzer Army Africa at Tobruk.

Jam-packed with incredible action sequences (such as Bergman crawling under a rolling German tank to attach a bomb, and Bergman eliminating German soldiers and tanks with a flame-thrower), *Tobruk* had George speaking German once again.

Even more importantly, in one of the best moments in the entire picture, Bergman has a brief conversation with Major Donald Craig (top-billed Rock Hudson) during which he makes clear to the Major just how serious the Jewish people are when it comes to holding onto, and preserving, their homeland of Israel. "For the first time since Jesus, we're beginning to think and feel as a people," he tells the Major. "The days of the wandering Jew are coming to an end. We're going home." "Palestine?" Craig asks. "Israel, Major, Israel," Bergman replies. "It's where we began. Anyone looking for trouble in the future will know where to find us."

Often cited as one of George's best performances, *Tobruk*'s depiction of him as as a man fiercely proud of his heritage, and, as a man subjected to the prejudice and discrimination of others, was a sign of things to come.

In 1968, George starred in three more features from Universal: *What's So Bad About Feeling Good?*, *House of Cards*, and *P.J.* In *Feeling Good*, which was produced, written, and directed by *Miracle on 34th Street*'s George Seaton, clean-cut George played a misanthropic, cynical Greenwich Village artist named Pete, who lives in a dirty dingy apartment with his girlfriend, Liz (the equally cast against type Mary Tyler Moore). After being infected with a "happy virus" by a toucan that has been smuggled through customs, Pete talks Liz into getting herself infected. Once she has, the two former hippies start thinking about cutting their hair, getting jobs, marrying, having children . . . in short, becoming adults and developing a sense of responsibility. Wanting their friends to experience this same happy feeling, Pete and Liz then pass

George Peppard and Gayle Hunnicutt in Universal's *P.J.* (1968).

the toucan on to them; naturally these friends, after being infected, introduce the bird to their other acquaintances. In time, the happy virus spreads all over New York City. This does not sit well with the politicians in New York, so they search for a "cure."

Location shooting in Paris and Rome, and a conclusion at the Roman Coliseum, were among the attractions in George's next feature, *House of Cards*. Also starring Orson Welles and Inger Stevens, George's first attempt at the international intrigue thriller had his down on his luck writer turned boxer Reno Davis learning of a plot by a Fascist organization to take over all of Europe. Though George was good in the part, he was much better suited to the detective drama *P.J.* In fact, there are some who believe that George's performance in this picture was a factor in his landing the role of Thomas

George Peppard and Gayle Hunnicutt in another scene from *P.J.* (1968).

Banacek. Given the content and style of the movie, they might have had a point. To begin with, there was his character's name, P.J. Detweiler. The P.J. stands for Peter Joseph. P.J., not Peter, was what others called him.

Then there were the opening credits: these featured George with an attractive young woman in bra and panties. As any watcher of *Banacek* knew, the opening credits of that series always featured Banacek with, or meeting, one or more women in a somewhat risqué situation.

P.J. also had the title character making such observations as "A butterfly will zap a bull elephant if the moon is high and the price is right." That sounded like one of those "old Polish proverbs" later uttered by Thomas Banacek.

Adding further *Banacek* parallels: George Furth's fussy "Sonny Silene" called to mind Thomas Banacek's fussy competitor Henry DeWitt (Linden Chiles), and the movie's plot had P.J. working for millionaire William Orbison (Raymond Burr). Insurance investigator Thomas Banacek often took cases where millions are at stake. The Polish sleuth would certainly have been right at home in the sequence where Detweiler and Orbison's sexy mistress Maureen Preble (Gayle Hunnicutt) make love on a bed covered with money!

He also would have enjoyed the wild party where two bikinied girls are shown swimming in a giant champagne glass!

One year after *P.J.*, audiences saw George in the motion-picture *Pendulum*. This one examined the flaws and advantages of the U.S. Justice System through the experiences of its lead character, Washington, D.C. police captain Frank Matthews. Shot on location in Washington, D.C. with scenes at such famous landmarks as the Capitol, the Jefferson Memorial and the Washington Memorial, the movie's portrayal of Washington D.C. politicians and lawyers was less than flattering.

Entering the 1970s by performing yet more roles in the action genre, George continued to display his versatility and willingness to try new things. *Cannon for Cordoba* (1970) was a WWI-era Western. George played Captain Rod Douglas: a soldier assigned to a suicide mission by General John "Blackjack" Pershing.

In *One More Train to Rob* (1971), George played Harker Fleet, a former train-robber, who, upon his release from prison, comes to the aid of Chinese workers that are being exploited by his former, double-crossing partner-in-crime, Timothy X. Nolan (John Vernon). Presaging George's soon-to-be casting as one of the *NBC Mystery Movie* crime-solvers was his leading lady, *NBC Mystery Movie-McCloud* semi-regular Diana Muldaur.

In yet another sign of things to come, in January 1972, George made his TV-movie debut with *The Bravos* as Major John David Harkness, a frontier cavalry commander who must protect his fort and its temporary shelter-seeking wagon train passengers from 2,000 Kiowa Indian warriors that seek revenge. The pilot for a proposed Western series, *The Bravos* was produced by Universal Studios, the makers of *Banacek*.

Around the same time, George appeared in two theatrical spy thrillers, *The Executioner* (1970) and *The Groundstar Conspiracy* (1972). In *The Executioner*, a tale of agents and double-agents told in flashbacks within a flashback, George's Michigan background was worked into the biography of his character: British-born, American-raised secret agent, John Shay.

In *The Groundstar Conspiracy*, George's leading lady was future *Banacek* leading lady Christine Belford. According to one reviewer, *The Groundstar Conspiracy* was originally intended as a TV-movie-pilot for a possible George Peppard series. Whether this was true or not, two months after he made his TV-movie debut in *The Bravos*, audiences saw him in his second TV-movie/pilot called *Banacek*: "Detour to Nowhere."

Peppard and Judy Geeson in Columbia Pictures' *The Executioner* (1970).

*Colonel Newcom had built the two-story log house, "Newcom's Tavern" (the oldest standing building in Dayton) in 1796. He went on to become Dayton's first inn-keeper, first bank president, and first sheriff in Montgomery County. (Dayton is part of Montgomery County.) Irene D. Newcom was Colonel Newcom's grand-niece. George Peppard referenced his connection to Colonel Newcom in Peggy Hudson's book, *TV 73*.

**According to the MGM theatrical trailer; the other two were George Hamilton and Luana Patten.

***At the time, the average motion-picture cost less than $3 million.

****Harold Robbins was the son of Russian and Polish immigrants.

[1] Film Score Monthly CD: *Home From the Hill*

[2] Jack D. Hunter, "The Blue Max Revisited," "Over The Front," *The League of World War I Aviation Historians,* Volume 13, Number 3, Fall 1998

George Peppard and Ralph Manza.

Chapter 2

George Peppard as...
BANACEK

"As the workman, so the work." –Polish proverb

In the preview scenes preceding the *Banacek* series 1972 pilot, "Detour to Nowhere," future employee Jay Drury says to his boss, "Hey, Mr. Banacek, didja ever think of changing your name? Nobody would ever think you was Polish."

"I would," the self-employed super-sleuth replies.

With that, George, his long-time friend (and executive producer) George Eckstein, and the regular cast and crew of *Banacek* were on their way towards overturning one of the longest-held stereotypes presented in popular culture: that of the dumb Polack.

Setting the whole thing in motion was series creator Anthony Wilson. The son of MGM writer/producer/narrator Carey Wilson, Anthony had done quite a lot of work in television by the time he created *Banacek*. In addition to serving as the story editor on Irwin Allen's *Lost in Space* and Alan A. Armer's well-regarded 1968-1970 CBS-TV Western, *Lancer*, he had written for *Bonanza* and *Have Gun, Will Travel*. He had also penned episodes of situation comedies (*Bewitched* and *Gidget*), war dramas (*Combat*), and dramas (*Mr. Novak*, *The FBI*, and *The Twilight Zone*.) So skilled at detail, he could make hour episodes into two-part shows, such as with "Landscape with Running Figures" in *The Fugitive*, and turn out impressive series pilots, such as "Beachhead" in *The Invaders*, Anthony also had a knack for diplomacy. Had he not, Irwin Allen might never have gotten the green-light from the CBS network execs to make *Lost in Space*.

Like other writers in television, Anthony eventually became a series producer. Leslie Martinson, series director on the September 24, 1970–September 8, 1971 ABC-TV science-fiction drama, *The Immortal*, has good memories of his professional association with Anthony. "Tony Wilson was an extraordinary guy, a wonderful producer," states Martinson. "A producer with whom any director would want to work. He was one of the more erudite, knowledgeable, meticulous producers. We had lots of meetings and there were boundaries. When things came up, what he thought was arbitrary, they would be discussed. He set the do's and the don'ts. Like the reactions of (series star Christopher) George—what he would and wouldn't do, the boundaries of the action to the situation. So the characters were well established on *The Immortal*."[1]

This same meticulousness and painstaking attention to detail was very much evident in *Banacek*. Creating a brilliant Polish super-sleuth "specifically to counteract a long-running series of (dumb Polack) jokes,"[2] Anthony (and George Eckstein) made *Banacek* even smarter, through the unusual story framework they developed for the program. This framework was modeled on insignificant details, such as the number of letters in a word, or the number of words in a sentence. Details like a single word, such as "submarine." This framework ensured that characters, things, and places would reflect the title character in some way; that dialogue would be written in a measured and precise fashion; that the writers of the episodes would give the audience clues as to what they were doing through repetition of words and phrases, rhyming, etc.

The *Los Angeles Times*' Kevin Thomas didn't know how right he was when he pointed out how the pilot which "obviously offers limitless series possibilities," "demands close attention."[3]

George being a man cognizant of the tiniest and most insignificant details, he and the *Banacek* concept were a perfect fit. "It amazes me to see a woman sit down," he told *TV Heroes*' Caroline Boucher during their lunch at the Beverly Hills hotel. "It takes about eighteen separate movements. Most men will pull out a chair and sit on it. Women will look at the chair, arrange the dress, the sleeves, the napkin—it's instinctive, and it's like a bird ruffling its feathers."[4]

In another instance of George's quick intelligence and mathematical mind, years earlier, he was doing an interview with film critic Rex Reed as part of the promotion for his late-1960s feature, *The Blue Max*. During the interview in George's hotel room, the two men heard a plane flying over the treetops in Central Park. Curious to see how close the plane was to the trees, George rushed to the window and looked out. According to Reed, George estimated the distance between plane and treetops with a cocktail napkin held at arm's length.

George was just as matter of fact when it came to the dinner parties and other social events he and former wife Elizabeth Ashley hosted. As noted by Ashley in her biography, *Actress*, he always wanted such occasions plotted out before they took place. Thus, each Friday evening, Ashley would show him their plans for the next week—what they would be doing, whom they would be entertaining as guests, what courses the couple would serve, etc. Since *Banacek* was executive produced by George Eckstein, it should have come as no surprise that the show displayed the same sort of precision, exactness, and mathematical thinking as its star.

George Peppard very much approved. "I like the character and I like the capers," he told the *Los Angeles Times*' Cecil Smith. "The capers intrigue me. The explanations are reasonable and logical. I can live with them. The character is reasonable and logical, too. He cuts his hair the way I do, smokes the same cigars I do*, likes the wines I like. I can live with him . . . ."[5]

One reason he could live with the character—he added a great deal to the role.

"The turtlenecks and all of that were all George's contribution," says George Eckstein. "The character was always as it was portrayed—he was always sort of elegant, and sophisticated, but some of the detail work George contributed. George himself wasn't sophisticated and elegant, not necessarily, that wasn't his off-screen persona. He was not necessarily a hell-raiser, but he was one of the guys; certainly not the sophisticate portrayed on screen. But he enjoyed doing that; he really enjoyed that character."[6]

There were a variety of reasons why. Chief among them: *Banacek* was the first Polish character series where the character both embraced and celebrated his Polish heritage.** Then there was "the individualism Banacek displays," George noted. "The fact that he likes older things rather than new things, is nice. The objects we surround ourselves with reveal a lot about a man."[7] Playing a minority was appealing, too. "It's important that we remind ourselves that we're all immigrants," he told *The Philadelphia Inquirer*'s Harry Harris. "I think the ethnic trend is healthy, and it makes my character more human. Poles are supposed to be very independent, and so is Banacek."[8]

The character's "toughness" and "sense of humor" was another attraction. "He's whimsical," noted the actor. "His attitude toward life is real."[9] Curious as to why his character was Polish, George asked about this very early in the proceedings. "The answer I was given is that the American-Polish today are a distinct minority more representative of minorities than say, the Irish or Italians, who've been absorbed to a large extent and may have lost a lot of their identity," the actor explained.

George worked hard to become a Polish character; he felt that he succeeded. "People tell me that as Banacek, I work like a Pole, or German," he told *The Philadelphia Sunday Bulletin's* Rex Polier. "I keep my head down and plow straight ahead. I get down to cases with no nonsense. I work long and hard... and with few complaints. Also, I don't say a lot. I'm not a Pole myself. But I grew up among them and worked alongside them in Detroit where my father was a building contractor. I know them. Matter of fact, the other day I just got my first fan letter in Polish."[10]

While there were those such as the *Los Angeles Times*' Don Page who thought highly of *Banacek*: "in one season, (it) could destroy all the tired Polish jokes,"[11] there were some Poles who saw creator Anthony Wilson's decision to give his proud Polish title character a non-Polish name*** as something of a slap in the face.

Such was not the reaction of the Polish-American Society. In fact, the organization was so happy with the pilot movie, *Banacek*: "Detour to Nowhere" when it aired in March 1972, they urged their members to write NBC and ask the network to please add the series to their 1972-1973 schedule.

Grateful for such enthusiasm, George was more than happy to tour as spokesman for the Polish people in America when he was asked. He also took a protective stance when it came to the people he was representing. "Don't try any Polish cracks on him," warned Rona Barrett's *Gossip* magazine during the series' original run. "Not that Peppard's Polish. He isn't, but don't try it, Peppard would be the last one to laugh."[12]

A number of actors found this out years later when George was being considered for the recurring role of Blake Carrington on Aaron Spelling's prime-time soap, *Dynasty*. At one point, George overheard some of his colleagues telling a Polish joke. Informing his fellow performers that he was a Pole, he made it very clear to one and all he did not care for such humor. In light of this behavior, more than likely it was George, not the *Banacek* writers, who inserted all the clues to Polish people, places, and things in the *Banacek* scripts.

"George was very serious about acting," states George Eckstein. "Very serious. He had done Broadway work, and he was not just a pretty face; he was devoted to the craft."[13]

As George made very plain to *TV Week's* Harry Harris, "To an actor it doesn't make any difference where they're going to project his image. The camera's the same. My attitude has always been to do the best work I can in whatever medium employs me—and to make as much money as I can!"[14]

He was not "at all contemptuous of television," says George Eckstein. "I mean George came to a point where the movie career was not really happening. And he was very close to (Universal Studios') Monique James; I think she recommended that he do this."[15]

Guaranteed a salary of $250,000, plus part-ownership of the program, George spent twelve hours a day working on the show, doing eight 90-minute episodes in five months. He had worked a twelve-hour/five-month schedule years earlier on *The Blue Max*, but that had been for a feature of two or so hours. In *Banacek*, he was shooting far more film in less time.

There was also the new acting challenge of being the lead regular in a television series. "In a film, when the film ends, so does the character," he pointed out to *The News Press/Daily Review*. "But in a series, the character continues, meets other people and does other things."[16]

Another motivation for taking on the series was that George would have more time to spend with his family. Troubled that his children were growing up without their father's influence (the movie offers he received always seemed to require going on location to other countries for long periods of time) George liked the idea of working a regular job near home. Even better—because he was part owner of the show—he could begin to develop his talents as a director. "Being an actor is the least creative thing in making a film," he noted to the magazine, *Photoplay*. "The director, writer, cameraman, producer, editor—they're all more creative than the actor. Directing is really where the creativity is, and that's what I hope to do someday soon."[17] During the first season, an opportunity to direct the majority of one *Banacek* episode would present itself****; in the second season, he would assume second-unit chores, for which he would receive on-screen credit. "There was some second-unit out of Boston—that was about it," recalls Eckstein. "George did the second-unit in Boston. That was his choice. He was fine at it. Certainly got everything we needed. He loved it. I don't know whether there was much second-unit used in the first season."

Which was not to say George didn't keep his hand in when it came to the writing of the show. "He put in a lot of time, paid a lot of dues, and George was a very bright man," says Eckstein. "We'd discuss the episodes . . . I'd get these two o'clock in the morning calls from him, and if he called, there was probably a reason. He'd be complaining about the script, didn't think this was strong enough or whatever. (Such late-night calling) was not a big thrill for my wife (actress Selette Cole), but George was George, and there was a lot of late-night drinking going on. He was drinking pretty hard. But it never seemed to interfere with his work. I had really very few problems with George. They were annoying when they happened, but they weren't serious. He eventually got over that (the drinking), but it was very bothersome at night. But there was a reason for the calls; it wasn't just arbitrary."[18]

Indeed if George Peppard was calling George Eckstein at such hours, it was definitely very important to hear him out; when it came to the *Banacek* stories, he was quite impressed with their quality. "The scripts are carefully written to involve you," he told *The Bulletin*'s Rex Polier. "You're absorbed into plots and character. The main attraction is to see if you can solve the mystery. We try our damndest to give everyone realistic clues. I look forward to seeing how the plot is put together."[19]

In the British publication, *TV HEROES*, he was even more specific. "It's the preparation of the Banacek stories," he told the magazine, "they are so outstandingly good. I rate them unique stuff for this kind of series. It's certainly far better stuff than most scripts that were ever submitted to me for major film productions for the cinema."[20]

Responsible for all of that "unique stuff" were *Banacek*'s George Eckstein, first season story editor Paul Playdon, and, second season story editor Robert Van Scoyk.

* The cigars Banacek smoked were quite special. The Puncheon Selection Slendores cigars Universal bought for George were made by 21 Club Selected Items, Ltd., N.Y., N.Y.

** *Banacek* was not the first television series to headline a Polish character. That honor went to Brian Keith's October 7, 1955-December 28, 1956 half-hour CBS/Revue Studios series, *The Crusader*. In *The Crusader*, Keith played Matt Anders, a freelance writer dedicated to helping people living under dictatorships, or Communist rule, escape to free countries. Anders had a very personal reason for undertaking such dangerous missions: after overthrowing the Polish government, the Communists had kept his mother in Poland and sent her to a concentration camp. There she had died. Not wanting others to suffer her fate, Anders went out of his way to help them.

*** See "Decoding *Banacek* Part One: The Games from the Names": the special section preceding this book's episode guide.

**** George Peppard said he would insist on directing at least one of the segments of *Banacek* if the show went into a second season.

[1] Leslie Martinson-2004-interview-by telephone

[2] Lawrence Laurent - "New NBC Series is Tough on Criminals – Banacek" – pg - R-48

[3] Kevin Thomas – *TV MOVIE REVIEW* – "Bounty Hunter Key in 'Banacek'" – *Los Angeles Times* – March 21, 1972, pg F14

[4] *TV HEROES* –"*BANACEK*" pg. 38

[5] Cecil Smith – "George Peppard: he can live with his Banacek character" – *Los Angeles Times* – Aug 27, 1972 – pg. U2

[6] George Eckstein – telephone interview, November, 2009.

[7] *News-Press/Daily Review, TV Week*-October 7, 1972 – "COVER CLOSE-UP - BANACEK … FIRST NAME THOMAS" – pg. 16

[8] Harry Harris – Screening TV – "Peppard's Not Polish, But He's Happy to Fake It" – *The Philadelphia Inquirer – TV WEEK* – February 4, 1973 – pg. 3

[9] Peggy Hudson, *TV 73*, 1972, Scholastic Book Services, Scholastic Magazine. pg. 120

[10] Rex Polier, *Bulletin* TV Writer/Associate Editor, "Private Eye Peppard -Give George Dynamite … And Look Out!" *The Philadelphia Sunday Bulletin – TV Time* – May 6, 1973 –pg. 3

[11] Don Page – "TV Reviews" – *Los Angeles Times* – September 14, 1972 – pg. e23.

[12] Rona Barrett's *Gossip* – February, 1973 – Vol 1., No 3 – "Close Up – George Peppard – He's No Polish Joke!!!!" – pg. 39

[13] Eckstein-interview

[14] Harris-Screening TV-"Fake It"-*TV Week*-pgs. 3, 41

[15] Eckstein – interview, November 2009

[16] *News-Press/Daily Review, TV Week*- "BANACEK … FIRST NAME THOMAS" – pg. 16

[17] *Photoplay* – February 1973 – Vol 83, No. 2 – pg. 91

[18] Eckstein – interview
[19] Polier, *The Philadelphia Sunday Bulletin – TV Time* – "Private Eye Peppard" – pg. 3
[20] *TV HEROES* – "WHO IS THOMAS BANACEK?" pg. 40

Chapter 3

Writing
BANACEK

"Many men, many minds" –Polish proverb

By the time NBC's 'locked room/impossible mystery" movie series, *Banacek*, premiered in September 1972, some 1,200 locked room/impossible mystery stories or novels had made it to the public. This presented George Eckstein and his associates with a problem: Was there some new approach to the locked room/impossible mystery? After all, the locked room/impossible mystery had been around for more than 130 years; during this time, all types of variations and twists on the genre had been presented. Moreover, since murders were a commonplace in the genre, authors had devised all manner of ways in which to dispose of their victims: death by stabbing, death by shooting, death by blunt instrument. Murder victims could be gassed, poisoned, decapitated, strangled, electrocuted, or hung. They could have their throats cut, or perish from carbon monoxide. If a victim was asphyxiated, this meant they could have been gassed, choked, suffocated, or smothered—the latter was often accomplished with a pillow. A death could also result from heat stroke, fright, drowning, or defenestration.

Henry Kane's 1957 short story, "Watch the Jools," in his Peter Chambers collection, *Death on the Double*, worked an ingenious twist on the drowning angle by having the drowning in that story occur in a high-rise executive office. Besides presenting their murders in unusual ways, another favorite approach was to stage such murders in locked, inaccessible places—hence the title of Robert Adey's invaluable 1979 bibliography, "Locked Room Murders."

Banacek avoided this seen-it-all-before dilemma by presenting its many murders *after* the sleuth began his investigation into the "impossible" disappearance of the object or person. That solved that particular problem, but not the one of how to bring freshness to the impossible disappearance element of the locked room/impossible mystery. Once more, after some 1,200 stories in the genre, the creativity well had been drained dry.

Among the many clever variations on the disappearing person angle, there'd been the staff of a hotel disappearing; five men vanishing on five separate occasions each time an ancient book is opened; a man disappearing from an airplane flying at high altitude. In regards to the disappearing object storyline, fans of the genre had encountered the disappearance of diamonds during a club meeting, with all exits blocked; the disappearance of a briefcase from a locked room; the disappearance of an ancient harp from within a locked room; 40 gallons of gold vanishing from a tank; the disappearance of a baby grand piano from a second story room.

Not content to deal with just people or objects vanishing, some authors had presented their audiences with the disappearance of things that were very difficult to move or transport, such as buildings. Thus, there was the disappearance of an aerodrome, a toyshop, a house from open countryside, and the disappearance and reappearance of a mysterious room from an old house. This was not to say that stories about the vanishing of things that could move hadn't been done. Among such scenarios were the disappearance of a car from a guarded stretch of road; the disappearance of a bus in a restricted area; a large truck vanishing from a stretch of road under observation at both ends.

Creating another obstacle for Eckstein and company were the names who had tackled the locked room/impossible mystery tale in the past. These included Sir Arthur Conan Doyle, Agatha Christie, Ed McBain, Ellery Queen, S.S. Van Dine, Dorothy L. Sayers, Craig Rice, Erle Stanley Gardner, and Kelley Roos. Adding further difficulties was the fact that there were authors from other genres who had combined their particular genre with the locked room/impossible mystery scenario.

For example, while Poul Anderson's 1958 *Ellery Queen Mystery Magazine* short story, "The Martian Crown Jewels" had Martian detective Syaloch trying to determine how a collection of crown jewels had disappeared from inside an unmanned spaceship traveling from Earth to Phobos Station (the station was located on a satellite of Mars); Isaac Asimov's novels *The Caves of Steel* and *The Naked Sun* had detectives Lije Baley and Daneel Olivaw (the latter was a robot) investigating, respectively, a murder in the future and on an outer planet.

Not only science-fiction writers tried their hand at the locked room genre. *The Wizard of Oz's* L. Frank Baum made a go of it in 1897 with *The White Elephant* short story, "The Suicide of Kiraros." As did novelist Joseph Conrad in 1935 with "The Inn of the Two Witches" in *The Complete Short Stories of Joseph Conrad*.

About that same period, Hollywood's Ben Hecht had published the "Mystery of the Fabulous Laundryman." Another Hollywood-connected name, MacKinlay Kantor, was also trying the genre in the 1930s. Kantor's attempts (presented in the *It's About Crime* series) included "The Light at Three O'Clock," "Nobody Saw Him Fall," and "Wolf! Wolf!"

A couple of decades before this, Sax Rohmer's detective Nayland Smith had investigated a death by poison in a study under constant observation in *The Mystery of Dr. Fu Manchu* (a.k.a. *The Insidious Dr. Fu Manchu*); around the same time, humorist P.G. Wodehouse (creator of the Jeeves and Wooster comedic novels) was going for a darker tone with the 1914 short story, "The Education of Detective Oakes" (a.k.a. "Death at the Excelsior"). Even stripper Gypsy Rose Lee got into the act with her 1941 novel, *The G-String Murders* (a.k.a. *The Strip-Tease Murders*).

Adding insult to injury, in addition to not being the first television series to feature a positive Polish character, *Banacek* wasn't even the first prime-time network series to work with the locked room, impossible mystery concept. Years earlier, *77 Sunset Strip* had dabbled with the format in three episodes, "Appointment with Fear," "Death and the Skylark," and "Now You See It." All three were television adaptations of stories *77 Sunset Strip's* Roy Huggins had previously published in *Esquire* and *The Saturday Evening Post*.

Presenting a further challenge to Eckstein and company, for six seasons, television audiences had witnessed some of the most outrageous thefts and vanishings of both objects and people on the popular CBS-TV series, *Mission: Impossible*. Included in that series' more outlandish schemes were throwing a false bed top over the team's mark and inflating it so that the man seems to disappear (the first season's "The Traitor"); stealing $2 million worth of platinum bricks from the base of a pool table and replacing them with inflatable copies (the second year's "Charity"); recreating their mark's private offices on the floor below and rigging his penthouse elevator to stop at their suite, rather than his (the fourth season's "The Double Circle"); stealing the entire take from a syndicate casino vault which is seemingly impenetrable to burglary (the sixth season's "Casino").

Fortunately for *Banacek*, many of the writers that worked on *Mission: Impossible* wrote a script or two for the *Banacek* series. Among them were Harold Livingston, Howard Browne, Shirl Hendryx, Stephen Kandel, and of course, first season story consultant Paul Playdon.

Even more fortunately, George Eckstein was a fan of the locked room, impossible mystery genre. That gave him one advantage when it came to tackling the overworked format. Eckstein had already dabbled with the genre in his previous television work. Two of his most clever efforts came with the second-season *The Invaders* episode, "The Trial," and the 1970 TV-movie/pilot, *The House on Greenapple Road*. The latter was an adaptation of the Harold Daniels novel, *The Red-Kitchen Murder*. As for the former, in many respects, *The Invaders* "The Trial" was something of a test run for the *Banacek* series. It even had a Slavic-named detective, Sgt. Bert Wisnovsky (William Zuckert).

One of the more realistic episodes of the 1967-1968 Quinn Martin series, "The Trial" partially resulted from Eckstein's "problem all the way through with the (*Invaders*) concept. The premise bothered me," he explains. "Maybe that's just me. But I thought if these aliens were so superior, and so dangerous and so powerful, why didn't they just kill him?* So I would try to avoid the superhuman qualities when I could."[1]

One way to do so was to take the aliens' normal way of dying (when they died, they burned up and left no trace) and present such a death as a murder where the victim's body might have been disposed of in a blast furnace. Thus the pre-opening credit teaser for "The Trial" concluded with David Vincent's old friend Charles Gilman (future *Banacek* guest Don Gordon) being found near a blast furnace inside a factory building by Vincent and Sgt. Wisnovsky; no trace of Fred Wilk, the *man* Gilman had pursued inside the building, could be found. Gilman's explanation: Wilk was an alien, so he had burned up when Gilman had struck him with a pipe in self-defense. Since Gilman was standing near the furnace when Vincent and Wisnovsky found him, for all anyone knew, Gilman's burned up statement might have been an unconscious admission from the man that he had disposed of Wilk's body in the furnace. The only way Vincent could clear his friend of murder was to prove Gilman had killed an alien, not a human being. Easier said than done. For, as he began to collect evidence for his friend's defense, David Vincent encountered road-block after road-block. To begin with, Fred Wilk was married. But his wife Janet might have been an alien too. But Janet was the former girlfriend of Charles Gilman. And the Wilks had a baby. Plus Charles Gilman, who still loved Janet, had followed the couple to the new town where they'd settled; a short time before his fatal altercation with Fred Wilk, he'd beaten the man up in public. There was still more which might cause one to dispute Gilman's claim that Wilk was an alien from outer space. Fred Wilk had a job, friends and was an active member of the community. He came from a small Indiana town, and his birthday was July 7, 1933; his mother and father, Fred Wilk, Sr. showed up in court with his birth certificate to prove it. The police also had Wilk, Jr's high school transcript and college records.

If Fred Wilk was an alien, he certainly had assembled one of the best covers any alien posing as a human had ever assembled on *The Invaders*. Co-written by Eckstein and the series' associate producer, David W. Rintels, "The Trial" was classic, locked room, impossible mystery stuff.

More than two years later, George Eckstein tackled the murder-without-a-body scenario again, in Quinn Martin's first TV-movie, *The House on Greenapple Road*. Once again featuring a Slavic-named detective, Sgt. Charles Wilentz, *The House on Greenapple Road* had Santa Luisa detective Lieutenant Dan August, and his partner, Wilentz, investigating what they believed to be the murder of one Marian Ord, which was a logical conclusion given the seven pints of blood splattered all over the floor, walls, refrigerator, etc. in Mrs. Ord's home (there were about ten pints of blood in the human body) and, given that Mrs. Ord had the same blood type O as that spilled in her kitchen; she also had disappeared. How she was killed was another question. Ditto how a killer could have left her home in broad daylight and not caught anyone's attention. As Sgt. Wilentz observed, "No body. No witnesses. No weapon. Except for that mess in the kitchen, it's like it never happened." Making Wilentz and his co-worker August's task even more difficult… Marian's husband, George Ord (future *Banacek* guest Tim O'Connor) was missing. As was Lillian Crane, the one person who could give George Ord an alibi. There were plenty of suspects to go around as well.

Having worked on two locked room, impossible mystery-type television stories, by his own admission possessing a "low threshold of boredom," it was therefore a certainty that when George Eckstein was assigned *Banacek*, he would come up with a new way to present the series. Not too surprisingly, Eckstein's solution relied considerably on his self-deprecating sense of humor. Throughout his TV career, he had displayed a penchant for poking fun at himself, at what series he was doing at present, at what series he had done in the past, and at those people he knew.

Casting his actress-wife Selette Cole as a shrewish sort of character in the *Banacek* episode, "The Two Million Clams of Cap'n Jack," making fun of *The Fugitive* being a TV series by having its title character, Dr. Richard Kimble, watch a re-enactment of his murder trial on a college TV station in *The Fugitive* episode, "Man in a Chariot," this was typical George Eckstein humor. As was Janet Wilk's "This isn't *Perry Mason*" retort to David Vincent in *The Invaders*: "The Trial." As was Sgt. Wilentz's "A detective. That's what I want to be when I grow up" remark in *The House on Greenapple Road*. Television being a performance art form where the repeat was a constant, particularly when it came to the weekly series, why not build a television series based on the TV repeat, Eckstein might have reasoned. A TV mystery series was the perfect vehicle for such an approach; in the mystery, the detective usually solved whatever the crime was by recreating, or repeating, the steps in the crime. As to how to write this repeat series, Eckstein and company found their formula in the one man so crucial to the *Banacek* series success: George Peppard.

To begin with, the full name George Peppard was a repeat of that of the show's creator, Anthony Wilson, at least when it came to the number of letters in each man's name: thirteen. Thirteen being considered an unlucky number, building portions of his lead character's biography from this number certainly would have appealed to Eckstein's smart-aleck sense of humor. The fact that Eckstein and George also had the same first name gave the series executive producer another repeat, as did the fact that both George Peppard and Anthony Wilson shared a six when it came to one part of their name (in the star's case, the first name, George, in the creator's, the last name Wilson), as well as a seven (in the star's case, the last name Peppard, in the creator's, the first name Anthony.)

As if these repeats weren't enough, the full name George Peppard repeated the number three. There were three syllables in the full name, three letter Es in the full name, three letter Ps in the last. Given these numbers and given that George often looked at things in a mathematical and precise way (the reader will recall his previously mentioned "eighteen separate movements" a woman goes through in seating herself observation), Eckstein and his associates decided to write this repeat series' scripts and dialogue in a mathematical, precise way, too.

As George Eckstein reveals, this is exactly what he and his regular writing staff of Paul Playdon and Robert Van Scoyk did. Says Eckstein, "Very often what would happen is, people would come in with a story, and we would approve the story; then they would write the script and turn in the first draft and that was the last we would see of them. Then we would take the script, either Bob and I, or Paul and I, and redo it in our own 'image' so to speak. Because that's what the series was about. Because the series was so dependent on character, on George's personality and all of that, we sort of had to do it that way."[2]

The whole thing got underway on March 20, 1972 with the *NBC Monday Night at the Movies* premiere, *Banacek*: "Detour to Nowhere."

---

*By him, Eckstein was referring to the series protagonist David Vincent, an architect trying to warn his fellow man that alien beings from another planet had come to the Earth for purposes of conquest.

[1] Eckstein-interview-2009
[2] Ibid

Decoding BANACEK

Part One: The Games from the Names

"Each mind has its own method" –Polish proverb

As we have previously noted, while the *Banacek* series was created to put to an end to dumb Polack jokes, the name Banacek itself was not Polish. University of Illinois professor Jana I. Tuzar more than proved this in February, 1974 when she published the essay, "An Introduction to Selected Aspects of Slavic Orthography – Or Why Banacek Can't Spell" in *Esquire* magazine. A teacher of Slavic language and literature for five years at the University of Illinois, Jana I. Tuzar knew what she was talking about.

Orthography is the art of writing words with the proper letters, according to accepted usage. Presenting to her readers the argument that Banacek spelled and pronounced his name in the Czech fashion (he spelled his name as Banacek, pronounced it as /banachek/ and accented the first syllable), Tuzar's essay showed how she had arrived at this conclusion. First, she pointed out that in Polish, the letter c is pronounced as /ts/ as in "tsetse fly," while the /ch/ sound as in "check" is written as cz. Then she explained that since Banacek spelled his name as "Banacek," the Polish pronunciation of the name would be /banatsek/. But the character pronounced his name as /banachek/. Because of this, the Polish spelling would therefore be: Banaczek.

Going on to note that in Polish, the accent is always on the second to the last syllable, Tuzar then revealed why she believed the character's name to be Czech. First of all, only in the Italian, Czech and Croatian languages would the c in Banacek be pronounced /ch/. Secondly, since the character was obviously not meant to be Italian, this left only the Croatian and Czech languages. While the Croatians belonged to the Southern Slavic groups, the Czechs, like the Poles, belonged to the Western groups. Given that the ek ending in the surname Banacek was typical of the Western Slavs, given that the accent on the first syllable was typical of the Czech language (in Czech, there is a fixed stress on the first syllable), it was clear to Professor Tuzar that the name Banacek was Czech. Obviously, when it came to Polish surnames, as far as Jana Tuzar was concerned, the men who made *Banacek* were pretty ignorant.

Brilliant and logical as was her argument, what Professor Tuzar did not take into account was the amount of repetition, and matching that was presented through the Banacek character in the series pilot. This repetition and matching came from the numbers 3, 6, 7, and 13.* That George Eckstein and Anthony Wilson were able to create so much biographical detail from just four numbers was nothing short of remarkable. These biographical details are presented below, starting with 13.

13s (including thirteen letter names, places, etc.)

Character's name: Thomas Banacek

State where character lives: Massachusetts (One of the original thirteen colonies*, and the only one of those colonies whose name begins with the thirteenth letter of the alphabet: M)

Neighborhood where character grew up: Scollay Square. (Note the alliteration of Scollay Square. Note too that the "Scoll" in Scollay is pronounced the same as the "scull" in the verb, sculling. When Banacek is first seen, he is sculling on the Charles River.)

Make of vehicle character drives: Packard Darrin

Address number of character's residence: 85 (8 + 5 = 13)

Type of proverb character quotes: Polish proverb (Note the alliteration of Polish proverb.)

Job character's father had when he came to the United States: mathematician.

7s (Including seven-letter names, places, etc.)

Character's last name, and how he prefers to be called: Banacek

Where character is first shown: The Charles River. There are seven letters in the name Charles.

Character's stock phrase: There's an old Polish proverb that says . . . .(There are seven words in the phrase.)

Name used when referencing character's automobile: Packard (Note that the last three letters in Packard are the same as the last three letters in Peppard.)

6s (Including six-letter names, places, etc.)

Character's ethnicity: Polish-American. He is very proud of his (six-letter) Polish heritage. He always identifies himself as Polish.

What character's friend Felix calls him: Thomas. Felix is the only recurring series character to call Banacek by his first name. Why just Felix? The name Felix begins with the sixth letter of the alphabet.

Country of character's father's birth: Poland

Polish city where character's father worked: Warsaw

U.S. city to which character's father moved: Boston.

Street where character now lives: Beacon Street (There are six letters in the first word "Beacon," six letters in the last word, "Street."

Address of character's club: 46 Beacon Street (Note that the six-letter words "Beacon" and "Street" follow the number 6. This is one of the clues Wilson and Eckstein give the audience as to what they will be doing in their planned television series.)

Sport character plays at his club: Squash.

Individual character encounters after exiting club: Carlie Kirkland. The first name Carlie contains six letters.

3s (Including three-letter names, places, etc.)

Number of syllables in character's last name: Three: It's pronounced Ban-a-cek.

Number of letters in third syllable of character's last name: Three. The first of these three letters is C: the third letter of the alphabet.

Character's home-town: Boston. The original name of Boston was "Tremountain" or "Trimountaine." Both names mean "Three hills."

Character's neighborhood: Beacon Hill. Beacon Hill is one of the "Three hills" of Boston.

Character's street address: 85 Beacon Street. The number 85 is three syllables; the street where the character lives, Beacon Street, is three syllables.

River where character indulges in one of his favorite sports, sculling: The Charles. The name of the river begins with the third letter of the alphabet.

Character's boyhood home: Scollay Square. Scollay Square is three syllables.

Last name of character's long-time friend/assistant: Mulholland. There are three syllables in the name, Mulholland. There are also three Ls. The first L is the third letter in the name, counting three from this L, we arrive at the second L. Following the third L are three letters: a, n, d.

Character's chauffeur/assistant: Jay Drury. There are three syllables in the full name, Jay Drury. The first name Jay is a total of three letters.

Character's chief rival: Carlie Kirkland. The name Carlie begins with the third letter of the alphabet. Note that the C in Carlie is pronounced like the K in Kirkland. Carlie's Christian name is Caroline. There are three syllables in the name Caroline.

Character's most frequent employer: Cavanaugh. The last name begins with the third letter of the alphabet. There are three syllables in Cavanaugh. Like Carlie, Cavanaugh makes his first appearance in the pilot episode.

Character's stock phrase: "There's an old Polish proverb that says . . . ." The third word in the phrase is the three-letter "old."

Again, that George Eckstein and Anthony Wilson were able to create a full biography for their lead character on the basis of just four (repeated) numbers was astonishing. That Eckstein and his story editors Paul Playdon and Robert Van Scoyk were able to write a total of sixteen scripts on the basis of this repeating numbers premise, was even more amazing. Whether Eckstein and his associates' heavy emphasis on repeating threes was also deliberately carried over into the series broadcasting history only they could say. At any rate, the broadcast history of the series definitely bore the mark of the "three."

---

*In time, the repetition and matching would expand to include other numbers such as 14 (the total number of letters in the names George Eckstein and Robert Van Scoyk) 11 (the total number of letters in the name Paul Playdon) and 4. The term "four-letter word" usually referring to an obscenity, the idea of writing a line or sentence with four four-letter words in a row, such as "they," "can't," "deny," and "that" was just too irresistible for the tongue-in-cheek George Eckstein and his associates to pass up.

(Note: The author is not saying there was a line in the show where the words "they can't deny that" were used. He is simply using these four words as an example to illustrate what sort of writing George Eckstein and company were doing.)

**The other thirteen colonies were (in alphabetical order): Connecticut, Delaware, Georgia, Maryland, New Hampshire, New Jersey, New York, North Carolina, Pennsylvania, Rhode Island, South Carolina, and Virginia.

The three male regulars of *Banacek*: left to right: Murray Matheson, George Peppard, Ralph Manza

Decoding BANACEK
Part Two: The Sign of the Three

The three-syllable *Banacek* is one of three rotating series in the 1972-1973 series, *NBC Wednesday Mystery Movie*. The other two series are: the three-syllable *Madigan* and the two-word, three-syllable *Cool Million*. All three of these series aired on NBC (one of the three television networks at the time) on Wednesday (the third day of the work week). *Banacek* starring the three-syllable George Peppard was the first *NBC Wednesday Mystery Movie* series to air. It was followed by *Madigan* starring the four-syllable Richard Widmark, which in turn was followed by *Cool Million* starring the five-syllable James Farentino. In other words, a three-syllable star's series premiere was followed by a four-syllable star's series premiere which was followed by a five-syllable star's series premiere. This made for a perfect numerical progression of three, with three as the first number. The Banacek character's first appearance came in March, 1972 (the third month of the year) in the three-word premiere episode, "Detour to Nowhere." This pilot movie aired on Monday, March 20. In 1972, the 20th was the third Monday in the month.

"Detour to Nowhere" features a total of three actors who are to be regulars on the 1972-1974 series: George Peppard, Murray Matheson, and Ralph Manza. Each of these three regulars has a three in his real name, and a three in his character name. The three-syllable George Peppard has the three-syllable, character last name Banacek. Banacek, not Thomas Banacek, is what the character prefers to be called. The three-syllable Ralph Manza plays the three-syllable Jay Drury; his character's first name Jay is a total of three letters. As for Murray Matheson, the actor's last name is three syllables; his character Felix Mulholland's last name is three syllables.

Also appearing in the pilot film is the series' future leading lady, Christine Belford, and future semi-regular George Murdock. Both Belford and Murdock are threes in real life; their characters are threes as well. Belford's first name begins with the third letter of the alphabet; her character's first name, Carlie, begins with the same letter. In the pilot, Carlie tells Banacek that her Christian name is Caroline; there are three syllables in the name, Caroline. In regards to George Murdock, like George Peppard and Ralph Manza, the actor's full name is three syllables. On the series, his character will go by his three-syllable last name, Cavanaugh; Cavanaugh begins with the third letter of the alphabet. George Murdock is the third "George" billed in the opening credits of the pilot; the other "Georges" are George Peppard and George Eckstein.

Three months after the Banacek character's introduction, in June 1972, George Peppard did the first of four *Password* guest-shot weeks that occured during the two-season run of *Banacek*. In three of these four Peppard-on-*Password* weeks, the other celebrity contestant was an actress whose first name begins with L. In all three cases, this "L" actress was, or at some point in her career, had been, three-named. The first of these actresses was the three-named Lynda Day George. Lynda Day George is best known for her role as "Casey" on the 1966-1973 series, *Mission: Impossible*. She was the third leading lady in the series. Her last name, George, was a direct match to actor Peppard's first name. George Eckstein also appeared on *Password* during the run of *Banacek*. This makes for a total of three *Password* "Georges" connected to *Banacek* and George Peppard.

The next "L" actress to do a "Peppard-on-*Password*" week was Linda Kaye Henning. Her first two names complete the match that was begun in the first Peppard-on-*Password* week. The actress' first name, Linda, is pronounced the same as Lynda; her second name, Kaye, rhymes with the second name Day. This left the third name, Henning. Like the last name, Peppard, Henning contains seven letters. Just as with her *Password* predecessor Lynda Day George, Linda Kaye Henning is best known for her work as a "three." On the 1963-1970 situation comedy, *Petticoat Junction*, she played (the three-named) Betty Jo Bradley, the third and youngest daughter of (the three-named) Shady Rest Hotel owner Kate Bradley.

The same month *Banacek* aired its final original episode (the three-letters-apiece-in-the-first-three-words) "Now You See Him, Now You Don't" (March 1974,) the third "L" actress appeared with George Peppard on *Password*. She was Lee Meriwether, earlier in her career, the three-named Lee Ann Meriwether. Like the name George Peppard, the name Lee Meriwether contains a total of thirteen letters. At this point in her career, Lee Meriwether was doing her third television series as an actress: *Barnaby Jones*. Her two previous series were *The Time Tunnel* (1966-1967), and *The New Andy Griffith Show* (1971). Her first name, Lee, is a total of three letters.

During its two-season run,* *Banacek* was to air a total of three episodes where the word, "Million" was part of the title. These episodes were, in order of their broadcast, "A Million the Hard Way," "The Two Million Clams of Cap'n Jack," and "The Three Million Dollar Piracy." "The Three Million Dollar Piracy" was the third-aired episode of the 1973-1974 *Banacek* second season. It aired in November, the third month of the 1973-1974 TV season on Wednesday, the third day of the work week. Airdate of this episode was November 21. In November 1973, the 21st was the third Wednesday in the month.

Three was truly the magic number on *Banacek*. Not only did Banacek live in Boston (a city which began as a "three"), not only were his closest associates and most frequent competitors and employers "threes," most of his cases had him recovering and restoring "threes."

In the first season, this included an "Experimental Safety Vehicle," "The Ten Kings," "Book of Hours," a "Cross," a "Collection," and "Clams"; in the second season, "Man in Harmony," "MAX" (a.k.a Maximum Data Coordinator), a "Coach," and a "Chalice." Moreover, even when the object or person Banacek sought to restore was not a "three," it was somehow strongly connected to a "three." This the reader will learn through the episode guide that follows.

---

*There were plans for a third season!

Three and a Match:
An Episode Guide to BANACEK

"He that has the spice may season as he pleases."
—Polish proverb

[Author's note: Accompanying the production credits and original airdate for each episode are two sections. *Section One: Matches* gives *some* of the matches presented in each episode; this includes on-screen Matching in Series Credits, Matches through Physical Production and Editing, Matching through Numbers, Alliteration and Future Matches.

[*Section Two* is composed of: Behind the Scenes anecdotes, The Polish Connection (references in the show which connect to Polish people, places, and things), *Banacek* Trivia, Inside Jokes and References, and Notes. With the exception of the pilot, following *Section Two* are seven *Banacek* Challenges which have been drawn from the episode. In order for the reader to solve these, it is crucial that he watch the episode, and look and listen carefully to each story. The answers to the *Banacek* challenges conclude the book. I thought it vital to create these challenges, as I believe they will help *Banacek* fans realize just what a clever and complex series George Eckstein and his associates gave the television audience.]

George Peppard and Christine Belford in a scene from the pilot episode, "Detour to Nowhere"

The *BANACEK* pilot:

March 20, 1972 *NBC Monday Night at the Movies* premiere: *Banacek:* "Detour to Nowhere"

"There's an old Polish proverb that says, 'If your socks are not in your shoes, don't look for them in heaven.'" –Banacek to Carlie

Credits:
George Peppard as Banacek
Also starring Christine Belford – Carlie Kirkland
Don Dubbins – Sheriff Jessup
Murray Matheson – Felix Mulholland
Russell Wiggins – Earl Lewis
Charles Knox Robinson – Arthur Patrick McKinney
Ralph Manza – Jay Drury
George Murdock – Cavanaugh
Guest Star Ed Nelson – Geoff Holden
Co-starring Bill Vint – Mackey
Vic Mohica – Indian Joe (Joe Hawk)
With
Lou Frizzell – Denny
J. Pat O'Malley – Hank
Gene Dynarski – Loser Griffin
Mario Machado – 1st Newscaster
Larry Burrell – 2nd Newscaster
Dee Gardner – Sharon
Uncredited
Lonny Chapman – Bartender

Produced by George Eckstein
Written by Anthony Wilson
Directed by Jack Smight

Associate producer – Steven Bochco
Music – Billy Goldenberg
Director of Photography – Sam Leavitt
Art direction – George Webb
Set decorations – James M. Walters
Assistant director – Brad Aronson
Unit manager – Henry Kline
Film editor – Robert Watts
Sound – John Carter
Titles and optical effects – Universal Title
Technicolor
Editorial Supervision – Richard Belding
Music supervision – Hal Mooney
Costumes by Grady Hunt

Exteriors/Filming Locations: Boston:
Back Bay, Back Bay Skyline, Charles River, Customs House, Longfellow Bridge, Beacon Hill, Copley Square, Prudential Center, Trinity Church, Financial District, Government Center, Boston Common, Massachusetts State House, aerial view of Boston possibly including Nantasket Peninsula,

Exteriors/Filming Locations: California:
Universal City Studios Stage 29, Salton Sea Area of California, perhaps Death Valley National Monument (The area in which the theft of the armored truck occurs looks quite similar to Death Valley, and its well-known locale, Zabriskie Point.)

SECTION ONE: MATCHES

Matches in series credits:
　*The title of the series is the three syllable *Banacek*: the name of this premiere pilot episode is the three-word "Detour to Nowhere."

*The second word in the episode title is the two-letter word "to." The word "to" and the number "two" are pronounced the same.

(Although the episode title is "Detour to Nowhere," the episode title is never shown on screen. Sources such as *Alvin H. Marill's Made-for-TV-Movies, 1964-1979*, do list this pilot episode as "Banacek: Detour to Nowhere.")

*The three letters in his first name, three syllables in his full name Don Dubbins is the first of three actors billed in the same frame. The other two actors are Murray Matheson (three syllables in his last name) and Russell Wiggins (three double consonants: SS, LL, GG in the full name.) Like Russell Wiggins, both Don Dubbins and Murray Matheson have double consonants in their names: Dubbins a BB in his last, Matheson an RR in his first. Because both the alliteratively named Don Dubbins and the alliteratively named Murray Matheson have their last names aligned with their first, a vertical reading of this particular frame's credits gives us a DD and an MM. In other words, thanks to the presentation of these particular credits, the producers create a total of seven double consonants in one frame. Seven is of course the total number of letters in the pilot's on-screen title, *Banacek*.

*Following the three names in one frame of Don Dubbins, Murray Matheson, and Russell Wiggins is another three names in one frame. The names in this frame are, from top to bottom, Charles Knox Robinson, Ralph Manza, and George Murdock. Note that the three-named Charles Knox Robinson follows three names.

*The name Charles Knox Robinson contains a total of three threes. The first: the full name is composed of three names, the second: the first name Charles begins with the third letter of the alphabet; the third: the last name Robinson is a total of three syllables.

*The five-letters in his first name, five letters in his last name Ralph Manza is the fifth actor billed after actress Christine Belford.

*Excluding Christine Belford (who is an *actress*, not an actor!), the opening credits bill a total of eight actors. The eight letters in his full name Ed Nelson is the eighth actor billed.

*In the closing credits, both Bill Vint and Vic Mohica make for match credits. In the case of Bill Vint, his full name makes for a match; there are four letters in the first name, four letters in the last name. As for Vic Mohica, his actor name is a match to his character name, Indian Joe. In addition to both names being a total of nine letters apiece, one part of the name is three letters, the other part is six. That George Eckstein and company intended a match to Mohica's name in the credits is inarguable. In the story, Mohica's character is either called by his first name, Joe, or his full name, Joe Hawk. Not at any time in the story is he referred to as Indian Joe. Moreover, whenever Mohica received billing in other productions, he was almost always billed as Victor Mohica. Had he been billed this way in *Banacek:* "Detour to Nowhere," there would have been no match to his screen-credited character name, "Indian Joe."

*Thirteen names after the thirteen-letter George Peppard, the alliteratively named Mario Machado receives his billing. As mentioned earlier, M is the thirteenth letter of the alphabet. Mario Machado is the third alliteratively named actor in the pilot; preceding him, are, in order, Don Dubbins and Murray Matheson. Mario Machado is another "three" performer in the pilot. His first name, Mario, is a total of three syllables, ditto his last name, Machado. In the pilot, he is billed as "1st newscaster." "1st" is a total of three letters/characters.

*There are three three-letter names in the "With" portion of the credits. They are, in order: Lou (as in Lou Frizzell), Pat (as in J. Pat O'Malley) and Dee (as in Dee Gardner.)

Matches through Physical Production and Editing:

*The teaser features three vehicles: the armored truck, the Texas police car, the Oklahoma police car.

*Each vehicle contains two men: two guards in the armored truck, two officers in the police cars.

*Excluding Banacek, there are a total of seven people in the teaser (the two armored truck guards, the two Texas police, the two Oklahoma police, and the unseen sniper—we only see his arm.)

*The teaser contains seven desert sequences featuring the (soon to disappear) armored truck, and seven sequences of Banacek sculling on the Charles River. Since the teaser switches back and forth between the desert and Boston sequences, these two "sevens" are difficult to detect.

*By the time the movie ends, the audience has heard a total of seven shots fired.

*In the conclusion, in which the armored truck is found, there are a total of six people in the final crowd shot: Carlie, the reporter interviewing her, his cameraman, a policeman, a man in a suit, and a construction worker. As the scene continues, a woman reporter or photographer then enters the scene, making it a seven.

*The insurance company National Meridian is located on the tenth floor of the high-rise office building in Government Center. In the offices of National Meridian, Banacek asks the receptionist to make him a copy of something; a copy costs a dime. A dime is ten cents; in other words, at a company located on the tenth floor, Banacek is having something copied for ten cents.

*As the name on the door shows, the eight-letter McKinney heads the eight-letter by eight-letter by eight-letter Property Recovery Division of the eight-letter by eight-letter insurance company, National Meridian.

*At Banacek's home in Beacon Hill, there is a brass nameplate on the front door. The name on this plate: T. Banacek is eight letters. When Banacek turns into the driveway of his home, we see the number of his address; the first number in the address is 8.

*The license plate on the armored truck is O-4821. This makes for a match of fifteen. O is the fifteenth letter of the alphabet; when we total the numbers on the plate (4+8+2+1), we arrive at fifteen.

*The first paper Banacek looks at is the fifteen-letter *Vantage Sentinel*. The name George Peppard, Jr. makes a total of fifteen letters.

*In both the *Vantage Sentinel* and *Daily Assurance Reports*, Banacek is interested in the information in the third column.

*Banacek cuts out the top story in the third column of *Vantage Sentinel*. The story begins with the seven-word headline, "Vantage Man Killed in Attack on Sheriff." Note that the seven-letter word "Vantage" begins this headline, and that it concludes with the seven-letter word, "Sheriff." The person clipping out this seven-word headline is the seven-letter Banacek.

*Going down the claim number listings in the (three-word) Recoveries and Rewards column, which is in the third column on Page Three of the three-word newspaper, *Daily Assurance Reports*, Banacek stops and circles (in red) the seventh claim number listing. The claim number is SR-376-B. As we know, the three numbers 3, 7, and 6 are key numbers in the *Banacek* series.

*On the back page of the *Vantage Sentinel* is the story, "She's 3rd Brightest But Hard Gal to See." The story is at the left. On the front page of *Daily Assurance Reports*, is the story, "Three Claims Are Under Investigation." It too is at the left.

*During the course of the movie, the audience sees seven specific Boston exteriors featuring, or tied to Banacek. They are: 1. The Charles River, 2. Beacon Street, 3. Government Center, 4. Boston Common, 5. Boston Union Club, 6. Massachusetts State House, 7. Banacek's house in Beacon Hill

*When the sleuth arrives in Vantage, the audience is treated to seven more specific exteriors tied to him. They are: 1. The Site of the theft, 2. The *Vantage Sentinel* building, 3. The sheriff's office and jail; 4. Banacek's hotel, 5. The general store, 6. Joe Hawk's shack, 7. Geoff Holden's place.

*Excluding the two places where Banacek lives: his home, and his hotel room, the sleuth is shown in a total of seven interiors. These are: 1. The outer office of National Meridian, 2. Felix's bookshop, 3. The squash court, 4. The bar in Vantage, 5. The Vantage sheriff's office and jail, 6. The general store. 7. Joe Hawk's shack.

*Banacek wears a total of thirteen outfits in the movie.

*The sleuth's investigation takes place in two cities/towns: the six-letter city of Boston and the seven-letter town of Vantage.

Matching through numbers:

*The Christian name of Banacek's chief rival is Caroline Kirkland. There are eight letters in the first name, eight letters in the last.

*Caroline Kirkland works for the eight-letter McKinney at the eight-letter by eight-letter insurance company, National Meridian.

*The thirteen-letter Thomas Banacek is investigating the disappearance of an armored truck which disappeared somewhere between the Texas/Oklahoma border; total number of letters from the combination of Texas and Oklahoma is thirteen.

*Geoff Holden (five letters in the first name Geoff) speaks the five-letter word "paper" five times in a row.

*When Banacek blows Carlie's cover and identifies McKinney as her boss, he calls the man by his full name: Arthur Patrick McKinney. There are six letters in the first name Arthur, seven in the middle name Patrick, eight in the last, McKinney. This makes for a perfect numerical progression of three.

*There are three syllables in the third and last name McKinney.

*During the conversation between the three-syllable McKinney and his three-syllable superior Cavanaugh, three numbers are mentioned: 11, 22, and 66. As we can see, in all three cases, each double digit number: 11, 22, 66, is composed of the same single digit number: 1, 2, 6.

*The second two numbers referenced: 22 and 66 are multiples of the first number 11.

*11 is the number of investigators from National Meridian who have been sent to Texas on the armored truck disappearance. Two more investigators connected with the company: Banacek and Carlie are to join the search. This brings the total number of investigators to thirteen.

*22 was the number of investigators on the earlier Fairfield Diamond Case; McKinney and Banacek also worked on this case. The recovery cost for National Meridian on that case was 22%.

*McKinney admits that Banacek has a good success rate: 66%. Both McKinney and Banacek have first names which are a total of six letters.

*Geoff Holden's "special friend" Sharon, whom Banacek meets at the wealthy Texan's spread was first runner up to Miss Guam in the 1967 Miss Free World Beauty Contest. She received her M.A from Baylor University in 1970. Note that both the years 1967 and 1970 can be connected to Thomas Banacek, in terms of numbers.

*In addition to two years in which she did significant things, Sharon is one of two beauty contestants referenced in this episode. The other is the former Miss America pictured in Jay's wallet photos.

*The former Miss America is one of several women whose picture Jay shows to police deputy Denny. He only references one other in his conversation with Denny however: the girl who lives next door to him.

*When Banacek begins his investigation of the armored truck disappearance, it has been nearly two months since the disappearance. Two sets of legal authorities are investigating the disappearance: the FBI and the Texas police.

*Joe Hawk is one of two men jailed by Sheriff Jessup; the other is Joe's friend, Charlie Burns, the town drunk. Joe Hawk is sentenced to a total of two months on the county work gang.

*Two-bit hustlers are the type of criminals McKinney says waste the time of National Meridian. Two weeks is the amount of time McKinney wants to solve the armored truck disappearance.

*There are two versions of the conversation which has Jay wondering why Banacek hasn't changed his name from the Polish "Banacek" to something more American-sounding. The first version comes in the scenes from the pilot segment which precedes the pre-credit teaser. The second version is of course in the pilot film. Towards the end of the story, Jay tells Banacek he owes him two days rental on the limousine.

*Banacek encounters Carlie twice in one day. (He specifically mentions this.) Carlie twice misrepresents herself as Mrs. Banacek.

*Two news reporters mispronounce the sleuth's name as "Banasek." The first is the *Vantage Sentinel*'s Earl Lewis; the second is the newscaster portrayed by the alliteratively named Mario Machado. Because he is the second character to mispronounce Banacek, newscaster Mario Machado twice mispronounces the name. Banacek twice corrects his mispronounced name, but the second time (at the end of the movie), he's not making the correction to the person's face.

*Felix tells Banacek he is trying to play chess with a "third-rate" chess manual; when Felix makes this remark, there are three people in the shot (Banacek, Felix, and a customer who's on the second floor of Felix's bookshop.). A line or so after Felix asks Carlie the three-word question, "You play chess?" Carlie tells Felix she can win the chess game in just three moves. (Note that the three-word "You play chess" question begins with the three-letter pronoun "You," and concludes with the word "chess," which begins with C: the third letter of the alphabet. Note too that when Felix poses this three-word question, there are again three people in the shot: Felix, Banacek and Carlie. Further note that the question "You play chess?" is a perfect numerical progression of three: three letters in "You," four in "play," five in "chess.")

*The stolen armored truck is a "four-month special." The total number of deaths connected to the armored truck robbery is four. Felix mentions four books that might help Banacek in solving the robbery. Two of the books have four-word titles.

Sevens, and other numbers in dialogue:

One: When Sheriff Jessup meets Banacek, he says to the sleuth: "Now don't tell me. You're T. Banacek." There are seven words in this line. The seventh and last word is the seven-letter surname, Banacek.

Two: Geoff Holden greets Banacek with the question/comment, "So you're the pro from Boston, huh?" Again there are seven words in the line. Within the line, there are two references to Banacek: "you're" and "the pro." "You're" is the second word in the line. This first *two* is matched by the second reference to Banacek: the two-word, "the pro." These two words are followed by two more words: "from Boston" which tell us where Banacek lives. Note that the six-letter town name "Boston" is the sixth word in the line. Note too that at the end of the word, "you're" (which of course refers to Banacek) there are a total of seven letters, and that with the two words "the pro" (which again refers to Banacek), we have a total of six letters.

Three: Another seven comes through the brief exchange between Banacek and Joe Hawk towards the end of the story. After Joe delivers the two-word question/line, "Banacek. Is that you?," Banacek gives the single sentence answer, "Yeah, it's me." Within these three lines are a number of threes. Joe's first sentence is the single-word, three-syllable "Banacek." He follows this with the three-word question, "Is that you?" The three-letter pronoun "you" is the third and last word. Banacek matches Joe's threes with his three-word "Yeah, it's me" reply. Like the pronoun "you," "me" refers to Banacek. Like Joe's "you," "me" is the third and last word in Banacek's sentence.

Alliteration:

Below is an alphabetical list of the alliterative words used during the course of the pilot. Again, alliteration is the practice of beginning the second word with the same letter that began the first word.

A: Adjusters Attend; and above all; another adventure; armed assault
B: Banacek. Boston; Be Back (sign on door of the *Vantage Sentinel*); Brightest But; Brink's Bandits by; Burlington Beach
C: cold concrete; Collateral. Cross-collateral; Crumbine Corporation
F: For forty
G: Gold, Greed
H: hang here; hear Hawk has; Here. He; Hippies. Hippies?; homestead here
I: Important Issues; insurance investigator
J: Just junk
L: Living like
M: maintenance man; make me; man-made; Martin-Marietta; myself. Mr.
N: Nader nightmare; No no no no; Not now
O: on over
P: Paper. Paper, paper, paper, paper; percentage player; Polack? Polish; Polish proverb

S: Say, say; Scollay Square; Security Systems; simpering schoolgirl; Somethin' so; Store, Sheriff; stupid Scotch

T: talk. That's; teach tone-deaf; then talk to; time tells; to talk to; to turn this town; To too; two truck;

V: Vantage. Vantage?

W: We're way

Y: Yeah, you.

Double alliteration

O&T: One of the top thirty

Future Matches:

*The scene of Banacek driving down the street and turning into the driveway of his home; someone, often a girl, walking on the sidewalk in front of his home at the same time. (Note, these scenes will be new sequences, not stock footage from previous episodes!)

*Banacek driving down the street, turning into his driveway, removing his scarf from his neck, sorting his mail

*The *Vantage Sentinel's* headline "Cries for Vote Reform in Congress"

*The scene of Banacek watching videotapes on his big-screen TV

*Eight weeks, four days (This is the amount of time since the disappearance of the armored truck.)

*Banacek's father being replaced by a computer.

*Carlie losing her temper and storming out of Banacek's home

*Someone asking Banacek why he saves his cigar stubs. His making the same reply.

*An attractive woman catching a pajama-wearing Jay by surprise in a hotel room

*The fairytale, "Puss n'Boots."

* Earl Lewis' description of his duties concerning the *Vantage Sentinel* (Earl is editor, writer, printer, maintenance man, and delivery boy of *the Vantage Sentinel*.)

*The *Sentinel* newspaper name

*Carlie's Ralph Nader reference
*The armored truck's Texas license plates.
*McKinney's Superman reference
*The fictional book, *Brink's Bandits*

SECTION TWO

Behind the scenes:
George Eckstein:

"I was at Universal from 1970 to 1980. Universal moved me into producing. I enjoyed it tremendously. It was a very supportive atmosphere when I was there, at least most of the time. It was very gratifying, and Sid Sheinberg, at that time, the head of the television department, was a wonderful boss. I mean he was supportive and did not micro-manage. It was just a very creative atmosphere. That show might have been in pre-production by the time I got into it. It certainly wasn't shot in Texas. I wasn't there – I never got to Boston (either). You get yourself nailed down to multiple project kind of things, and I was not able to get there. It was not a happy time; George getting charged with rape, which was not a wonderful thing."[1]

Behind the scenes: George Peppard and the rape charge:

The sculling scene, which was the one scene to appear in both seasons of the credits, was shot on a cold January morning in 1972. The scene required George to go sculling on the Charles River wearing nothing but a sweat suit. "The temperature was only 10° above, and those sculls capsize easily unless you hit the oars just right," he stated. "It was a tough scene and I knew it."[2]

Things were about to get a lot tougher. During a pause in the shooting, George began talking to twenty-four-year old aspiring actress Joan McLaughlin, who had responded to a Universal studio call for extras when the *Banacek* company came to Boston to film. After George finished with the sculling shots and lunch was called, McLaughlin came in and sat down at his table. The table seated twelve. Following lunch, George went back to his hotel. A little bit later, he and his sixteen-year-old son and a friend went out to dinner. George returned to the hotel after that.

Soon after his return, George received a call from Joan McLaughlin, who was in the lobby. She asked him if she could come up to his room. He said that was fine. According to George, after he and McLaughlin talked in the living room of his suite, she asked him if she could go in his bedroom to phone her roommate. He agreed. When McLaughlin came out a good bit later, she was wearing George's pajama tops, and very little else. Suddenly, she bit George on the cheek, and ran. Realizing he'd been framed, he immediately contacted police.

After the police arrived and heard George's side of the story, no action was taken. Nonetheless, fears of bad publicity had Universal beginning to think about settling with McLaughlin for $25,000, although George believed it could have been settled for a fifth of that, or even less. Knowing he'd done nothing wrong, he was determined to fight the accusation.

The next day, George finished the location shooting in Boston. Since nothing was heard from McLaughlin in the next few days, it looked like the trouble was over, so he returned to California. Then, said George, "All of a sudden, my business manager phoned and told me that the Commonwealth of Massachusetts wanted me on charges of assault and battery, and assault with intent to commit rape, preferred by this girl. (The date of the charge was February 2, 1972.) Even then I probably could have settled out of court, and the girl would have withdrawn her charges, but I chose to hire Paul Smith, a top criminal lawyer in Boston. And I flew back for my day in court."[3]

By choosing not to settle out of court, George guaranteed himself quite a bit of bad publicity. Testifying that the star invited her to his hotel room for a drink and made sexual demands of her, McLaughlin claimed that when she refused, George jumped up on top of her, started punching her on the face, and choked her. Her story was carried in newspapers all over the country. Under cross-examination however, McLaughlin then began changing that story. She also admitted to using a number of different names while working as an exotic dancer.

Cleared of all charges by Judge Elijah Adlow, who said the only one assaulted was George Peppard, George shared the judge's compassion for Joan McLaughlin. For upon returning to Los Angeles, he received a letter from her, which he described as "rambling." It seemed that Joan McLaughlin was on welfare and had a baby to support.

Behind the scenes: guest star Ed Nelson:

Shortly after filming the *Banacek* pilot, guest star Ed Nelson ran for city councilman of San Dimas, California. Five other candidates were seeking the same position at the time. In early March 1972, Nelson appeared in an episode of NBC/Universal TV's horror anthology, *Night Gallery*. He was on screen for a total of eleven minutes and fifty seconds. Because Section 315 (a) of the Federal Communications Act's Equal Time Law required that a TV or radio station offer equal time to any political candidate when any of his opponents appeared on a program that was not a newscast or news show, KNBC, the NBC Los Angeles affiliate that had aired the program, had to give each one of the other five candidates running for the position, exactly 11:50 air time. As a result, the station lost 59:10 of prime-time programming.

KNBC being a major television station in the country, they could have reached a potential audience of 10,000,000 viewers each day. Only 16,000 of this potential audience lived in San Dimas. As a result, by airing these 59:10 of political programming, KNBC was thus running the risk of annoying 9,984,000 uninterested viewers.

When KNBC learned that Ed Nelson had appeared in the *Banacek* pilot, "Detour to Nowhere," and that the movie was scheduled to air on March 21, they did not want to go through the same experience again; they canceled the upcoming broadcast and replaced it with other programming. Because of this action, Ed Nelson, the actor, became a liability; as long as he was a political candidate, his presence in a movie or show carried with it the potential of causing a TV station to air some unwanted programming. Not wishing to give up his acting career at that particular time in his life, he dropped out of the city councilman race. Once he did, KNBC put *Banacek*: "Detour to Nowhere" back on their schedule.

The Polish Connection:

#1: As we learn in the pilot, Scollay Square, Boston's most multiethnic neighborhood, is where Banacek grew up. In 1958, in an early example of urban renewal, Scollay Square and the adjoining West End were leveled, uprooting 2,800 apartments and boarding houses. These demolished buildings and houses had been the homes of 7,000 Polish, Italian, Greek, Irish, Albanian, Lithuanian, Russian, and Ukrainian immigrants. Thomas Banacek references this displacement in the pilot.

#2: When Banacek and Felix discuss how the theft was accomplished, the sleuth makes a reference to the famous fictional detective, Sherlock Holmes. Creator of Sherlock Holmes was Sir Arthur Conan Doyle. Doyle's "Exploits of Brigadier Gerard" (a series of comic short stories about a vain Hussar in the French Army during the Napoleonic Wars) featured Polish characters.

Trivia:

*During the sequence where Banacek retraces the path the armored truck took towards the rim of the 600-foot chasm, at times the camera pulls so far away from Banacek (through the aerial views) that he becomes little more than a dot on the landscape. This kind of aerial photography was the way creator Anthony Wilson's series, *The Immortal*, concluded every episode.

*The headline in the *Vantage* newspaper, "Diplomats Feted as Important Issues Go By the Board," had been used on television before in the "Wings over Hooterville" September 14, 1966 second season premiere of the popular CBS sitcom, *Green Acres*. This same headline appeared in the show's fictional newspaper, *The Hooterville World Guardian*.

*The headline in the *Vantage* newspaper: "She's 3rd Brightest But Hard 'Gal' to See" appeared years later in a 2011 Traveler's television commercial.

*The aerial footage of the armored car was later used in episodes of other Universal series, including Farrah Fawcett's second *Six Million Dollar Man*, "The Peeping Blonde."

*Jack Smight's other 1972 TV movie, *The Screaming Woman*, featured *Banacek's* "Detour to Nowhere's" co-stars Ed Nelson, Charles Knox Robinson, Lonny Chapman, and Russell Wiggins.

Inside Jokes and References:

*At the Golden Years Rancho (the retirement community Holden plans to build) is the sign, "Grand Opening Next September" (*Banacek*, of course, premiered a few months later, in September.)

*Above the claim number posted by National Meridian in the "Recoveries and Rewards" column of the "Daily Assurance Reports" is a claim number posted by the Crumbine Corporation. Dr. Samuel J. Crumbine—a pioneer in public health—was a doctor in Dodge City, Kansas. Dr. Crumbine was the model for Doc on *Gunsmoke*. *Banacek*'s George Eckstein wrote for *Gunsmoke*; the first episode he wrote for the series: "Doctor's Wife."

*As previously noted, Felix Mulholland mentions four books that might give Banacek some information that will help him solve the armored truck disappearance. The books are *Hijackings, Past and Present* by Peter Allen Fields, a writer who worked with George Eckstein on *The Name of the Game*. *Brink's Bandits* by Hargrove & Irving, (this referred to) Eckstein's fellow *Name of the Game* producers, Dean Hargrove and Richard Irving, *Gold, Greed and Guns* by Rupert DuMarney, and *Nancy Drew and the Great Payroll Robbery*. The last two books display no connection to Eckstein; they are simply there to create a match of four to the stolen armored car, "a four-month special" as previously noted.

Notes:

The scenes presented in the trailer that precedes the teaser sequence gives the audience a good sense of what the series will stress: first: Banacek's pride in being Polish; second: Banacek's reputation as a professional; third: the sleuth's healthy ego; fourth: his cool demeanor and sense of humor; fifth: his taste and sophistication; sixth: his seduction of women; seventh: his always getting the better of his competitor. That the show is to be based on matches, usually of numbers, is made very clear in the teaser. The Texas Highway Patrol car 0202 contains two officers in the front seat; the third number on the Oklahoma state route sign 703 is three. That the numbers in the show will come primarily from its lead character Thomas Banacek is also made plain in the teaser. For example, the unseen sniper is the seventh and last character to appear in the desert sequences; his action of firing the rifle and temporarily stopping the Texas Highway Patrol car brings to a close the first desert sequence; following this we see the first Banacek sculling on the Charles sequence. Continuing the numbers theme, the seventh and last Banacek sculling on the Charles sequence segues into the opening credits. After a total of seven actor names have followed that of star George Peppard, the seventh credit frame lists the second "George" in the series: producer George Eckstein.

From this point on, the show presents one clever match after another, giving its audience only the slightest and briefest of hints as to what it is doing, thus conforming to all the proper etiquette and rules of the locked room, impossible mystery format.

Although Thomas Banacek has many positive qualities, he also exhibits traits that are rather off-putting, including a lack of humility, a fairly big ego, and a strong inclination for womanizing. George, having delivered some of his best performances playing less than likable individuals, imbuing Thomas Banacek with a number of negative traits was a shrewd move by Anthony Wilson and George Eckstein.

---

[1] Eckstein- interview, 2009
[2] "George Peppard: I Did Not Attack That Girl" as told to Jim Bacon -*Photoplay* – Vol. 81, No. 5, pg. 115.

Reviews and Publicity: *Banacek*: "Detour to Nowhere":

March 10, 1972 – *Los Angeles Times* – "TV'S EQUAL TIME – A Sledgehammer for Swatting a Fly'" – by Maury Green – pg G23 – (article about actor Ed Nelson, in which the *Banacek* movie-pilot is referenced.)

March 13, 1972 - *NBC Monday Night at the Movies: Banacek*: "Detour to Nowhere" pre-empted by Bob Hope special. In one skit, Bob plays a Polish detective!

Publicity preceding the series' fall debut:

*April 8, 1972—"The Doan Report" –Richard K. Doan – *TV Guide* — Vol. 20, No. 15, Issue #493: NBC announces fall prime-time schedule for 1972-73 season. Doan reveals that *The NBC Wednesday Mystery Movie* may include the series: *Banacek, Cool Million, Madigan, Heck* (later *Hec Ramsey*, which became one of *The NBC Sunday Mystery Movie* segments), and *The Judge and Jake Wyler* (Bette Davis and Doug McClure starred in the series pilot of the same name.)

*May 1972—"George Peppard Found Innocent of Attempted Rape Charge" by Anissa Mulligan – *Movie Mirror* – Vol. 16, No. 7

*May 6, 1972—"As We See It"–*TV Guide*—Vol 20. No. 19, Issue #497: *Banacek* mentioned in a story about Ed Nelson candidacy for San Dimas, California councilman. The magazine reveals that Nelson's *Marcus Welby/ Owen Marshall* two-part guest shot, "Men Who Care" (the first of two *Welby/ Marshall* two-part dramas) is in danger of being canceled by ABC because of the equal-time rule. Calling the controversy over Nelson's candidacy "foolish," *TV Guide* points out that Section 315(a) of the Communications Act which applies to the actor's situation says nothing about equal time; rather it specifies "equal opportunities." They further note that Ed Nelson appeared as an actor and not a political candidate in *Banacek, Welby,* and *Marshall*, and point out that all three programs were filmed months before Nelson threw his hat in the ring.

*June 5-9, 1972: *Password*: George Peppard and Lynda Day George are the guests on ABC-TV's popular game show, *Password*.

*June 27, 1972: *The Tonight Show with Johnny Carson*, NBC: Johnny returns from a stint in Las Vegas. Scheduled guests are George Peppard and Rodney Dangerfield. (The *TV Guide* listing makes it clear that *Banacek* will be premiering in the fall of 1972.)

*July 19, 1972: "*Los Angeles Times*"—pg. G14. The *Los Angeles Times* announces that NBC sport-casters Curt Gowdy and Charlie Jones, the San Diego Chargers David (Deacon) Jones, and the Oakland Raiders Ben Davidson have now been added to the guest cast of *Banacek*'s premiere episode, "Let's Hear It for a Living Legend." Pro-football players John Brodie and Gene Washington have already been cast.

*July 29, 1972: *TV Guide* — Vol 20, No. 31, Issue#509: "TV Teletype: Hollywood—Joseph Finnigan Reports": Finnigan reveals that San Francisco 49ers John Brodie and Gene Washington will be guest starring on George Peppard's new NBC series, *Banacek*, and that the 203 lb Brodie's first name was misspelled as "Joan."

*August 5, 1972: *TV Guide*—Vol. 20, No. 32, Issue#510: "TV Teletype: Hollywood—Joseph Finnigan Reports": Finnigan discloses that Marty Ingels will play a talk-show host in one of the *Banacek* episodes.

*Aug 27, 1972: *The Los Angeles Times*: Cecil Smith, "George Peppard: He can live with his Banacek character"

*September 2, 1972: the *Banacek* pilot movie repeats.

*September 2, 1972: *TV Guide*—Vol 20, No. 36, Issue#514." In "This Week's Movies" in her review of the pilot film, *TV Guide*'s film critic Judith Crist states that *Banacek* will premiere the next week, and that NBC is handing out promotional buttons stating: "You don't have to be Polish to like Banacek!"

September 9, 1972: *TV Guide*—Vol. 20, No. 37, Issue#515. pg. 54: the stars of *The NBC Wednesday Mystery Movie*: George Peppard (*Banacek*), James Farentino (*Cool Million*), Richard Widmark (*Madigan*) are pictured.

Season One

Episode #1: Let's Hear It for a Living Legend, September 13, 1972

"There's an old Polish proverb that says, 'If you're not sure that it's potato borscht, there could be orphans working in the mines.'" –Banacek to Quillery

Opening Credits
Writer: Del Reisman
Director: Jack Smight
Guest Stars

Stefanie Powers	Angie Ives
Madlyn Rhue	Holly Allencamp
And Robert Webber as	Jerry Brinkman

Special Appearance by John Brodie as Ritchie Mulligan
And

Ben Davidson	Mangine
Deacon Jones	Joe Fabian
Tom Mack	Ed Wolinski
Gene Washington	Clay Mills
Clancy Williams	Walt Hicks

Co-starring

Conrad Janis	Quillery
Michael Lerner	Bartender
Jock Mahoney	Albert Bates
Curt Gowdy	
Charlie Jones	
Marty Ingels	
As Themselves	

Closing Credits
With

Chuck Morrell	Hank Ives
Anitra Ford	Susan
Colby Chester	Corliss
John Finnegan	Lt. Hallohan
Russell Arms	Ambulance Attendant
Peggy Walton	Dr. Judy Forrest
Byron Morrow	Grant
Bart Burns	1st Reporter
Bud Furillo	2nd Reporter
Chris Forbes	Debbie
Not Billed – Marv Goux	Coach

Executive Story Consultant: Paul Playdon
Music Score: David Rose
Wednesday Mystery Movie Theme: Quincy Jones
Director of Photography: Sam Leavitt, A.S.C.
Art Director: George Webb
Film Editor: Robert Watts, A.C.E.
Set Decorations: John Austin
Sound: Earl Schwarz
Assistant Director: Jack Barry
Unit Manager: Chris Christenberry
Editorial Supervision: Richard Belding
Music Supervision: Hal Mooney
Costumes by Grady Hunt
Main Title Design: Wayne Fitzgerald
Titles & Optical Effects: Universal Title
Technicolor

Exteriors/Filming Locations: opening credits: Boston's Charles River, the Longfellow Bridge, Boston Common, Government Center, near city hall.

Exteriors/Filming Locations: Boston: Logan International Airport, Boston Expressway

Exteriors/Filming Locations: Los Angeles: NBC Studios, Los Angeles Coliseum

SECTION ONE: *MATCHES*

Matches in series credits

Opening and closing credits:

*The title of the series is *Banacek*; there are seven letters in the title; the title of the episode is "Let's Hear it for a Living Legend"; there are seven words in this title.

*The last two words in the episode title are "Living" and "Legend." Both words begin with the same letter: "L."

*The sixth word in the episode title: "Living" is a total of six letters.

*Like the sixth word, "Living," the seventh word, "Legend" contains a total of six letters.

*The three-letter word, "For" is pronounced the same as the number four. "For" is the fourth word in the episode title.

*In the screen presentation of the title, above the fourth word, "for" is the four-letter word, "Let's."

*Following the four-letter word "Let's" is the four-letter word "Hear."

*In the guest cast, following the six-letter last name "Powers" (as in Stefanie Powers) is the six-letter first name "Madlyn" (as in Madlyn Rhue.)

*Robert Webber is the third performer listed. The six-letter first name Robert matches perfectly with the six-letter last name Webber.

*Tom Mack is the seventh guest star credited. There are seven letters in the full name Tom Mack.

*There are two performers named Jones in the credits. The six letters in his first name Deacon Jones is the sixth guest-star credited; if we count seven names from Deacon Jones, we arrive at the second Jones: the seven letters in his first name, Charlie Jones.

*There are six co-stars in this episode: Conrad Janis, Michael Lerner, Jock Mahoney, Curt Gowdy, Charlie Jones, and Marty Ingels. The first of these six co-stars: Conrad Janis, has a six-letter first name; the sixth and last co-star: Marty Ingels, has a six-letter last name. Note that performers Conrad Janis and Marty Ingels also match in fives: the last name "Janis" is five letters; the first name "Marty" is five letters.

Closing credits

*The third billed actor in the "with" credits: Colby Chester has a first name that begins with C, a last name that begins with a C, and a character name that begins with C. C is of course the third letter in the alphabet.

*There are eight letters in the last name of actor John Finnegan; there are eight letters in the last name of his character: Lt. Hallohan. Note that in both last names, "a," and "n" are the last two letters; note that in both last names, there is a double consonant: "nn" in Finnegan, "ll" in Hallohan.

*In the fifth "with" credit, the last name "Arms" (as in Russell Arms) is followed by a two-name character: Ambulance Attendant; all three names begin with the same letter: "A." In the character name, "Ambulance Attendant," there are nine letters in the first name, nine letters in the second name.

*The last three actors in the "with" credits: Byron Morrow, Bart Burns, and Bud Furillo all have a first name that begins with "B." Note that starting with the first name, "Byron" there is a reverse numerical progression of three with "five" as the first number.

Matches through physical production and editing

*Thirteen seconds into the show, we see that the live football game is being watched on a television. The thirteen-letter Thomas Banacek is watching the television.

*In addition to one of the Boston Rebels sporting a jersey with the number 76, and one of the Philadelphia Cougars a 67, the teams themselves are sixes and sevens. There are six letters in the team name "Rebels," seven in the name "Cougars."

*There are a total of seven men (five Philadelphia Cougars and two referees) on the football field when Banacek (and the audience) realize that Hank Ives has disappeared.

The seven men on the football field.

In addition, the number on one of the Cougars' jerseys is 67. (67 is the reverse of 76.) (The Cougar player in question is second from the left.)

*Early in the show, the seven-letter Banacek enters Jerry Brinkman Enterprises, and walks past a group of people. The moment he is out of the shot, we see that there are seven people in the scene.

*In the sequence at the NBC TV studio, the camera slowly tracks over five people before stopping on the sixth: Thomas Banacek. During this sequence, Banacek learns from the director Quillery that there were six cameras covering the game.

*When Banacek and Quillery review the footage of the game at the studio, Banacek's right index finger is near the number on a Boston Rebels' football jersey. The number on the jersey is 76. (7+6 = 13) (Note how Banacek's hand is hiding part of the 6 on the jersey.)

Banacek and Quillery review the footage from the game.

*At the end of the show, after the assistant coach (Marv Goux) asks Banacek the three-word thirteen-letter question, "Are you Banacek?," Banacek delivers the three-word, thirteen-letter reply, "Yeah, I'm Banacek." At the time of this exchange, excluding Banacek, there are thirteen people in the shot.

Matching through numbers:
THREES:
*Hank Ives (the football player for whom Banacek is searching) was three years old when his father was killed.

*Hank lost his father's dog tags three weeks ago.

*Jerry Brinkman has been paying $300 a week for a bodyguard for Hank Ives.

*For the last three days, Ritchie Mulligan has been trying to figure out how Ives disappeared.

*Jerry Brinkman is given three days to raise the two million demanded by the kidnappers.

*In his first meeting with Boston Rebels owner Jerry Brinkman, Banacek suggests the disappearance of Hank Ives might be one of the owner's famous publicity stunts. The sleuth can remember three such stunts: One, in 1968 in Pittsburgh, there was the icy field; Two, in 1970 at the press party, Brinkman introduced his new lady quarterback; Three, in the 1971 playoffs, Brinkman released twelve poodles on the field.

*Admitting that Banacek has a point, Brinkman offers the sleuth three possibilities in regards to Hank Ives' disappearance: One, "It could be an insurance fraud," Two, "It could be a publicity stunt," Three, "Or it just could be a kidnapping." (Each time Brinkman gives Banacek a possibility, he repeats the same three words: "it" "could" and "be.")

*There are three "Cougars" to whom Banacek talks: Fabian, Mangine, and Wolinski. Banacek is the third interrogator to question the trio; he was preceded by the Boston police and the news reporters.

*The three-syllable Wolinski tells Banacek there are "three pieces" of a (three-letter) "guy" a football player can grab when it comes to the kind of tackle he and the three other Cougars performed on Hank Ives: first, an arm, second, a leg, third, "whatever you can get to." Wolinski also tells Banacek how difficult this sort of tackle is when you have "three other guys jumping on your back."

*During their conversation, Holly Allencamp (three syllables in the last name Allencamp) talks to Banacek about a drink which she describes as a "crazy concoction" of three things: One, Cognac, Two, Crème de Cacao, Three, Milk. Note that there are three C's in the three-syllable word, "concoction."

*Holly's full name is Hollis Barker Allencamp. Note that "camp," the third syllable in the three-syllable last name Allencamp begins with C: the third letter of the alphabet.

*The three-named lip reader Dr. Judy Forrest watches the tape of Jerry Mulligan talking to Hank Ives three times.

*Banacek references three U.S. presidents (George Washington, Thomas Jefferson, and Abraham Lincoln) in the fictional autobiography he gives Angie Ives at the end of the show. Thomas Jefferson, the third President of the United States, is the last president Banacek references.

FOURS:
*The last time anyone saw (the four letters in his first name, four letters in his last name) Hank Ives, he was being tackled by four Philadelphia Cougars.

*Quillery, the TV director of the football game where Hank Ives disappeared, tells Banacek he was back filming the game in four seconds after a slight interruption in the play.

*It took Quillery four hours to collect for Banacek the appropriate footage of the above game.

*Hank's father was killed in WWII (four letters/characters in "WWII") in 1944.

*When Hank goes on Marty Ingels' television talk show, there are four empty chairs on the set.

*The (four syllables in his full name) Joe Fabian, who was one of the four Cougars who tackled Ives has gone thirty-four years without an accident.

*84 is the number on Fabian's football jersey. (Eight is of course a multiple of four.)

*Holly Allencamp gives Banacek a piece of information which proves invaluable in his locating the missing Hank Ives. Banacek finds Holly in the fourth bar he enters.

*Together, Banacek and Hank Ives overcome the villains; key to their success is a play Banacek gives to Hank: "It's fourth down and long yardage."

*Some of the dialogue from Hank Ives' appearance on the Marty Ingels talk show is presented in fours, such as Ingels's line, "Hank, enough of this chit-chat. Let's play football, okay?"

(Following the four-letter name "Hank" are four words, "Enough of this chit-chat." This is followed by a four-word question, "Let's play football, okay?")

SEVENS:

*During the course of this episode, Jay uses an emphatic and repeated "Mr. Banacek!" so as to capture the sleuth's attention. The number of times Jay says "Mr. Bancek" totals up to seven.

*In the teaser, Banacek references the famous magician Houdini. There are seven letters in the name Houdini.

*Also in the teaser, after Banacek says, "Big words don't impress me," his girlfriend replies, "Don't worry. I know what does impress you." The repeated word "impress" is a total of seven letters. In between the first and second "impress" are a total of seven words.

*In another seven, after the policeman asks the one-word question, "Banacek?" the sleuth makes the two-word, seven letter reply, "That's me."

EIGHTS:

*The eight-letter Hank Ives appears on the Marty Ingels television talk show in August. August is the eighth month of the year. (See the Notes section for another clever use of eights as regards the TV talk show sequence.)

THIRTEENS:

*Both Jay and Felix speak the same words: "Thomas, in case you're wondering how I managed to get them so quickly...." The total number of words is thirteen.

*After Wolinski tells Banacek, "You look more like a halfback, fancy," Banacek replies, "All right, like a fancy halfback." Total number of letters in "fancy halfback," or its reverse, "halfback, fancy," is thirteen. Total number of words in this exchange between the two Polish characters is thirteen.

Alliteration:
Alliterative words used in this episode:
B: Beautiful Beautiful; Be back; Being buddies; Boston backfield; Boston bartender; Brinkman Building
C: Couldn't cope; Crazy concoction; Cross-connect

F: Female fans; Fife furniture; Finder's fees; Football's finest; Free for
G: Gotta get
H: Hank has his; Hicks had
I: Injury, illness
L: Living Legend; Looked like; Looks like
M: Man Mulligan; Maybe maybe; Mr. Mulligan; My mind's; My mouth
N: Nervous now; Network news
P: Pass pretty; Press party; pile-up peeled
S: Say something; Some sort; Start screaming
T: Talk to; television tape; Tend to; took the time to try
W: Wouldn't want; Well, we went; Why what
Double alliteration:
B&C: Bring Boston Casualty's congratulations
W&T: What were they talking

Matches to previous episodes:

*Jay's solution as to how football player Hank Ives disappeared is similar to Banacek's actual solution of the armored truck theft in the pilot film "Detour to Nowhere."

*In the pilot film, eight weeks and four days have passed since the disappearance of the armored car; in this episode, the character who has disappeared is the eight-letter Hank Ives; Hank's first and last names both contain four letters.

*In the pilot, Geoff Holden's girlfriend Sharon (a former beauty contestant) possesses a Master's Degree from Baylor University; in "Legend," football player Ritchie Mulligan has a Master's Degree in Business Administration.

*In the pilot, Felix mentions the book, *Brink's Bandits,* to Banacek. In this episode, Banacek goes to work for his old friend Jerry Brinkman.

Future Matches:
*Jerry Mulligan's glass knee.
*Jerry Brinkman's "could be"
*Marty Ingels' "chit-chat"
*Guest star Stefanie Powers
*Guest star Conrad Janis
*Banacek's reference to George Washington.
*Holly's middle name "Barker"
*The episode title, "Let's Hear it for a Living Legend."
*Boston Rebels owner Jerry Brinkman.

*Angie Ives says she was once told that the only difference between a man and a computer is that a man doesn't count. A variation of this "computer counts" joke will be used later in the series.

*Holly Allencamp wears a large letter "A" on her scarlet dress. In Nathaniel Hawthorne's *The Scarlet Letter*, the character Hester Prynne wears a large scarlet "A". The name, "Hester Prynne" will be mentioned later in the series.

*Banacek being introduced watching a football game on TV.

SECTION TWO

Behind the scenes:
Executive producer George Eckstein:

"George and I had a long history. We worked together as college students (at the Ashland Shakespeare Festival in Oregon), and we went back to 1951. The one (play the two did together) I remember the most is *Henry the IV-Part II*. I played the part of Justice Shallow, and he played the part of Davy, who was the servant to Shallow, and so we had all these scenes together. We had a very good time."[1]

George Peppard:

For two weeks, in mid-August, George Peppard worked in the Los Angeles Coliseum with football players John Brodie (Ritchie Mulligan), Gene

Washington (Clay Mills), Deacon Jones (Joe Fabian), and Clancy Williams (Walt Hicks).

Former high-school football player George in the NBC-TV/Universal *Banacek* season premiere, "Let's Hear it for a Living Legend."

When Peppard went to Boston to film the exteriors for "Legend," not wanting to run into another Joan McLaughlin-type situation, NBC and Universal sent a private detective to accompany him. George had a four day break between the sequences in the Coliseum and the exteriors in Boston. He planned to use the off-time to go trout fishing in the Sierras.

The Polish Connection:

#1: Guest Star Stefanie Powers: Born Stefania Zofia Federkiewicz, Polish-American Stefanie Powers is proud of her Polish heritage. In 1995, she was Grand Marshal of New York City's Pulaski Day Parade (Often called the "father of American cavalry," during The Revolutionary War, Poland's Casimir Pulaski saved the life of George Washington.) Three years after leading the Pulaski Day Parade, Powers appeared in the PBS documentary, *The Polish Americans*. In that documentary, she described leading the 1995 parade as her "greatest thrill."

#2, 3 & 4: As previously noted, at the end of this episode, Banacek gives Angie Ives a fictional autobiography referencing presidents Washington, Jefferson, and Lincoln. All three of these presidents have connections to Polish generals who served in The Revolutionary and Civil Wars. General Pulaski's connection to George Washington has already been noted in the above profile of Stefanie Powers. Pulaski's contemporary, Tadeusz Kosciuszko also had connections to Washington, and Jefferson.

Chief engineer of the defenses that were mounted at (the later military academy) West Point, Kosciuszko planned the defense for Saratoga as well; The Battle of Saratoga proved to be a turning point in the American Revolution. Appointed Brigadier General and awarded the Cincinnati Order Medal in 1783 by George Washington, seven years earlier Kosciuszko became friends with Thomas Jefferson shortly after he arrived in Philadelphia, and read the Declaration of Independence. Emotionally moved by what he read; everything Jefferson said in the Declaration matched what Kosciuszko firmly believed, the general was determined to meet Jefferson. Discovering how similar their philosophies were, the two men eventually became the closest of friends.

Civil War general Wlodmierz B. Kryzanowski also played an important part in American history. First cousin to the Polish composer Frederic Chopin, Kryzanowski enlisted as a private in the Union Army two days after President Abraham Lincoln called for volunteers. The company of Polish immigrants Kryzanowski soon recruited was one of the first companies of Union soldiers. Later, after becoming a Colonel in the 58th Infantry Division (listed in the official Army Register as the "Polish Legion"), Kryzanowski fought in the battles of Cross-Keys, Bull Run, Chancellorsville, and Gettysburg. In time, President Lincoln promoted him to general. More than fifty years after his death (January 31, 1887), Kryzanowski's remains were transferred from Greenwood Cemetery in Brooklyn, New York to Arlington National Cemetery in Washington, D.C. During this period, President Roosevelt broadcast his tribute to General Kryzanowski on the radio; Poland's president, Ignacy Moscicki, transmitted his from Warsaw.

Trivia:

*The Brinkman Building named after Boston Rebels' owner Jerry Brinkman is the same building that housed Banacek's previous employer: National Meridian.

*Curt Gowdy and Charlie Jones were announcers for NBC football at the time of this episode.

*This episode also features: two San Francisco 49ers: quarterback John Brodie and wide receiver Gene Washington, three Los Angeles Rams: defensive back Clancy Williams, left guard Tom Mack and former defensive end Deacon Jones plus one Oakland Raider: defensive end Ben Davidson.

*USC assistant coach Marv Goux also worked in "Legend."

*"Let's Hear It For a Living Legend" marked the premiere of *The NBC Wednesday Mystery Movie*. It was also the second season *The NBC Mystery Movie* aired on Wednesday. To make room for *Banacek*, *Madigan*, and *Cool Million*, the three new *Mystery Movie* series airing on Wednesday, NBC took

the three original *Mystery Movie* series *Columbo*, *McCloud*, and *McMillan and Wife*, and moved them to Sunday, where, along with *Hec Ramsey*, they aired under the revised series title, *The NBC Sunday Mystery Movie*.

Inside Jokes and References:

*The television character Thomas Banacek is introduced watching a TV program.

Notes:

The series' September 13, 1972 season opener starts on a biographical note, thanks to the football game that Banacek is watching on TV. As mentioned in "Chapter One: Starring George Peppard," the actor had been the captain of his high-school football team. Kicking off a series that was to rely so heavily on numbers with a story where so many of the key characters were wearing numbers (the aforementioned football jerseys) was both a self-deprecating move on the part of the writers and an important clue to the audience as to how the show was to be written. An even stronger clue is the fact that Banacek is looking for a "match" character: the four-letter-by four-letter Hank Ives. Finally, since one of *Banacek*'s primary objectives was to give the Polish people a pro-Polish series, the casting of proud Polish-American Stefanie Powers as the lead guest in the series premiere was a very smart way to demonstrate this.

Reviews and Publicity:

Sept. 14, 1972: Don Page: *Los Angeles Times*, pg e23:

"The seed was cleverly planted; you had to stay with it." "Director Jack Smight did an extraordinary job in getting remarkable performances" from the football players.

Three and a Match: An Episode Guide to *Banacek*   85

BANACEK Challenges

(Author's note: It is highly recommended that when the reader tackle these challenges, that he have both seasons of the *Banacek* DVDs at hand. While some of the challenges can be solved without the DVDs, the only way to complete all seven challenges per episode is through the viewing of that episode. At times, such as with the "Dmitri's letter to Felix" challenge in the premiere episode, "Let's Hear It For a Living Legend," the reader will find it necessary to move to the particular sequence that is being referenced and pause or freeze the picture so as to solve the challenge that is being given him.)

"Let's Hear It For a Living Legend"

#1: Why is Jerry Brinkman Banacek's first client?

#2: During the course of this episode, Jerry Brinkman delivers the following line: "No one fears for the safety of Hank Ives more than I do." Can you find the four fours in the above line?

#3. As part of his investigation, Banacek watches a videotape of an interview Hank Ives did at a TV station. Can you detect the three sixes presented during this interview?

#4. As noted earlier, during this TV interview, talk-show host Marty Ingels says to Hank Ives, "Hank, enough of this chit-chat. Let's play football, okay?" Excluding that Ingels' line is delivered to Hank, in what three other ways does the line directly connect to the football player?

#5. Hank is a nickname for the missing football player's true first name, "Henry." Shortly after Banacek and Ives' former wife Angie finish watching Hank's TV interview, the sleuth asks her to dinner. Angie wonders if Banacek is using the invitation as an excuse to keep asking her questions about her former husband. To which Banacek replies, "Henry? Henry? Henry who?"

Excluding that Banacek's reply makes for yet another four-match to the missing Hank Ives, can you identify the three remaining matches that are presented in the line?

#6. At one point in the story, Felix receives an envelope from his Russian friend Dmitri. The two have been playing chess by mail. The envelope shows four fours. Can you identify them?

#7. During this episode, *Banacek* creator Anthony Wilson is acknowledged through an on-screen, inside joke. Can you identify it?

Episode #2: Project Phoenix –September 27, 1972

"Read the whole library, my son. But the cheese will still smell after four days. That's an old Polish proverb." –Banacek to Felix

W: David Moessinger
D: Richard T. Heffron
Guest Stars

Joanna Pettet	Christine Verdon
William Windom	Harry Wexler
Herb Edelman	Joe Thaddenhurst
Bert Convy	Douglas Ruderman
Percy Rodrigues	Falvo

Special Guest Star
Peter Mark Richman   Andy Cole

And:

John Fiedler as	Paddle
With	
Bruce Kirby	Collier
Stafford Repp	Police Chief
Warren Finnerty	Whitey
Isaac Fields	Fats
Seamon Glass	Deke

Exteriors/Filming Locations: Santa Fe Railroad Station

SECTION ONE: MATCHES
Matches in series credits:
Opening and closing credits
(See "Project Phoenix" Banacek challenges #1 and #2)

Matches through physical production and editing

*In the sequence where Banacek's helicopter lands and Jay is there to meet him, two matches are presented. The first is a matching of vehicles: a white car with a black top is followed by another white car with a black top; the second match is with colors: an orange car is parked alongside a fence of the exact same color.

*When Banacek and Jay pay a visit to the hippies, hoboes, and hophead's camp, at the left, there are two people sitting on cushions; at the right, also sitting, are a mother and her baby. Standing further away and closer to the approaching Banacek car are two people at the left; they are complemented by two people standing at the right.

*In the teaser, we see three men (Falvo, Ruderman, Wexler) standing on three steps between three railing posts. Since Falvo's right leg is on the bottom step, and his left on the second, the three-by-three match is not perfect, so it is a trick match. In the final standing on the steps scene, the trick is discarded; now, Falvo has both feet on the second step.

*In a later scene, Wexler says he can think of three people alone in the past ten months whom their competition: Horizon Engineering, tried to lure away. At the time Wexler speaks this "three," he is standing alongside a three-light fixture on the wall.

*In the Laundromat sequence, the owner, Collier, talks about the woman customer clogging up Washer#4. At the time, there are four people, including Banacek, on the right side in this scene. Nearby Collier, who is working on unclogging Washer#4 is a box of soap: (the four-letter-by-four-letter) STAR SOAP to be specific. Collier, by the way, is the only undertaker within forty miles.

*Towards the end of the story, Banacek captures three criminals. Complementing the four people in this scene are four gunshots: fired by one of the three crooks. These are the only gunshots fired.

*To help solve the mystery of the missing Phoenix, Banacek purchases an electric train set. The number on the train which is pictured on the cover of the box is "1405." On the box are five words: "READY TO RUN TRAIN SET."

*There are two five-letter words in the above: "READY" AND "TRAIN." In between these two "fives," are the two words, "TO RUN." Total number of letters from TO RUN: five.

*Learning from the hobo Paddle that another hobo named Whitey might be able to provide him with some valuable information regarding the night the Phoenix disappeared, Banacek spots the latter in the freight yards. Believing that Banacek means him harm, Whitey takes flight. Banacek finally locates the man in the third railroad car he looks into; on the outside of this car are three letters: RGR.

*Six minutes into the story, the characters Falvo and Thaddenhurst hear the sound of a helicopter. As we learn within seconds, in that chopper is Banacek. The name on the outside of the helicopter is DECAIR. There are six aerial scenes presented from Banacek's POV (point-of-view) in the sequence where the sleuth (in the helicopter) retraces the route of the missing Phoenix.

*Seven guards are shown boarding the train carrying the (seven-letter) Phoenix. When the guard tells Lt. Keenan that the (seven-letter) flatcar to which the (seven-letter) Phoenix was secured is gone, there are a total of seven guards (including Keenan and the guard talking) in the scene.

*The seven-letter Banacek walks past a freight car with seven numbers, which read vertically.

Matching through numbers:
TWOS:

*In the series' second aired episode, the two-word "Project Phoenix," Banacek says "old Polish proverb" twice. (He gives only one Polish proverb, however.)

*There are two safety cars in which Concord Motors has expressed interest: one is the seven-letter Phoenix, the other is the A-20-G. (G is the seventh letter in the alphabet.)

*Up till two years ago, Christine Verdon was working for (the two-word) Horizon Engineering. Two months ago, things got bad for Christine. When fired by R&W (R&W stands for the two last names Ruderman and Wexler), Christine wasn't even given a two-week notice.

*There have been two unsuccessful SEC prosecutions of Andy Cole. Posing as a reporter/publisher, Banacek tells Cole his new magazine's first publication will be in two months.

(MULTIPLES OF TWOS):

There are three sentences in the following line, delivered by Banacek to Christine Verdon, "Of course. Early American drill press. It's always been one of my favorite styles."

The second and third sentences are both multiples of twos. The second sentence, the four-word "Early American drill press," is double the number of words in the first sentence: the two-word, "Of course." The third sentence, the eight-word "It's always been one of my favorite styles," is double the number of words in the aforementioned second sentence.

THREES

*The object for which Banacek is looking is a (three word) "Experimental Safety Vehicle." Banacek says he saw three junkyards during the helicopter trip where he was retracing the route of the missing ESV (ESV is the abbreviation for Experimental Safety Vehicle.)

*The three-syllable Thaddenhurst mispronounces Banacek's three-syllable last name as "Banasek" three times.

*Banacek's (three-syllable) great uncle Enescu was an engineer on the (three-word) 20th Century Limited. He is mentioned three times in (the three-named) E.D. Lerner's book, *Great Trains and Trainmen*.

*The three-syllable Ruderman tells Banacek that originally his three-word company (Ruderman and Wexler) could have gone to such real companies as (one) GM, (two) American, and (three) Chrysler.

*Wexler lists three things (engineering, design, performance) when he tells Banacek that he and Ruderman had their competition beat in every area. He can think of three people whom Horizon tried to lure away from R&W in the past ten months.

*Obtaining copies of all the small-town newspapers located along the eighty miles of track between Middlefield and Boston, Felix has found only three stories from them which reported unusual events the night of the Phoenix's disappearance. They are, in order, and as quoted by Felix (excluding the information given in parentheses):

One: "(A three-letter) Dog poisoned by irate neighbor."

Two: "Itinerant, victim of (the three-word violation/crime) hit-and-run."

Three: "Three juveniles arrested for possession of marijuana."

*Felix has three new locks installed on his door

*Andy Cole, whose last name begins with the third letter of the alphabet, has a "long history" of three things: One: Corporate buccaneering; Two:

Stock manipulation; Three: Personnel raids. *The "3-H" club refers to three types of people: One: Hippies; Two: Hoboes; Three: Hopheads.

*Collier, whose last name begins with the third letter of the alphabet, tells the woman at the Laundromat, that he has three signs posted on the walls.

*Because he has (the three-word condition of) low blood sugar, Jay Drury needs three cups of coffee a day, with three teaspoons of sugar in each cup.

*To find the Phoenix, Concord Motors gives Ruderman and Wexler thirty additional days. Wexler says it might as well be thirty years.

*On the Route 27/126 road sign, each route will take the driver to three separate places. Route 27 leads to Sudbury, Maynard, and Acton; Route 126 leads to Lincoln, Rte. 2, and Concord.

FOURS

*The (four letter/number) A-20-G was born at Horizon Engineering four years ago.

*Jay asks Banacek how his helicopter trip went; the sleuth tells him he saw four things: One: A lot of railroad tracks; Two: Three junkyards; Three: A hobo jungle; Four: A polluted lake. Each of the four places Banacek describes has a word which is either four letters: hobo, lake, or is a combination of two four-letter words: "rail" and "road"; "junk" and "yard." "Yards" is of course the plural of "yard." By pluralizing "yard," George Eckstein and his story editor Paul Playdon disguise from the audience the four-by-four match they have just presented to them.

*When the flatcar is being dredged up from the lake, there are four people watching the retrieval: Banacek, Jay, Thaddenhurst, and Falvo. During this sequence, Thaddenhurst says to Falvo, "He (meaning Banacek) said he'd help me if I'd help him." The last four words are alliterative: two "I" words: "if I'd" followed by two "H" words: "help him." Note that the first "help" is the fourth word in Thaddenhurst's line. Note too that when we count four from this "help," we arrive at the second "help."

FIVES:

*The five-letter character Falvo speaks two sentences: "I know that, Mr. Wexler. I know," in an exchange with Wexler following the Phoenix's disappearance. The first sentence is a total of five words. It is followed by the two-word second sentence, "I know." Total number of letters in the second line is five. By repeating this five-letter "I know," Eckstein and company are giving their audience a clue as to what number they are matching in these two sentences.

*It is also during this sequence when Wexler delivers his own "five" when he says to Falvo: "Funny? You think this is funny?" The five-letter word "Funny" precedes the five-word question, "You think this is funny? Once again, through the repetition of a word/words, Eckstein and associates drop another clue to the audience as to what number match they are doing.

*A more obvious clue comes with Thaddenhurst's line, "Forty. Forty-five all the way." Here the number "five" follows two-five letter "Forty's."

SIXES

*(The six-letter) Paddle tells Banacek that Denver Sam (six letters in Denver) came from (the six-letter state of) Oregon, and always traveled with (the six-letter) Whitey.

*Before boarding the helicopter, Banacek tells Thaddenhurst "You did my investigating for me." "Me," which refers to Banacek, whose first name is (the six-letter) Thomas, is the sixth word in the line.

SEVENS:

*The two cars in this story: the Phoenix, and the A-20-G are both "sevens." Phoenix is seven letters; G is the seventh letter of the alphabet.

*To get to Rensler (seven letters in the last name Rensler) Tool and Die, Banacek and Jay make a left through Sudbury (seven letters). Rensler Tool and Die went bankrupt seven years ago.

*About seven miles east of the jungle, Whitey and Denver Sam hear something unusual.

*Falvo drives seventy miles to the spot where Thaddenhurst (and Banacek) expect to find the seven-letter Phoenix.

*At one point, Andy Cole declares to Banacek, "It'll corner even better than the G." G is the seventh character/word in this sentence.

*Falvo says to Thaddenhurst, "Look, I know how you feel about Banacek." Preceding the seven-letter name Banacek are seven words.

THIRTEENS

*The train carrying the Phoenix is to make its first stop at Boston (six letters). Its second stop will be Detroit (seven letters).

*The thirteen-letter Concord Motors is the company interested in the Phoenix.

*Banacek tells Felix he'll get him a couple matches at (the thirteen-letter, two-word) Boston Gardens.

*The (six-letter) boxcar is attached to the (seven-letter) flatcar.

FIFTEENS

*The fifteen-letter Douglas Ruderman tells Banacek that Concord Motors was offering $15 million for the rights to the best designed safety car. (Note the sign on Ruderman's office door which is shown moments before Ruderman gives Banacek the above piece of information.)

*Sometime back, Banacek recovered stolen Rembrandts for the (fifteen-letter) Cleveland Museum. The fifteen-letter Joe Thaddenhurst was also working on that case.

Alliteration:
B: Banasek. Banacek!; been brewing; blueprint business; body buried; be bought
C: Choo-choo
D: doesn't do
E: ESVs? Experimental; Easy. Easy; engineer? Electrical; Enterprising enough

F: Forget. Funny; Forty. Forty-five
G: getting good; Gonna give
H: hate him; he'd help; hitchhike; Hoboes, Hippies; hophead
I: insurance investigator; isn't it
L: line like; little luxury
M: machines, man; make me; miss my; more money
N: Nope. Nothing; Not necessarily
O: okay, okay; Out of
P: phony pitch; pizza parlor; police, photographers; pores. Pathetic; Project Phoenix
R: railroad; record results; ruined Ruderman
S: saw something; seems sort; since she; single sighting; so scared; Southern Serves; STAR SOAP; steal some; stepson; still smell
T: talked to the three; that thing; That's that; to trot; truck. Trucks
W: Where's what?; Which way?; while Whitey; woman working; would, wouldn't

Double alliteration

I&H: if I'd help him
L&S: Looks like some sort
L&I: Look lady, it is
M&A: me more about Andy
P&T: phony pitch this time
W&M: We wanted money, man
W&S: Why was she stopped

Matches to previous episodes:

*In the previous episode, the last two words of the title are alliterative: "Living Legend." In this episode, the first two words (and the only words) of the title are alliterative: "Project Phoenix."

*In Let's Hear it For a Living Legend," the top billing went to an actress, whose last name began with a P; the name contained a total of six letters: "Powers," as in Stefanie Powers. In this episode, the top billing goes to an actress whose last name begins with a P; it contains a total of six letters: "Pettet," as in Joanna Pettet.

*After telling Banacek he hasn't talked to Christine Verdon in two years, Andy Cole tells the sleuth he can either believe that, or "punt." "Punt" is of course a football term, and the first Banacek episode, "Let's Hear it For a Living Legend," dealt with football.

*About a year ago, Banacek and Thaddenhurst tangled while both were working to retrieve stolen Rembrandts for the Cleveland museum. In the previous episode, football player Hank Ives lost his deceased father's dog tags a day after the Cleveland game.

* In the pilot film, *Brinks Bandits* is one of the books Felix suggests to Banacek when the two are discussing the armored truck disappearance which Banacek is investigating. In the premiere episode, "Let's Hear it For a Living Legend," Banacek is working for Jerry Brinkman. In this episode, already suspected of stealing the Phoenix, Christine Verdon jokes to Banacek that when she was accused of that, she then expected to be accused of being one of the famous Brinks robbers.

*In the pilot film, Jay asks Banacek why he saves his cigar stubs. "They're expensive," the sleuth replies. In this episode, Banacek says exactly the same words when Thaddenhurst asks him exactly the same question.

*In the pilot, McKinney objects to Cavanaugh's agreement to let Banacek tackle the armored car disappearance. "The man's no Superman," McKinney tells his boss. In this episode, Joe Thaddenhurst paraphrases part of the famous catchphrase from the *Superman* TV series ("Is it a bird? Is it a plane? No, it's Superman") as a means of insulting Banacek; he changes "man" to "Pole."

*In this episode, as previously noted, Banacek and his rival Joe Thaddenhurst have a "fifteen" in common: the Cleveland Museum; in the previous episode, "Let's Hear It For a Living Legend," the sleuth and Jerry Brinkman exchange a "fifteen": Banacek tells Brinkman he'll arrive at the Brinkman Building in fifteen minutes; a short time later, Brinkman tells Banacek he's fifteen minutes late for a trucking merger.

Future Matches:

*Guest star Joanna Pettet.

*Thaddenhurst's Superman reference.

*Thaddenhurst's mispronunciation of Banacek as "Banasek."

*The last name "Collier."

*Jay's three cups of coffee.

*Freight cars.

*Banacek's description of engineer Christine Verdon as "electrical."

*Actor Seamon Glass

*The fictional company Concord Motors

SECTION TWO

Behind the scenes:

Executive producer George Eckstein on co-stars Murray Matheson and Ralph Manza:

"They were both good. Felix was an elegant character, and Manza ... it was somebody for George to play off of, sort of take away the extreme polish and bring somebody in who wasn't polished, and to serve as contrast."[2]

Behind the scenes: "The Phoenix":

The Experimental Safety Vehicle in this story, "The Phoenix," was actually a 1969 AMX that George Barris customized for the show. The car was lowered and its body heavily modified. The roof was chopped almost five inches and the car was lengthened by eighteen inches (460 mm). The AMX name came from the "**A**merican **M**otors e**X**perimental" code used on a concept vehicle and then two prototypes shown during the company's "Project IV" automobile show tour in 1966. One was a fiberglass two-seat "AMX," and the other a four-seat "AMX II." Thus, the episode title, "Project Phoenix" may have been inspired by the real life "Project IV."

BANACEK extra: Comments from real life insurance and property claims men regarding *Banacek*:

Early in the series' run, the *Los Angeles Times* interviewed real insurance investigators concerning the accuracy and realism of *Banacek*. Below are these men's comments:

Chris Wilson: New York Claims Surveyor for Lloyds of London: "We get quite a laugh out of it." Describing such *Banacek* episodes as "Let's Hear it For a Living Legend," and "Project Phoenix" as "far-fetched," Wilson added that the life of a real insurance investigator is "sort of humdrum. You don't meet a beautiful woman at every door." Wilson later pointed out that most claims investigations were pretty routine; they hardly required the sleuthing abilities of someone like Banacek.

George Cretney: Second vice-president in charge of property claims at Hartford's Traveler's Insurance Company: Found the series concept unbelievable. "We have several thousand claims men on our staff. We do not hire freelance people, nor do we encourage or deal with people who are freelancers."

Carl Maser: Claims supervisor at Fireman's Fund American: "This fellow's a special investigator, really. I doubt whether any claims manager has ever had cases similar to his."[3]

Trivia:

*This episode was mentioned by George Peppard in his interview with the *Los Angeles Times'* Cecil Smith.

*A "top-of-the-line" Atlas O F-9 set is the train set Banacek uses in reconstructing the theft of the experimental car and flat-car.

*At the end of this episode, George, who had done a great Jimmy Stewart impersonation in *How the West Was Won*, does a fine imitation of W.C. Fields, complete with cigar.

Inside jokes and references:

*When Banacek tells Felix "Read the whole library, my son . . . ." and concludes with "That's an old Polish proverb," Felix replies, "Well, maybe it just takes an old Pole to understand it."

*After Banacek pays his first visit to Christine Verdon, Jay asks him, "How was the lady engineer?" "Electrical, but not civil," Banacek replies. As noted earlier, when George went to college, he studied civil engineering.

*At Felix's bookshop, Banacek is heard talking to someone named Monique. Monique James was George's agent at Universal Studios.

*On *Batman*, Stafford Repp played the role of Gotham City Police Chief O'Hara. In *Banacek* "Project Phoenix," Repp is cast as the town police chief! His character also works as a filling station attendant.

Notes:

In his first *Banacek*, director Richard T. Heffron foreshadows who will hire the sleuth by having the character Falvo walk past a total of seven oil cans in the opening shot. (At the same time, through this shot, Heffron plays off the number of letters in his own first and last name). The seven by seven Richard Heffron being a perfect "match name," this episode therefore gives us some memorable "match" scenes: among them: the three by three by three featuring Falvo, Ruderman, and Wexler, the visit to the hippie/hobo jungle by Banacek and Jay, and the four gunshots to four characters scene preceding Banacek's reconstruction of the crime.

Later, in the Laundromat sequence, Eckstein, Heffron, George, et al drop two clues as to how they are playing tricks on the audience through the dialogue. The first is Bruce Kirby's annoyed and irritated Laundromat owner Collier telling the woman customer he has three signs, "and they're written in English, and they're hidden from view." The second: Banacek's telling Collier "things aren't always what they seem."

The number four having been of great importance in the previous episode, this episode builds on that with a number of fours, among them: four people (including Banacek) in the freight yard fight sequence, four people (including Banacek) at the retrieval of the flatcar scene, and four people (excluding Banacek) in the sleuth's front hallway at the conclusion of the story. The episode also opens with a first line, which contains a number of fours.

George Eckstein and his associates often doing their matches through series continuity, like the previous episode, "Let's Hear it For a Living Legend," this story has a thirteen-letter actor repeating the first word he speaks. In the previous show, this was the thirteen-letter George Peppard speaking the nine-letter word, "Beautiful"; in this episode, it's the thirteen-letter William Windom repeating the four-letter word, "Easy." Note that when nine and four are added together, the result is thirteen.

Note also that the alliteratively named-actor William Windom is the first person heard in this alliteratively titled episode, "Project Phoenix." William Windom's character, Harry Wexler will also connect "Project Phoenix" to the next episode: "No Sign of the Cross."

George Eckstein's earlier statement that the writing in *Banacek* was based on George Peppard and his character is also vividly demonstrated in this episode. For example, the seven-letter "Phoenix," which was being transported from Middlefield to Boston on a seven-letter flatcar, is the object which the seven-letter Banacek hopes to retrieve. Accompanying the Phoenix on its journey was a total of seven special guards. As for thirteens, the seven-letter flatcar was positioned between two six-letter boxcars, and, the company that expresses strong interest in purchasing the Phoenix is the thirteen-letter Concord Motors. Joanna Pettet's Christine Verdon is the first in a long line of non-insurance company, successful, highly intelligent women with whom Banacek becomes romantically involved. As can best be determined, this episode mentions no historical or cultural person, place or thing which can be connected to anyone or anything in Polish history or culture.

Reviews and Publicity:

October 7, 1972: In "The Doan Report," *TV Guide* – Vol. 20, No. 41, , Issue #519, it is revealed that *Banacek* has placed Number 20 in the ratings; in the same issue's "TV Crossword," 1 Down is "Warsaw citizen"; Bert Convy's guest shot on *Banacek* is mentioned in Joseph Finnigan's "TV Teletype: Hollywood."

BANACEK Challenges: "Project Phoenix"

#1. This episode features a very clever double reference to the father of the modern detective story. Can you identify it?

#2. Including both the opening and closing guest casts, there are six matches that can be drawn from the top-billed name, Joanna Pettet. Can you find all six?

#3. Can you find the twos, threes, and fours in the following line spoken by the special guard: "Hey, Lieutenant. Lieutenant Keenan. It's gone, Lieutenant. The whole damn flatcar."

#4. Can you find the fours and fives in the below line spoken by Harry Wexler: "Easy. Easy on that fender. Take your time, Fred. They're gonna wait for you. Don't worry about it."

#5. At one point Banacek says to Christine Verdon, "Of course. Early American drill press. It's always been one of my favorite styles." Thanks to the way this line is written, a certain number is present in all three sentences. Can you identify it?

#6. In this episode we hear Joanna Pettet's Christine Verdon saying to Banacek: "Oh, that's right. That's what you do, isn't it?" Later in the series, we will hear this same dialogue from Banacek to another character. In what episode is this dialogue repeated and to whom?

#7. What are the three reasons this performer's character is the recipient of this dialogue?

Episode #3: "No Sign of the Cross," October 11, 1972

Banacek: "Twelve good horses and silver candlesticks won't stop the snow falling in Bialystock. It's an old Polish saying."
Alicia: "Is there an old Polish translation?"
Banacek: Well, I think it means there are some things money can't buy."

Teleplay by Robert Presnell, Jr.
Story by Howard Browne and Presnell
D: Daryl Duke
Guest Stars

Broderick Crawford	Gilbert De Retzo
Louise Sorel	Alisa Donato
Gordon Pinsent	John Weymouth
Jack MacGowran	Michel Lanier

Special Guest Star

Victor Jory	Paul Andros

Co-starring

Ned Romero	Chief Mendoza
Ahna Capri	Mme Pompadour

And
Peter Donat as Robert Morgan

Kermit Murdock	Archbishop
Peter Brocco	Cardinal

And

Annette Cardona	Cecelia Gomez

With

Alan Fudge	Father Cass
Ruben Moreno	Colonel Perez
Julio Medina	Padre Borda
Alfonso Tafoya	Anselmo Gomez
Francisco Ortega	Padre Guillermo

Pedro Regas   Old Mexican
Adele Yoshioka   Receptionist
Erica Hagen   Bikini Girl
Paul Gleason   Border Guard

Exteriors/Filming Locations: Exterior of Church in Boston; LAX – Los Angeles International Airport

SECTION ONE: MATCHES
Matches in series credits:
Opening credits:

The title is presented in this fashion:

NO SIGN
OF THE CROSS

Because of this presentation, there are two NO words (one reading horizontally and one vertically), as well as two OF words (again, one reading horizontally and one vertically

If we take the episode title and match only letters, we find just three: N, O, and S. This is the third-aired episode.

Opening and closing guest credits:
*There are three performers: Broderick Crawford, Ahna Capri, and Annette Cardona whose last name begins with a C. In each case, the performer's character name is a three of some kind. Crawford's three is a three-part name: Gilbert De Retzo; Capri's character is a double three: the character's first name is the three-letter Mme (standing for Madame); her last name, Pompadour, is three syllables. Annette Cardona's character name is also a double three. The character's first name Cecelia, begins with a C: the third letter of the alphabet; the name Cecelia contains three syllables.

*Supporting guest Peter Donat's role as Robert Morgan also allows for matches. The actor's first and last names contain the same number of letters

(five) his character's first and last names also contain the same number of letters (six). Last-billed Erica Hagen and Paul Gleason also create a match; the first name of the actress' character begins with a B; ditto the actor's; the last name of Hagen's character begins with a G; ditto Gleason's.

Matches through physical production and editing:
　*There are two sequences featuring the two-named Bikini Girl.

　*During the sequence where Alisa drives Banacek to her grandfather's home in Mexico, we see (in the background) two identical yellow cars with black hardtops going in opposite directions; when the two visually intersect, we also see two parallel arrows on a road in the background. The arrows are both pointing up.

　*The process of transferring the cross from Gilbert de Retzo to the archdiocese in Los Angeles requires a nighttime rendezvous between two pairs of men: Mexico's Padre Borda and Colonel Perez with the United States' Father Cass (from Los Angeles) and a U.S. Marshal. During the rendezvous, we are treated to such twos as: two flashlights, two separate hands holding things, two nods of one man's head; one nod is directed to the Mexicans, the other to the U.S. figures, the sight, and/or sound of a car's driver and passenger side doors opening and closing, etc.

　*About three minutes into the teaser, director Daryl Duke gives us an alignment of three: Padre Borda, Colonel Perez, and the border guard.

　*At Andros' fitness club, Banacek, Andros, and the attendant are twice reflected in the mirror at their left, in other words, there are "three" shots of each of these three men.

　*In the four words painted on the police headquarters in the small town of Live Oak: LIVE OAK POLICE DEPT., we can find twos, threes, and fours. OAK, the second word begins with an O; O is the second letter in the following word, POLICE. This third word POLICE begins with a P; P is the third letter in the next word, DEPT. There are four letters in this fourth word.

　*In this episode's opening sequence, we are shown first one, then two, then three cars. The third car is a police car. On it are three words: EJER-

CITO NACIONAL MEXICANO. Each of these words contains exactly the same number of letters: eight.

*In the teaser, we are introduced to the characters Colonel Perez and Padre Borda. There are five letters in the latter's first name, five letters in the last. To the right of the five-by-five Padre Borda is a candelabra containing a total of five lit candles.

*Walking through the terminal at LAX, Banacek and Jay pass a sign that says ARROW TOURS. Later, at the Gomez home, Banacek sees the tombstone of Alfonso's deceased wife, Maria. In addition to the five-letter by five-letter name, Maria Gomez, the year of death: 51, is the reverse of the year of birth: 15.

*The show also plays off the five-letter cross through groupings of people. For example, there are a total of five men of the cloth: the Cardinal, the Archbishop, Padre Borda, Padre Guillermo, and Father Cass; later, when the Gomez's travel to Mexico to visit the Virgin of (the five-letter) Avila, we see five women praying at the shrine; then, at episode's end, five people (Banacek, Alisa Donato, Michel Lanier, the Archbishop, and Father Cass) are present when the recovered cross is verified as The Cross of Bayonne.

*At the athletic club, we see Paul Andros lifting fifteen pound weights.

Matching through numbers:
TWOS:
 *Two former 1930s gangsters both connected to the title object
 *Two Padres
 *Two members of the family Gomez: Anselmo and Cecelia.
 *Banacek mentions two of DeRetzo's best "salesmen" (killers), both of these "salesmen" have three-part names
 *Banacek's second wonder
 *Two fives on the same tombstone

THREES:
 *In the teaser, DeRetzo does three things with the cross: one: he wraps it

up in red velvet, two: he puts the red velvet covered cross in a gold bag, three: he puts the gold bag in a briefcase.

*Following this, Weymouth does three things with the briefcase: one: he locks it; two: he seals the briefcase, three: he handcuffs the briefcase to Padre Borda.

*Gilbert De Retzo has a three-part name.

*DeRetzo mispronounces Banacek's name as Bananacek: there are three "a's" in the three syllable word, Banana.

*Paul Andros talks to Banacek about his three pleasures. The first is smoking; he gave that up about three years ago. Second: about the same time, the pleasure of sex (three letters in the word) gave him up. This left only a third pleasure for Andros: food, which he enjoys to this day.

*During the course of the show, we learn of three historical event parties thrown by art collector Robert Morgan. One was a victory celebration for Julius Caesar, another was a Garden of Eden party; the third, at which Banacek is present, is the day before the French Revolution.

*After Banacek and Jay pass a farm, the sleuth speaks three words, "Nice little farm." Jay replies he'd much rather see a "nice little restaurant." A little bit later, Jay repeats the three words "nice little restaurant," after telling his boss what they'll find in the "California whistle-stop" town of Live Oak: "(one): a vegetable stand, (two): a gas station, and (three) no nice little restaurant."

FOURS:

*When Father Cass discovers the Bayonne Cross has been snatched from under his nose, he exclaims, "Dear God in Heaven. It is not possible." As we can see, there are four words in the Father's first sentence, four words in the second. Why? His last name, Cass, is a total of four letters.

FIVES:

*The title of the episode is five words. The object for which Banacek is searching (cross) is five letters.

*During the early thirties, Gilbert DeRetzo was one of the five most dangerous gangsters in Chicago

*Cecelia Gomez, whose last name is five letters, suffers from the five-letter disease of polio.

*When Banacek and Weymouth are discussing who might have taken the cross, the sleuth lists five people: Lanier, Morgan, De Retzo, Andros, whomever.

*During the course of the story, Banacek mentions a certain make of car: Rolls Royce. In addition to being alliterative, each word of this two-word automobile make contains a total of five letters.

A THREE, FOUR & FIVE in a SEVEN:

During Banacek's reconstruction of the crime for Weymouth, he repeats the words "here" and "here's" as shown below in the following **seven** sentences:

"Here, I'll show you.

"Now, here's De Retzo's house.

"Here's the road.

"Here's the archdiocese.

"Here's the border.

"Here's the rendezvous point.

"And here we are."

As we can see, the five-letter word, "here's" is spoken a total of five times, there are four four-word sentences, and three three-word sentences. Note that the third sentence, "Here's the road" is the first of the three three-word sentences.

SEVENS:

*There are seven letters in the word, "Mexican." This episode features a total of seven (speaking-part), Mexican characters. They are, in order of appearance: one: Padre Borda, two: Colonel Perez, three: Chief Mendoza, four:

Anselmo Gomez, five: Cecelia Gomez, six: Padre Guillermo, seven: Enrique Rojas (in the credits, Old Mexican)

*Frank Mendoza is the police chief in the seven-letter town of Live Oak.

*The last name of the seven-letter Anselmo and the seven-letter Cecelia begins with G-the seventh letter of the alphabet.

*In director Daryl Duke's aerial view of the walk-and-talk sequence between Banacek and Weymouth, the two-word, seven-letter "Could be" is spoken a total of five times. When Banacek speaks the last "Could be," it is seven sentences after his first "Could be."

Alliteration:
A: Andros! Andros!; anything about
B: Banacek. Banacek?; Banacek but; Bananacek. Banacek.; bikinis by; Boston. Better be
C: California coast; call came; can't confess; Casualty company; Cecelia; collector's collector; commission. Congratulations
D: Digging. Digging?; double dealings
F: fast freight; finder's fee; foot fence
G: Generation gap
H: have him; haven't heard; her husband; how high
L: late last; like Lancelot looking; little less; lot less; lousy life
M: me Mr.; me much; Morgan makes; Mr. Michele; more materialistic; murders more
N: not necessarily
O: other offer; other's only
P: perfect place; private place
R: really remarkably; Rolls Royce; Roman ruins; romantic restaurant
S: seen something; servants said; Sparta, Spanish; special seal; special shrine
T: that the thieves; That's that; to talk to this; to their touching; these things; trying to tell
U: upon us

W: Well, we wouldn't want; what were we; Who wasn't? Who wasn't?; Willya, willya?; wondering why; woodworker; would we?
Y: You. Yeah

Double Alliteration:
A&T: after all this time
H&F: Hated him for forty
H&M: He hates me more
L&A: Look like an attempted
P&A: Probably pull an atheist
T&I: the time it is
W&B: we will be back
W&H: want what he has
W&T: was willing to top

Matches to previous episodes:

*In "Let's Hear it For a Living Legend," Banacek makes a reference to Thomas Jefferson at the end of the story. In this episode, Banacek is seen standing near a copy of the Jeffersonian-written document, "The Declaration of Independence."

*In "Legend," Jerry Brinkman repeats the two words "could be" in one line after another. In this episode, Banacek repeats the words, "Could be" in one line after another.

*In the previous episode, "Project Phoenix," the story dealt with freight cars. In this episode, Banacek talks about a man being killed under a "fast freight."

*Towards the end of his reconstruction of the crime in "Project Phoenix," Banacek says the line, "And that's that." Towards the end of this story, he speaks the same three words.

Future Matches:

*The term "woodworker"

*A String quartet playing

*The first name Gordon

*Director Daryl Duke's walk-and-talk sequence

*The three-part named gangsters Gilbert De Retzo and Paulie "The Nail" Anderson

*The saying on the cross of Maria Gomez: "Duarme en los Brazos de Jesus"

*Alisa's final words to Banacek (and the final words in the episode): "Welcome to Los Angeles, Mr. Banacek."

*Art collector Robert Morgan's comment about "inquisitional tortures."

*Banacek's walk through the Gomez's cemetery.

*The road sign indicating that there are three miles to the town of Live Oak.

SECTION TWO

Behind the scenes:

Executive producer George Eckstein:

"Daryl (Duke) was wonderful. I worked with Daryl subsequently on various projects (including the miniseries, *Masada*). I enjoyed the experience a great deal. With Broderick Crawford, you always had to write additional material, cuz he spoke so fast you ran out of . . . a scene that you hoped would run two and a half minutes ran a minute and a half, and so you always had to pad. I don't remember any specific problem (Crawford's drinking) but I'm sure he was. It would be very surprising if he wasn't."[4]

Guest commentary on guest star Broderick Crawford:

Actor Michael Forest, (who appeared on Crawford's 1950s series, *Highway Patrol*): "Brod Crawford! Oh, my God! There was a guy who could drink like crazy. Yet he could deliver lines like a machine gun. He could rattle off lines. Never forget—never forget. I don't know if he had a photographic memory, but the lines would come out of him like a machine gun; never heard anybody who could speak lines that fast and with that clarity. He was ... course,.he was this big tough-looking guy with a bent-in face. But he was a very good actor. I talked to people who knew him when he was younger; they saw him do *Romeo (and Juliet)*. Can you imagine Brod Crawford doing Romeo? They said he was wonderful; he just was very sensitive and rough when he had to be and they said he was wonderful. I thought, *My God. That's not a Brod Crawford that I know.*"[5]

Guest star Broderick Crawford with George Peppard in the Universal/NBC *Banacek* "No Sign of the Cross."

Writer/Producer/Director/Actor/Composer Andrew J. Fenady (discussing his hiring of Crawford for his 1976 TV-movie, *Mayday at 40,000 Feet*): "Broderick Crawford! I loved Brod Crawford. We had done three or four pictures together. He was always perfect. I get on the phone with Brod, and he says, (imitating Crawford), 'Yeah. Whattaya want? Whattaya want, Andy?' I said, 'Brod, I need you to be in Salt Lake City. Get down to the airport within the next hour.' He says, 'What'm I doing? What'm I doing?' I said, 'You're doing an air marshal.' He says, 'What about the wardrobe? Whattaya want me to bring?' I said, 'Well, bring an overcoat and suit.' He says, 'Anything else? Anything else?' 'No, no, that's all.' 'Okay, okay.' So I call his agent, make a deal. He gets to the airport just in time, and he lands in Salt Lake City, and he's got a whole suitcase he's carrying with him. I thought, 'Jesus Christ, he's bringing his Scotch.' And Salt Lake City is supposed to be dry. I said, 'Whattaya got in there, Brod?' He says, 'Well, I got some udder coats in case you want 'em and all that.' I mean he was that kind of a guy. More wardrobe. I said, 'What you got on is fine.' So we're shooting . . . we're there all that time in Salt Lake City, and he's great. Perfect. I mean he's innovative, he's wonderful. Ah, he was great, He was wonderful. He had a brilliant mind. He could look at the page of the script, look at it once, 'All right, let's go.' Photographic memory."[6]

The Polish connection:

#1: This episode has Banacek hunting for the Bayonne Cross. In the 1900s, in Bayonne, New Jersey, Our Lady of Mount Carmel Parish was founded to serve the ministerial needs of the enormous Polish immigration to America that was taking place during that time. Always maintaining a strong Polish element, in 2008, the Bayonne parish registered an 85% Polish presence.

#2: When Banacek finds the wheelchair-bound Cecelia and her father Anselmo, they are at the Virgin of Avila: a special shrine where people visit to pray at the statue of the Virgin Mary. In Poland, the Virgin Mary is viewed as the "Queen of Poland." The Black Madonna of Czestochowa (a painting of the Virgin Mary and Christ child, attributed to St. Luke the Evangelist) is one of Poland's holiest relics; it is also one of the country's national symbols.

In 1382, this painting was discovered at the recently founded Jasna Gora (Mountain of Light) monastery in Czestochowa. Czestochowa is about 140 miles south of Warsaw. In 1655, Sweden invaded Poland. For forty days, as the Swedes surrounded the monastery, the monks of Czestochowa prayed to the "Black Madonna" in the hopes of deliverance. Their prayers were answered. The siege failed, and the Poles succeeded in driving the Swedes out of Poland. In gratitude, Jan Kazimierz, the reigning monarch at the time, dedicated his throne, and the country of Poland to "the Virgin Mary, Queen of Poland." More than a half century later in 1711, the citizens of Warsaw went to Czestochowa to thank the Virgin for saving them from the bubonic plague. Since this time, the pilgrimage to Czestochowa has been a yearly rite for the Polish people.

#3: In the office of Chief Mendoza, we see a framed copy of the Declaration of Independence. During the conversation between Banacek and Mendoza, Banacek stands to the right of the Declaration. As previously noted in the discussion of "Let's Hear it For a Living Legend," the Declaration of Independence contained everything in which American Revolutionary War Polish hero Tadeusz Kosciuszko firmly believed.

#4: During the course of this story, Banacek attends a costume party at the home of eccentric art collector Robert Morgan. Morgan is dressed as France's King Louis XVI. Louis XVI's maternal grandfather, Frederick Augustus II of Saxony, also held the title, King of Poland.

Inside jokes and references:

*When Banacek accompanies Andros to the steam rooms, he says, "These places always remind me of *The Untouchables*." George Eckstein wrote quite a few episodes of *The Untouchables*.

Notes:

As made clear by guest commentators Michael Forest and Andrew J. Fenady, Broderick Crawford's colorful portrayal of former 1930s gangster Gilbert De Retzo is simply a case of Broderick Crawford being Broderick Crawford . . . at least when it comes to the manner in which the actor delivers his dialogue. Crawford's rapid-fire delivery, his habit of repeating himself when speaking makes him the perfect guest for a series where there is such a heavy emphasis not only on the repetition of words, lines, etc. but on the necessity of keeping said repetition from making too much of an impression on the audience. The drawback to the casting of such a performer as Crawford? Since the actor's style required more writing than usual from George Eckstein and his story editor Paul Playdon, the two didn't have as much time to insert the typical *Banacek* touches; thus, this episode does not reference past bits of business, etc. to the same degree as did the two preceding shows.

Despite this extra writing time, Eckstein and his associates obviously liked the idea of a character speaking rapidly; they presented such a character the second season. Also proving an inspiration for the second year was Daryl Duke's "aerial" walk-and-talk sequence featuring Banacek and John Weymouth. This sequence features a great deal of matching. Yet because of the way Duke stages and shoots this "walk-and-talk," the matching is difficult to spot. When *Banacek*'s second-season assistant director ,George Peppard, was to direct his own "walk-and-talk" sequence, he would more than top Duke. Duke's previously mentioned playing off of this episode's title object opened another potential creative door for Eckstein and company to explore as the series continued.

Reviews and Publicity:

October 14, 1972: *TV Guide* – Vol 20, No. 42 –, Issue#520 – "TV Crossword" – 1 Down – Answer: Pole.

October 21, 1972 : *TV Guide* – Vol. 20, No. 43 –, Issue#521 – "Letters" – reader Rosemary Byrd from Gary, Indiana asks "Where was George Peppard's mother when he was born into the world "alone?"

BANACEK Challenges: "No Sign of the Cross"

#1. In the opening credits, the names of guest stars Broderick Crawford, Louise Sorel, and Jack MacGowran all display the same characteristic. Can you identify it?

#2. In the first sequence featuring Banacek (the sequence where the sleuth arrives at the Boston church to talk to the cardinal), director Daryl Duke plays off the title object by giving the audience a total of five hard-to-detect "crosses" within seconds. Can you spot all five?

#3. Can you find the "three" in the character played by Victor Jory?

#4. Why is the "Old Mexican" named Enrique Rojas?

#5. At the Gomez home, in the graveyard, Banacek digs the ground with a shovel seven times. Why?

#6. Early on in the show, Banacek and DeRetzo have the following conversation:

> *De Retzo:* You see, he hates me. He hates me more than anybody hates anything else in the world. Except the way I hate him. I've hated him for forty years. Listen, I got enough hate left for forty more.
>
> *Banacek*: That's a lot of hate.

In addition to their both using the word "hate," Banacek and De Retzo both match in a second way as a result of this word. What is this second match?

#7. Why was the nail Paul Andros used to carry a total of eight inches long?

Episode #4: "A Million the Hard Way," November 1, 1972

W: Stanley Ralph Ross
D: Bernard Kowalski

Guest Stars
Margot Kidder	Linda Carsini
Don Porter	Arnold Leland

Co-starring
Don Keefer	Alex Loomis
J. Duke Russo (Barry Russo	Lester Sawyer

With
Claire Brennen	Betty Janus
William Bryant	Burns
Angela Greene	Marcia
Dolores Quinton	Edna Beach
Harvey Fisher	Andrews
Russ Marin	Flanders
Kathleen King	1st Girl
Inga Neilsen	2nd Girl
Stanley Ralph Ross	Larry Fields
Mark Harris	Chauffeur
Mary Ann Gibson	Florence

Unbilled
Judson Pratt	Jack Moses

SECTION ONE: MATCHES

Matches in series credits:
Opening credits:
*This is the fourth-aired episode; the fourth word in the episode title. "A Million the Hard Way" is the four-letter word, "Hard."

*There are the same number of letters: six, in the first name of the top-billed guest star Margot Kidder, as there are in her last.

Opening and closing credits:

*There are two guest actors (Margot Kidder and Don Porter) billed in the opening credits; there are two guest actors (Don Keefer and J. Duke Russo) billed in the co-starring credits.

*The first two guests in the "With" credits (Claire Brennen and William Bryant) have last names that begin with "B"

*The last two guests in the "With" credits (Mark Harris and Mary Ann Gibson) have first names that begin with "M"

*There are two Don's in the guest credits (Don Porter and Don Keefer). Both Don's have six-letter last names.

*Both Don Porter and Don Keefer play characters whose first names begin with "A"; both of these characters' last names begin with "L."

*There are two alliteratively named performers: Kathleen King, and Stanley Ralph Ross in the "with" credits. (The latter's middle and last names are alliterative.)

Matches through physical production and editing:

*There are two kaleidoscope shots of Las Vegas (they are the first and second shot in the episode). The first kaleidoscope shot is the "Welcome to Las Vegas" sign; the second: a nighttime view of the Las Vegas strip; two sets of women's legs (a waitress and a customer) follow the two kaleidoscope shots of Las Vegas.

*Betty Janus (who has the same number of letters in her first name and her last) is among the people standing near the slot machine, "Big Betty."

*There are two sets of couples who are photographed by Linda Carsini at the million-dollar exhibit: there are two $ signs at the million dollar exhibit.

*When Banacek's plane arrives in Las Vegas, two female crew members (the stewardesses) come down the steps; when Banacek's plane leaves Las Vegas, two male crew members (the pilot and the co-pilot) board the plane.

*The third shot in the episode presents three pairs of legs: two are women's: both of the women are walking; the third pair is a man's: the man is sitting.

*The three-syllable Banacek is the third passenger off the plane.

*When Banacek enters the barbershop in Jonathan Jackson's casino, the audience sees three photos of card decks on the wall. In the barbershop, there are three employees: two barbers, and one manicurist. Banacek's entering the barbershop makes him the third person in the shop who is not an employee of that shop: in addition to casino guard Jack Moses, there is another man getting his hair cut.

*On the Blackjack table, while there are clearly more than four players being dealt cards at the table, the camera shows us only four piles of cards; on the Blackjack table there are four four-letter words: two "MUST"s, the word, "PAYS," and the word, "DRAW."

*There are four people (Linda Carsini, Jack Moses, and the elderly couple) at the disappearance of the money. Over the exhibit is a small canopy, there are four striped poles holding up this canopy.

*Five words (PLAY ONE TO FIVE COINS) are followed by a five-digit dollar amount: $10,000 on the slot machine, Big Betty.

*Banacek is the fifth person off the plane, and the fifth person outside the gate at the Las Vegas airport.

*Six people in front of Banacek and Jay at the Las Vegas airport when they're leaving; Banacek gives Jay $600 in this scene.

*Six girls standing in the scene featuring Larry Fields. Six letters in the last name Fields. The name of Fields' photographer is Freddie. F is the sixth letter of the alphabet.

*Three number 7s is the winning number on the slot machine, "Big Betty"

*The seven-letter word "DOLLARS" follows the seven-letter word "MILLION"

*Seven people at the explanation scene (including Banacek)

*Seven girls with the seven-letter Banacek in the sequence featuring Larry Fields; six girls are standing, one is sitting.

*Seven overhead shots of Las Vegas in the episode.

*Banacek becomes the seventh person standing in the shot taken by Larry Fields' photographer; the other six people are the girls in bikinis.

*Seven pictures/photos (some in brochures) on the bulletin board in the Loomis kitchen.

*Banacek and Jay pass a (Union) 76 filling station sign on their way to Jackson's man Leland (7+6=13), before that they pass a TEXACO sign and a STANDARD sign (but the N in STANDARD is missing) so the six-letter sign TEXACO is followed by the seven-letter sign STA DARD.

*Six passengers are in front of Banacek and Jay in the airport departure scene, seven passengers are behind them.

A CALENDAR OF THREES:

The calendar in the Loomis' kitchen is a great example of the detail the producers went to when playing with numbers. In the case of the "Threes":

*Tuesday is the third day of the week; there are three Tuesdays in a row (the 6th, the 13th, and the 20th) where an event or appointment has been scheduled.

*On the calendar, the 3rd is a Saturday: there are three days between Tuesday and Saturday (Wednesday, Thursday, Friday), there are three Saturdays on the calendar where an event, or appointment, has been scheduled.

*There are three events or appointments, in the third line of the calendar.

*There are a total of 28 days on the calendar. Since the 3rd is a Saturday, and the first full week begins on Sunday the 4th, there are a total of three full weeks in the month shown on the calendar. In the third full week, there are a total of three scheduled events/appointments.

Matching through numbers:
TWOS:

*Banacek's solution of the mystery requires traveling to two different two-name cities: Las Vegas, and Los Angeles. In both cases, the first name of the city begins with an L and concludes with an S; in both cases, the first name is a total of three letters. Moreover, though the spelling is different, both cities are pronounced the same way.

*Both Banacek and Mrs. Leland say "Certainly" in response to the other's request.

*Betty Janus (who has the same number of letters: five, in both her first and last name) has a last name which means "two-faced"; Betty Janus rotates her "visits" to the Las Vegas hotels about once every two weeks.

*Linda Carsini came to Las Vegas two years ago to get married; Linda has a double order of (the two-syllable) scampi while in the two-named Los Angeles. Linda says (the two-syllable greeting) "Hiya" twice to Banacek. (The second time is on the phone.)

THREES:

*Jonathan Jackson owns thirty percent of: 1. Las Vegas, 2. Half of West Texas, and 3. Most of Arizona; Jackson's hotel/casino is in its third year of operation; during the course of the story, there are murder attempts on three employees of Jackson's.

*In the showgirls' dressing room, Banacek is given three nicknames for Linda Carsini: one: Black Roots Linda, two: Big Hips Linda, three: Dark, Luscious Linda Each nickname is a total of three words. Soon after Linda Carsini and Banacek arrive in Los Angeles, she frets about him having "a fat wife and three kids." A short time later when the two are flying from Los Angeles back to Las Vegas, Banacek tells Linda that all he had to eat for dinner was "three crackers and an after-dinner mint."

THREE THREES:

*The scene featuring Banacek and Miss Beach has Miss Beach speaking a total of three threes:

first, she offers the sleuth a cold drink-he has three choices: Cola, Root Beer, or Lemon, then, after telling him of the three labor disputes the casino faced: the waiters, the dealers, and the security people, she explains that three months ago, the sprinkler system malfunctioned and drenched everyone in the casino.

FOURS:

*In episode #4, Jay has done four things upon arriving in Las Vegas: one: rented the car; two: made the hotel reservations, three: gotten his suit pressed; four: dropped $22 in the slot machines. There are two 2s in the number 22. Add 2 and 2; the result is four.

*After Banacek remarks to Andrews, "Just you and me," Andrews replies, "Needs four separate keys." Note that the four-letter word, "Just" begins Banacek's four-word remark, and that Andrews' first sentence, which is a total of four words, ends with the four-letter word, "keys." Note too that in between Banacek's four-letter "Just," and Andrews' first-four-letter word, "four," are a total of four words: "you, and, me, needs."

*The four-letters in his first name Jack Moses tells Banacek that he has been through four changes of management at the casino/hotel.

*After Linda Carsini tells Banacek that she is a pilot, he gives her a fourth nickname: Smiling Linda, Daredevil of the Skies. Note that the second part of the nickname, "Daredevil of the Skies," contains four words and that it begins with D: the fourth letter of the alphabet.

SEVENS:

*Knowing that insurance company representative Andrews resents his being called in to investigate the disappearance of the money, Banacek at one point tells the man:

"Andrews, cheer up. Even Eisenhower needed Patton."

This seven-word line begins with the seven-letter name Andrews.

TEN:

*The ten-letter Frank Burns tells Banacek he's known Marvin Flanders for ten years. Then he tells Banacek he just saw Flanders, about ten minutes ago.

TWELVE:
*When Banacek arrives at Arnold Leland's office and asks Miss Beach if he's available, she tells Banacek that her (twelve-letter) boss is out on the golf course, and should be approaching the twelfth hole right about then.

FIFTEENS:
*Fifteen years ago, Arnold Leland met the fifteen-letter Jonathan Jackson
*Jack Moses tells Banacek he has been with the hotel fifteen years; a few moments later, he tells the sleuth he has fifteen more minutes before he needs to return to work.

TWENTY-FIVE:
Loomis has had the same job for twenty-five years; when in Las Vegas, his picture is taken by twenty-five-year-old Linda Carsini when he hits the jackpot at the casino.

Alliteration:
A: Absolutely. Astounding; afraid Andrews; after another; Alton Associates; always answer; and an after-dinner; and an all-around; any attention; around asking; at all
B: Banacek. B-a-n-a-c-e-k; baseball; been battling; better believe; Big Betty (name of the winning slot machine)
C: Car Checked (for Brakes-note on calendar in the Loomis home); Cheers. Cheers; classic cheating; come complaining; control. Clear.
D: daredevil; death dating; desert. Dries; dinner dating; doesn't drink
E: easy enough; Electrical engineer; Even Eisenhower; everyone else's ends
F: Florence. Florence; for fifteen; forty-five
G: guys get
H: Hardly. He; holding Harry
J: Jonathan Jackson
L: lemon. Lemon; like living: Linda. Linda?; Luscious Linda
M: magnetic machinery; male model; more minutes; much money

N: No no no no

O: out on

P: phone please; Physics problem; Picture please; plenty people

R: running resort

S: say so; say some; says she; sixty seconds; slurp soup; so sure; some smug; somebody standing; someone stole; sounds so sexy; sprinkler system; stays so

T: teetotalers; there till the time; Thirty? Thirty-five?; till the time; time to turn; turntable

W: wouldn't worry

Double alliteration:

B & O: be better off on

C&H: company could have handled

I&O: it is one of

T&R: teetotalers running resort

Matches to previous episodes:

*In the pilot episode, "Detour to Nowhere," insurance company representative McKinney told his boss Cavanaugh that Banacek was no "Superman." In "Project Phoenix," insurance company representative Thaddenhurst paraphrased part of the introduction from the *Superman* TV series when he referred to Banacek as "Super-Pole." In this episode, when Banacek introduces himself to Linda Carsini, she remarks, "One name, like Superman?"

*The premiere episode, "Let's Hear it For a Living Legend," featured Conrad Janis as one of the guest stars; this episode features a character named Betty Janus. The last names "Janis" and "Janus" are pronounced the same way.

*In "Project Phoenix," when Jay asks him "How was the lady engineer?" Banacek replies "Electrical, but not civil." In that episode, the word "Engineer" preceded the word "Electrical." In this episode, the word order is reversed when the term, "Electrical engineer" is used.

*The previous episode, "No Sign of the Cross" concluded with the spoken line, "Welcome to Los Angeles, Mr. Banacek." This episode opens with a shot of a sign saying, "Welcome to Fabulous Las Vegas, Nevada."

*In "No Sign of the Cross" a departing airplane carrying (an unseen) Banacek is the last shot in the episode; in this episode, an arriving airplane carrying (an unseen) Banacek marks the sleuth's entry into the story.

*In the previous episode, art collector Robert Morgan speaks to Banacek of "Inquisitional tortures"; in this episode, Linda Carsini calls Banacek "Mr. Torquemada" and asks the sleuth if the "Inquisition" is over. (Torquemada headed the infamous Spanish Inquistion.)

Future Matches:

*The character Betty Janus

*Actor Don Porter

*Director Bernard Kowalski's triple "leg" shot.

*Linda Carsini's safe landing of the sabotaged plane in Las Vegas, Banacek assisting.

*Banacek's remark about a church when Linda Carsini treats him to some frightening turns and spins in her plane.

*Linda Carsini's "two-and-a-half room apartment."

*The $10,000 jackpot

*Jay meeting Banacek at the Las Vegas airport.

*Jay gambling at the tables and rolling the dice wrong.

*Banacek's $100,000 fee.

SECTION TWO

Behind the scenes:

George Eckstein: "Stanley (Ralph Ross) was another story. Stanley came to me through Howie Horwitz, because Howie had worked with him on *Batman*. He liked to write parts for himself too, which is all right. There was always somehow a part that he could play in the show. He made a lot of money as a voice-over actor."[7]

The Polish connection:

#1: Polish-American Bernard L. Kowalski is director of this episode. Rather appropriately, Kowalski would direct more *Banacek* episodes than any other director on the series. One of the most common surnames in contemporary Poland, "Kowalski" is a derivative of the word, "kowal," which means the occupation of "smith," such as in "blacksmith."

#2: Linda Carsini's mention of Liberace. Las Vegas favorite Liberace was born Wladziu Valentino Liberace. His mother, Frances Zuchowska, was a Pole, his father Salvatore "Sam" Liberace an Italian. Playing the piano by age four and memorizing difficult pieces by age seven, Liberace studied the technique of the famous Polish pianist, and future family friend, Ignaz Paderewski. He met Paderewski when he was eight. During the course of his life, pianist Paderewski was also Prime Minister of the Republic of Poland, Minister of Foreign Affairs, and 2nd Prime Minister of the Second Republic.

#3&#4: After insurance man Fisher gives Banacek the information he has on the robbery, he makes it plain to the sleuth how much he resents his involvement. In response, Banacek tells him, "Fisher, cheer up. Even Eisenhower needed Patton." In 1944, U.S. Army General George S. Patton met with Polish Army General Wladyslav Anders on the warfront. During their meeting, the two men exchanged medals; Anders gave Patton two. One was a medal showing a white eagle with a crown (the Polish coat of arms, and Polish emblem). The other medal depicted a "mermaid." The mermaid was both the sign of the Polish capital city of Warsaw and the sign of the Second Polish Corps. For his part, Patton gave Anders a number of medals including one with the U.S. Army insignia. Like Patton, Anders was suspicious of their Russian Allies. Noted Patton on one occasion, "General Anders of the Polish II Corps told me laughingly that if he got between a German Army and a Russian Army, he would have difficulty deciding which they should fight."

As for General Eisenhower, in addition to recognizing the three Polish mathematicians Rejewski, Zygalski, and Rozcyki's breaking of the Nazi's seemingly unbreakable Enigma Code during WWII (to quote Eisenhower, "it has saved thousands of British and American lives"), on September 30, 1960, he addressed the Polish-American Congress in Chicago. Telling the Congress how happy he was to meet them, Eisenhower declared "the people of Poland have shown such a fierce dedication to the conception of liberty and personal freedom ... they have been an example for all the world." A few moments later, Eisenhower concluded his comments about Revolutionary War general Kosciuszko by noting "there has never been a time when the Polish people and Polish fortunes have been absent from the hearts and minds of the American people." For his service during WWII, the Poles awarded Eisenhower the Virtuti Militari, the Cross of Grunwald, and the Order of Polonia Restituta Chevalier.

#5: During their phone conversation, Banacek and Felix talk about Banacek's "physics problem," and mention is made of Albert Einstein. In 1938, Albert Einstein and his co-author: Polish physicist Leopold Infeld published their book, *The Evolution of Physics*. This book is a frequently read history of physical theory from the seventeenth to twentieth centuries. Infeld worked with Einstein at Princeton University. Like Einstein, Infeld was interested in the theory of relativity. The two scientists also co-formulated the equation describing star movements.

Trivia:

*The scene of the Las Vegas airport is stock footage, other Universal series, such as *Switch*, used this same footage.

*Felix's phone number has changed since the pilot film. It is now 617-QUINCY-67788.

*This episode features no "old Polish proverbs."

Inside jokes and references:

*When Banacek visits Loomis at his home in Los Angeles, wanting to keep his Las Vegas visit a hidden secret from his wife, Loomis gives Banacek the cover of insurance man. Given how he is almost always clashing with an insurance company's representative when investigating a valuable item's disappearance, Banacek finds this cover amusing.

*At the time Banacek visits the Loomis', Mrs. Loomis is watching a horror movie on the living room TV; Universal Studios was of course known for the horror movie genre; the studio also produced the first made-for-TV-horror movie: *Fear No Evil* (1969).

*On the way back to Las Vegas, the plane carrying pilot Linda Carsini and her passenger Banacek almost crashes. This causes Linda to remark to Banacek, "I didn't mean to give you cardiac arrest, my dear Red Baron." George Peppard's character, Bruno Stachel, met the Red Baron in *The Blue Max* (1966).

*In Linda Carsini's apartment, there is a cat statue; episode writer Stanley Ralph Ross wrote all of the Catwoman episodes of *Batman*.

*When first seen, the character Betty Janus is playing the slot machine, "Big Betty."

Notes:

Despite George Eckstein's misgivings concerning future episodes Stanley Ralph Ross was to write for the series, Ross would go on to pen more *Banacek* scripts than any other contributing writer to the show. Ross' scripts for *Batman* made him an ideal fit for *Banacek*. Like *Banacek*, *Batman* featured a great deal of alliteration; like *Banacek*, *Batman* contained a number of inside jokes. In the case of Stanley Ralph Ross for example, Lisa Carson, a character played by Lee Meriwether in one of the "King Tut" *Batman*s, was the name of Ross' own wife; Margot Kidder's character, "Linda Carsini," in "A Million the Hard Way" is something of a variation of this name. Moreover, given his love for word-play, his alliteratively-named *Batman* characters such as Zolta Zorba and Minerva Matthews, plus the lengths to which he would go when writing a show (for example, before writing the "Egghead" *Batman* episodes "An Egg Grows in Gotham"/ "The Yegg Foes in Gotham," Ross went to his thesaurus, and looked up every word beginning with "ecc" or "ex"), it's difficult not to believe that Stanley Ralph Ross was responsible for a good bit of the humor in "A Million the Hard Way." He certainly penned the "Why do women always answer questions with questions?"/ "Do we?" exchange between Banacek and Linda Carsini. Two years later, audiences heard a more elaborate version of this exchange between a female detective and a female psychiatrist in the 1975 TV-movie-pilot, *Mrs. R, Death Among Friends*.

This episode goes a long way towards dismantling two of the major criticisms concerning *Banacek*: first that the character's non-Polish surname was an insult to the Poles. Given his Polish heritage, it's not likely director Bernard Kowalski would have done *Banacek* had he believed the character's name an insult to the Poles. As for the second charge, the complaint that Thomas Banacek was sexist, if the latter was true, why then does the sleuth exhibit no objection, or make any smart remarks concerning Linda Carsini flying him to Los Angeles in her own plane? Moreover, when the plane develops mechanical troubles as it returns to Las Vegas, it is Linda who lands the plane safely, not Banacek. In fact, he doesn't even know how to fly a plane. Jay's placing his bets at the craps table on the number seven does more than reference one of the key numbers in the *Banacek* series; in Craps, if a player's come out roll (the first throw of the dice) turns up a seven (or an eleven), he automatically wins on his bet. Though the item stolen in this episode is not a "three," there nonetheless is a "three" connected to the theft; there are a total of three characters who pull off the robbery.

Reviews and Publicity:

November 3, 1972: *Life*, Volume 73, No. 18,. In his "TV Review," the magazine's "Cyclops" describes *Banacek* as follows: "Male chauvinist pigginess, rotten Polish jokes, plots dreamed up by bowls of spinach."

November 4, 1972: *TV Guide* – Vol. 20, No. 45 — Issue#523 – "TV Teletype: Hollywood: Joseph Finnigan Reports" – Finnigan reveals that Janis Paige and Kevin McCarthy will be guest-starring as a couple of coin collectors whose $3,000,000 is stolen in an upcoming episode of *Banacek*

November 5, 1972: *TV Channels*, The New Haven Register, R-48, "New NBC Series is Tough on Criminals." In his review of *Banacek*, *TV Channels* television critic Lawrence Laurent notes: "Series creator Anthony Wilson looked at the Polish joke craze and decided the time is right for a TV hero who is Polish and proud of it."

November 11, 1972: *TV Guide* – Vol. 20, No. 46 — Issue#524 – "TV Crossword" – 18 Across – Banacek to friends

BANACEK Challenges: "A Million the Hard Way"

#1. Other than the three that results from her full name, last-billed guest Mary Ann Gibson matches in three separate ways to other members of the entire guest cast. Can you identify each match, and the guest names to whom Gibson matches?

#2. Besides their both being located in the casino, what match does the teaser establish between the slot machine Big Betty and the Blackjack table?

#3. How does Banacek's introduction in this episode connect to both the episode title and the episode's first original shot? Note, the first original shot is in the casino.

#4. At one time when Banacek enters the casino, he finds Jay playing the crap tables, exclaiming, "A little seven will take me right to heaven. A little seven will take me right to heaven. A little seven . . . Big Daddy." The line "A little seven will take me right to heaven" contains a total of three sevens. The word "seven" is of course one of them. Can you identify the other two?

#5. Later in the story Jay delivers another rhyme: "Keep your eye on the queen. Prettiest little lady you ever seen" when playing a game of chance with the Leland's chauffeur. Other than this being the second occasion when Jay does a rhyme while gambling, what are the other two matches between this rhyme sequence and the "little seven" sequence?

#6. Excluding his looking at it, in what two ways does the calendar in the Loomis kitchen connect to George Peppard? Hint: This question is referring to George Peppard, not the character he is playing.

#7. When Banacek arrives at Arnold Leland's office, Leland's secretary, Miss Beach, is in the process of giving her boss the correspondence and other items he needs for that day. How many things does she put on Leland's desk before turning to speak to Banacek? Why?

Episode#5: "To Steal a King," November 15, 1972

"There's an old Polish proverb that says, 'A wolf that takes a peasant to supper probably won't need any breakfast.'" –Banacek to the Garson brothers

Writer: Stephen Kandel
Director: Louis Antonio
Guest Stars

Brenda Vaccaro	Sharon Clark
Kevin McCarthy	Allen Markham
Pernell Roberts	Matthew Donniger
Roger C. Carmel	Oliver Garson
Logan Ramsey	Roland Garson

And

Janis Paige as   Lydia Markham

Co-starring

David Spielberg	Wendell Church
Tod Andrews	Graves
William Traylor	Ballinger
Hope Summers	Mrs. Liddell
Irene Tedrow	Dr. Dora Bancroft

With

Will Hare	Grayson
John Finnegan	Lt. Hallohan
Anthony Eustrel	Butler

Unbilled

Don Pedro Colley   Samuels (Garson chauffeur)

SECTION ONE: MATCHES

Matches in series credits:

*This is the fifth-aired episode; though there are six guest stars, Janis

Paige is singled out from the other guests by her five-word–"And Janis Paige as Lydia" credit. Since Paige's credit follows the names of five guest stars, we therefore have five guest stars followed by a five-letter first name (Janis), which is followed by a five-letter last name (Paige), and then a five-letter character name (Lydia).

*In addition to the first name Janis, and the last name Paige, the guest credits also contain three five-letter first names: Kevin, Logan, and Roger. As a result, in episode #5, we have five five-letter actor names.

*Janis Paige is one of two performers in the opening credits whose last name contains the same number of letters as her first name. The seven-by-seven Pernell Roberts is the other performer.

*In addition to the match they enjoy through their characters' first names (each has a total of six letters), Roger C. Carmel and Logan Ramsey share five-letter first names, and six-letter last names.

*Roger C. Carmel is one of three actors in the opening credit cast to possess side-by-side Cs in his performer name. The other two performers are Kevin McCarthy and Brenda Vaccaro.

Matches through physical production and editing:

*Sharon Clark is standing below a sign that says "ROOM." When she walks past Matthew Donniger, he is show standing near a sign that says "ROOMS."

*Three shelves in the safe where Markham places his coins: the three-word, "The Ten Kings."

*Three sitting police officers at the alarm panels: the third officer is the one to push the button that releases the safe's time-lock

*Three people in the elevator (Allen Markham, Mrs. Liddell and Dr. Bancroft).

*Three towels in the bathroom in the Markham's suite.

*In the cemetery, Banacek and Donniger find the headstone of Donniger's ancestor Josephus Donniger. There are a total of six lines on the headstone. Each line contains a "three." In the first line, there are three words: REST

IN PEACE; in the second line, the three-syllable first name JOSEPHUS is followed by the three-syllable last name DONNIGER. The number 3 is the third number on the third line (1734-1776). In the fourth line, the three-syllable word HIGHWAYMAN describes what Josephus Donniger was. The last two lines: the three-word WHOSE ROAD ENDED (line 5), and the three-word ON A GIBBET (line 6) reveal his fate. Note that the six-letter word GIBBET is the last word on the six-line tombstone.

*Six people including Banacek (first name-the six-letter Thomas) at the reconstruction of the crime.

*The sixth tombstone shown in the cemetery sequence is the one with the six-letter last name GERARD.

*Seven people in the suite in the teaser

*Seven people, and seven park benches which Bancek and Sharon Clark pass in the walk-and-talk scene in the park

*There are a total of seven tombstones with names (or parts of names) shown in close-up or in the two-shots during the walk-and-talk scene with Banacek and Donniger.

*The first tombstone which Banacek and Matthew Donniger view together is that of the thirteen-letter Abraham Morris. On this tombstone, thirteen words (this includes the three-letter abbreviations Jan. and Mar.) precede the thirteen-letter state name Massachusetts.

Matching through numbers:
TWOS:

*After saying "Allen? Allen?" Lydia Markham then says "What is it? What is it?"

*Allen Markham says "My kings" twice, "Sorry" twice, "There's been a" twice.

*Allen Markham's middle name Arthur begins with the same letter as his first name, Allen.

*The line "What I did I did" is spoken by two separate characters. In other words, two "I did"s, two characters saying "I did I did."

THREES:

*The stolen item which Banacek is trying to recover on this occasion is a set of coins, known by a three-word title, "The Ten Kings."

*The safe works on a time-lock. Every guest who uses it needs to use a combination of three numbers.

*Markham enters the lobby at 9:03 a.m. to report the robbery.

*Markham speaks his wife's first name three times in a row; the second time he only says the first three letters, "L,y,d"

*Markham says "No" three times in a row.

*The catalog displaying the upcoming auction of the ten kings went out to thirty people; the opening bid of two million has cut the number of bidders to three (Sharon Clark, Matthew Donniger, and the Garson brothers)

*As a set, the ten kings are worth $3 million, maybe more.

*Sharon wonders why she's telling Banacek everything about herself in the first three minutes

*Already on the case, Church tells Banacek he at present has three "No's": "No clues, no leads, no anything."

*The Eagles, which Markham sold to Donniger at an earlier time, were worth less than $300,000.

*After she says, "I want" three times during her confession, Sharon Clark tells Banacek this confession should prove to him she is three things: trustworthy, honest, and sincere.

*In the cemetery as he and Banacek search for the grave of his Revolutionary War ancestor, Donniger mentions three ethnicities: Poles, Jews, and Swedes whom his search has revealed to have fought in the Revolution.

*Felix tells Banacek that in the three-syllable state of Nebraska, Matthew Donniger made his money in three ways: cattle, oil, and wheat.

*There are four coins shown in Felix's slideshow-the first three all share the same number-the three-digit 100.

FOURS:

*Sharon Clark is frightened by four things: spiders, bugs of all sorts, mug-

gers, and poverty; Sharon Clark has been competing with the Garsons for over four years.

*Felix tells Banacek that Matthew Donniger would like to be someone like a Rockefeller, an Astor, possibly a Cabot, maybe a Whitney; it is after Felix mentions these four elite American families that Banacek references the famous elitist group, "The Four Hundred."

FIVES:

*Both Allen and Lydia Markham have five-letter first names.

SIXES

*The last name Garson is a total of six letters. Both Roland and Oliver have six-letter first names, as does their grandfather, Edmund.

SEVENS

*Banacek wears $70 shoes.

*Seven months ago, the seven-letter Grayson, whose last name begins with G, the seventh letter of the alphabet, was fired for planning a burglary at the Stafford.

NINES:

*Allen and Lydia Markham occupy a suite on the ninth floor in the Stafford; the alarm is set for nine a.m. the next day. The last time the Markhams were at the Stafford was nine months ago.

TENS:

*The ten zloty is the last of the ten kings shown in Felix's slide presentation.

*Jay's made a deal with Banacek. If he helps his boss recover the vanished items he'll get ten percent of Banacek's ten percent of restoring the ten kings.

THIRTEENS:

*Allen Markham repeats his wife Lydia's first name three times in the teaser, but he says Lyd the second time. This triple alliteration of "Lydia, Lyd, Lydia" yields a total of thirteen letters

FIFTEENS:

*Banacek wears a $150 sport-coat.

*The Garsons, who expect to obtain The Ten Kings, and plan to exhibit them to a select group, have sent out 150 invitations for the event.

Alliteration:

A: account anywhere; administered after; Alan! Alan!; Alan Arthur; Alas, as; as an assistant

B: Banacek. Bearing; banking business; bankrupted by

C: can cause; chit-chattin; Clayton. Charming; coin collecting; coin collection; come close; company cannot; complete confession; crash course

D: Dr. Dora

E: everything else

F: feel free; furniture for

G: generally get; Going, going; great grandfather

H: happened, happened; However. However; hundred hotel

L: Lydia. Lyd?, Lydia?

M: magician Mr.; make mistakes; meeting Ma; million, Maybe more; Morning, "Missing Money" Mr., Mrs?; Might miss; motive?, Matthew; much money; my manners

N: no need; No, no, no; not necessarily

O: odds. Odds?; of owning; Oliver of; one? Officially; only open once

P: Peterman pulling; policy premiums: Polish proverb; purchase price

R: railroaded; Right, right; Roland. Right; ruby ring

S: SS; secret source; Security Suite; seven sharp; sixty seconds; so she; so sure; some selfish; some small scrap; some sort; Sorry. Sorry; still stands

T: take things too; taken too; talking to; that the two; things tend to; twenty-three; type to

U: us ungrateful

W: Well, will; Wendell will; were, walking; when we were; why we were

Y: Yeah, yeah

Double alliteration:

I&T: It's, it's the ten

Matches to previous episodes:

*In the premiere episode, "Let's Hear It For a Living Legend," talk-show host Marty Ingels says to Boston Rebels star player Hank Ives, "Hank, enough of this chit-chat" during their interview; in this episode, Matthew Doniger tells Banacek, "You don't come on chit-chattin."

*In "Legend," Banacek is put on the case by Boston Rebels owner Jerry Brinkman. In this episode, Allen Markham seeks Banacek's help on the advice of Jerry Brinkman.

*In "Legend," Holly Allencamp's middle name is Barker. In this episode, Sharon Clark makes reference to the notorious female gangster, Ma Barker.

*In "Legend," Conrad Janis was one of the guest stars in the opening credits; in the previous episode, supporting guest Claire Brennen played a character named Betty Janus (Janus is pronounced the same as Janis); in this episode, Janis Paige is one of the lead guests.

*In "No Sign of the Cross," Banacek walks through the small cemetery at the Gomez's farm; in this episode, Banacek walks through a large cemetery with Matthew Donniger.

*In "No Sign of the Cross," Banacek is working for the church. In "To Steal a King," Banacek is working against a character named Church.

*In "A Million the Hard Way," Banacek collects $100,000 as his fee for solving the disappearance of the $1 million from the casino exhibit. In this episode," Sharon Clark tells Banacek she placed a $100,000 bet on him.

Future Matches:

*The character Sharon Clark

*The Garson brothers

*The "Sullivan. Mr. Banacek." exchange between Banacek and policeman Sullivan.

*The side-by-side letter "c"s in the names Vaccaro, McCarthy, and C. Carmel.

*The last name Barker

*Guest star Janis Paige

*Lydia Markham's Maserati

*The words "What I did I did."

SECTION TWO

Behind the scenes: "To Steal a King" director Lou Antonio:

"I know I did one. It turned out very well. I have no idea whether they would have liked me (to do another). I remember Kevin McCarthy, Brenda Vaccaro . . . Kevin McCarthy was from the Actor's Studio. It was supposed to take place in Boston, and I had to make sure I missed palm trees. I go back a long way with George (Peppard). My very first Broadway play was understudying George and Arthur Storch. I was assistant stage manager in an N. Richard Nash play, with Pat Hingle, George, and Shelley Winters . . . . *The Girls of Summer*, not a success, but I understudied George, and we did scenes together in Lee's (Strasberg) private class. We got along swell. George Eckstein was a good writer. Knew just what he was doing. Very nice man. I remember on a *Fugitive* . . . this is how nice he was. I had an idea for a story, and I said to George, 'I'm gonna write a screenplay with this idea . . . an episode.' He said, 'Yeah. Go ahead.' And you can imagine the flood of scripts they would get because in those days they only had a story editor; they didn't have a staff of writers. So, I wrote the screenplay and sent it to him. Mind you, I'm living in New York. I'm no hotshot. And, son of a gun, if he didn't write the nicest note back saying why they couldn't do it. Took the time and even gave me some tips. Very nice man."[8]

Guest Star Don Pedro Colley on George Peppard:
"Georgie Porgie. I wouldn't call him that to his face. George was pretty much a one-dimensional actor, and so he had a sense of self-importance that was much greater than it should have been, but, of course he was Hollywood's pretty blond boy. After Tab Hunter and Troy Donahue. George was all right. George was all right for what he had to do. He was never a very sociable person. He had his own problems and he started drinking real heavy. I got to drive this incredible 1927 Rolls Royce: Silver Phaeton. Oh boy. As his chauffeur."[9] (Actually as the Garson's chauffeur bringing Peppard's Banacek to their home.)

The Polish connection:
#1: Banacek describes Ma Barker as "his first crush." Polish-American gangster Alvin Karpis was a member of the Barker gang.

#2: Felix goes to Banacek's home with a collection of slides showing different rare coins. One of the slides is of a ten złoty. The złoty is the form of currency in Poland.

#3: Felix talks about Władysław IV during his discussion of different coins. Władysław IV was king of the Polish Lithuanian Commonwealth from 1632 to 1648. He managed to keep the Commonwealth from becoming involved in the Thirty Years War and protected it from invaders. He was also in favor of religious tolerance, and carried out military reforms.

#4: In the cemetery, Donniger and Banacek are talking about history and such Revolutionary War locations as Valley Forge. The Polish were among those at Valley Forge.

#5: At one point, Donniger finds a grave where the headstone reads General Pilsudski, born in 1749. There was a General Pilsudski, but General Josef Pisludski lived in the twentieth century. General Pilsudski was considered by many Polish-Americans to be the "George Washington of Poland." He did more than any other Pole to achieve the independence of Poland after WWI.

Trivia:

Supporting guest star Irene Tedrow (Dr. Dora Bancroft) was married to Polish immigrant William Kent.

Inside jokes and references:

*The name of the hotel is the Stafford. Stafford, Indiana is the home of *The Fugitive* (a.k.a Dr. Richard Kimble.) George Eckstein was both writer and associate producer of *The Fugitive*.

*Church describes Banacek as the "great turtleneck Polish vulture."

*Banacek walks over to a tombstone with the last name of "Gerard." Lt. Philip Gerard (Barry Morse) was the Stafford, Indiana police lieutenant who was constantly pursuing Dr. Richard Kimble on *The Fugitive*.

*In an episode which features a scene in a cemetery, there is a character named Graves.

*At the end of the show, as Banacek and Sharon Clark walk down the sidewalk, above them, and to their right is a sign where the first two words are "The End."

*In (the eight-letters in his last name) Lt. Hallohan's office is a picture of his wife and three daughters. Executive producer George Eckstein (eight letters in the last name) and his actress-wife Selette Cole had three daughters.

Notes:

This episode is an excellent example of both Georges' points: the "realistic clues" George Peppard mentioned to *The Philadelphia Sunday Bulletin's* Rex Polier in an interview during the show's run, and the series being written "in our own image," as stated by George Eckstein earlier. Illustrating the former, in the teaser, the audience is given a clue as to the thief's identity through both dialogue and setting; the information Banacek later provides in his summation contains one word which immediately connects to both thief and setting.

As for the writing of the show "in our own image, the character Grayson's noting the cost of both Banacek's shoes ($70) and sport-coat ($150) is a case of Eckstein and company taking the number of letters in the last name Peppard, or Banacek, (seven in both cases) and the number of letters in the full name George Peppard, Jr. (fifteen) and multiplying these numbers times 10 (The Ten Kings is the object for which Banacek is searching on this occasion.) Having the seven-letter character Grayson, whose last name begins with the seventh letter of the alphabet, note the cost of the seven-letter Banacek's shoes and sport-coat is a tongue-in-cheek clue which Eckstein and company drop to the audience as to how they are writing the show. Other such clues include the name of the hotel (the eight-letter Stafford), the Hallohan character (the Lieutenant's eight-letter last name begins with the eighth letter of the alphabet), and the tombstone with the name Gerard. As noted in the Inside Jokes and References section, the names Stafford and Gerard are names associated with George Eckstein's earlier series, *The Fugitive*. Like the Margot Kidder character in the preceding *Banacek*, "A Million the Hard Way," Brenda Vaccaro's casting as a feminist bank representative to whom Banacek is attracted and vice versa, is yet more proof that Banacek's chauvinism was something of a put-on when it came to his dealings with feminists on- screen.

Reviews and Publicity:

November 18, 1972: *TV Guide*, Vol. 20, No. 47, Issue#525: "TV Crossword": 18 Across: Banacek to friends: Answer: "Tom"

December 2, 1972: *TV Guide*, Vol. 20, No. 49, , Issue#527, on page 44, in his review, Cleveland Amory describes *Banacek* stories as "exciting, absorbing plots that really have fascinating beginnings." Goes on to say that "after a series of good dramatic scenes," the climax will be "jarring and unreal." Mentions the fencing scene in "No Sign of the Cross" as "awful" and sees no need for it; says Banacek's explanations at the end are "very annoying," and he sounds like he's talking to a bunch of schoolchildren. Also says half the time the audience wasn't given the necessary clues. Hates the Polish proverbs.

December 16, 1972: *TV Guide*, Vol. 20, No.51, Issue#529: "TV Crossword": 8 Down: George Peppard's role

December 23, 1972: *TV Guide*, Vol. 20, No. 52, Issue#530: "TV Crossword": 8 Down: Answer: Banacek

January 6, 1973: *TV Guide*, Vol. 21, No. 1, , Issue#532: "TV Crossword": 1 Across: Polish Insurance Investigator

BANACEK Challenges: "To Steal a King":

#1. Besides their appearing in their respective teasers, and being present at the discovery of the theft, what three other things do "A Million the Hard Way's" Linda Carsini and "To Steal a King's" Allen Markham have in common? Hint: one is right in front of you.

#2. In the teaser, we learn two things, both of which we can immediately connect to the billing and character played by guest star William Traylor. What is this connection?

#3. In the teaser, Kevin McCarthy's Allen Markham repeats a number of words following his discovery of the theft. In three specific instances, the number of words Markham repeats matches the number of people in the scene. Can you detect these three matches? Hint: It's as easy as one-two-three.

#4. In the cemetery, the first tombstone Banacek and Matthew Donniger view together is that of Abraham Morris. The last is Donniger's ancestor Josephus Donniger. What is the other connection between these two tombstones?

#5. Also in the cemetery, the words on the tombstones which Banacek and Donniger view or pass create a numerical progression of three. Can you find this? Hint: this progression is in reverse.

#6. Can you find the four fours given in Felix's slide presentation?

#7. Midway through the story, Banacek talks to the cab driver Grayson. There are seven sevens connected to the character Grayson. Four have already been noted: one: the character's seven-letter name, two: the character's name beginning with the seventh letter of the alphabet, three: the character talking to the seven-letter Banacek, four: the character's guess that Banacek's shoes cost $70. Can you identify the three remaining sevens?

Episode #6: "Ten Thousand Dollars a Page," January 10, 1973

"There's an old Polish proverb that says, Just because a dress is red satin, doesn't mean it comes off easily." –Banacek to Glassman.

Writer: Paul Playdon
Director: Richard T. Heffron

Guest Stars
Stella Stevens	Jill Hammond
Joel Fabiani	Art Woodward
David Doyle	Elliot
Special Guest Star: David Wayne	Walter Tyson
and Richard Schaal as	Glassman
Co-starring	
George Lindsey	Lt. Bradshaw

Ted Cassidy	Jerry Crawford
Michael Masters	Steve Crawford
Uncredited	
Jamie Farr	Ludlow
Tom Reese	Policeman in video
Mark Russell	Policeman

Exteriors/Filming Locations: The Norton Simon Museum of Art, formerly the Pasadena Art Museum.

SECTION ONE: MATCHES

Matches in series credits:

*Since David Wayne is billed under Special Guest Star and Richard Schaal has a "And Richard Schaal as Glassman" credit, this leaves three performers: Stella Stevens, Joel Fabiani, and David Doyle who are billed under the "Guest Star" credits. Three is the exact number of performers in the closing credits: George Lindsey, Ted Cassidy, Michael Masters.

*The name David Doyle is a double match-there are five letters in both first and last name, and each name begins with the same letter.

*All three actors in the closing credits (George Lindsey, Ted Cassidy, and Michael Masters) have seven-letter last names; all three of these actors play characters with eight-letter last names (in the case of George Lindsey, Bradshaw, in the case of Cassidy and Masters, Crawford).

Matches through physical production and editing:

*Three guards in the Book of Hours room; three men (including two guards) in the medium shot/two-shot featuring the case containing the Book of Hours.

*In the scene in Lt. Bradshaw's office, there are three photos behind Banacek, and three file boxes in front of them; three pencils are in the cup in front of Lt. Bradshaw.

*Three boxes of slides on Felix's desk.

*Three men involved in the physical theft of the Book of Hours.

*Three colors: black, red, and brown, on the ransom letter sent to Tyson; three words: YOU'LL, BE, and CONTACTED on the third black line of the ransom letter.

*Five-word sign: A-ONE AUTO WRECKING CO; five dollar bills (presumably one-hundred dollar) placed under the hood by Banacek in the auto junkyard of the A-ONE AUTO WRECKING COMPANY.

*Six people in the Book of Hours recovery scene, including Banacek, following the ransom drop and pickup; on the close-up of the monitor of the Book of Hours Room, six control buttons can be seen: V HOLD, H HOLD, BRIGHT, CONTRAST, POWER, and another V HOLD.

*Six police cars pull up outside museum.

*Seven men at the murder scene of Ludlow-excluding Banacek.

*Seven shots of the monitor in teaser.

*Seven scenes/sequences Banacek watches on his TV as he runs the videotape footage of the robbery; as he watches the seventh sequence, he discovers a clue which he reveals to Lt. Bradshaw.

*When Banacek comes in the entrance hall, and spots Jill, there is a candlelabra/light fixture at the left; there are seven lights in this fixture.

*At the gas station where Banacek has been told he will find the Book of Hours, there are a total of seven large words which have been spray-painted on the window; Banacek is standing to the left of these words.

*In the ransom letter, there are seven words that precede the seven-letter word, HUNDRED.

*In the ransom letter, there are eight words that precede the eight-letter word, THOUSAND

Matching through numbers:
THREES:

*Banacek describes Elliott as heavy-set, gravel-voiced, and paranoid; Elliott describes Banacek as an "over-rated, overpaid showboat."

*Elliott tells Banacek that there were (one): no prints, (two): no forced entry, and (three): no alarms cut, inside or out; Elliott mentions three insurance company representatives to Banacek in their first meeting: one: the divisional vice-president, two: the district manager, three: himself.

*After Elliott tells Banacek there is just one door in the museum, and no windows, he tells the sleuth of the third possible entrance to the Book of Hours room: the ventilator openings; the openings are three by three inches. Next Elliott talks about three more parts of the room: the floor, the ceiling, and, the walls.

*When it comes to a previous success: the recovery of the Victoria Diamond, Banacek remembers three things about it: the Diamond, the finder's fee, and the company that employed his services: National Fidelity Insurance. To find out Walter Tyson is National Fidelity Insurance, Tyson tells Banacek he would have to go through: companies, sub-companies, and trusts.

*Louisa DeWitt (Walter Tyson's late wife) had a $3 million trust fund; Felix describes Tyson's formative years in three ways: orphanages, poverty, squalor. Three years ago, Tyson lost all feeling in his toes.

*The flashlight which is referenced in the story is a (three-digit) Mitchell 490.

*Three minutes after the squad cars arrived at the Tyson museum, a WBZ-TV news team appeared. (Note that there are three letters: W, B, and Z in this television station's call letters).

*Jill accuses Banacek of disappearing on her friend Kathy Summerfield three months after he took Kathy to Bermuda with promises of marriage.

*Jerry Crawford served three years for (the three-word) attempted armed robbery.

FIVES:

*Elliott calls Banacek at five in the morning to tell him about five people who work at (the five-word) A-One Auto Wrecking Company; the owner of the A-One Auto Wrecking Company is Fred Davis-five letters in the last name. Jerry Crawford (five letters in the first name) works at A-One Auto Wrecking Company; he was told to meet the crook at "Eight-o-five sharp"; for his time and trouble he picked up $500.

SIXES:

*In episode six, one of Banacek's clues is a sixth squad car at the robbery. When Banacek notes this clue with the sentence, "Six squad cars instead of five," he is delivering a sentence of exactly six words.

SEVENS:

*Jill Hammond (seven letters in the last name Hammond) tells Tyson that he stole seven years out of her life.

EIGHTS:

*The first sentence spoken by Lt. Bradshaw is "Eight tests." There are eight letters in the last name Bradshaw.

TENS:

*Tyson wants a progress report from Banacek, "every day at ten." Note that the total number of letters in the three words that specify how often Tyson wants the report: "every day at," is ten.

TWELVES:

*Louisa DeWitt's twelve letter name begins with L: the twelfth letter of the alphabet, L; her baby lived twelve hours.

Alliteration:
A: appearance again; as an added; ashes analyzed; attempted armed
B: Banarcek. Banacek; big bank; book because; burglary business
C: closed circuit; Come come; complete cooperation; corporate complexities
D: directly downstairs; drove down; dunderheads do
E: explosive electronically
F: finder's fee; first four; folder from; for four
H: Hart here; huge house
L: like lightning; little left; Ludlow. Ludlow
M: masterminded; my move
N: Night. Night; No no. No
O: out of Oliver: overrated, overpaid
P: phony policeman; Polish proverb; prayers probably pulled; pretty possessive
R: real reason
S: say so; she said she: simpering, self-righteous; six squad; social status; someone stole; something somehow; something? Someone; stole seven
T: Ten to the; time to time; TV transmission; twenty-three times
W: welcome wagon; well what; what went wrong?; what what
Y: Yeah. Yeah

Double alliteration:
G&T: gonna go through this
T&A: take that as a

Matches to previous episodes:

*In the pilot we see Banacek watching videotapes on his big-screen TV. In this episode, we see Banacek watching videotapes on his big-screen TV. The shots of Banacek watching the TV come from the pilot film.

*In episode two, "Project Phoenix," actor Seamon Glass was the sixth, and last billed in the closing credits. In this the sixth-aired episode, the last-billed actor in the opening credits is Richard Schaal. As the credits show, he plays a character named Glassman. Like the first name Seamon, there are a total of six letters in the last name Schaal.

*In episode three, "No Sign of the Cross," Banacek and Jay come upon a road sign at a turn-off. The sign notes that it is three miles to the town of Live Oak; to reach Live Oak, one must turn left. In this episode, at three a.m., Banacek is to leave the Tyson house, take Highway Ten to the White Oaks turnoff, and make a left.

*In the preceding episode, "To Steal a King," when Banacek enters the Markham's suite, and spots a policeman he knows, he greets him with the one-word, "Sullivan." "Mr. Banacek," the policeman replies. This same one-word exchange takes place between Banacek and Sullivan at the murder scene in Ludlow's home.

*In "To Steal a King," it is revealed that Lydia Markham owns a Maserati. In this episode, murder victim Stu Ludlow owns a Maserati

*In episode five, the four-word "To Steal a King," the five-letter Paige is the last name of the sixth-billed and last guest in the opening credits. In this episode, the sixth-aired episode, the four-letter word, "Page," is the last word in the five-word title, "Ten Thousand Dollars a Page."

*In "To Steal a King," the six-letter Garson brothers have first names of exactly six letters; in this episode, the eight-letter Crawford brothers have first names of exactly five letters.

Future Matches:
　*Art Woodward's remark about the Reign of Terror.
　*The "Sullivan"/ "Mr. Banacek" exchange
　*The solution to the robbery.
　*Banacek's remark about pyramids
　*Felix's statement that the Book of Hours changed ownership more than twenty-three times.
　*Elliott's description of Banacek as an overrated, overpaid showboat.
　*The three-by three inch ventilator openings Elliott mentions.

SECTION TWO

Behind the scenes:

Executive producer George Eckstein:

"The Polish proverbs were totally made up. I wrote most of them, I think. I don't know whether I have any favorites, but they were fun to do. I think there was one I liked, 'Just because it's a red dress doesn't mean it comes off easily.' They were really . . . I mean it was sort of a great escape doing those."[10] (Note: The Polish proverb that Eckstein cites, "Just because a dress is red satin, doesn't mean it comes off easily," is a total of exactly thirteen words.)

The Polish connection:

#1: When Felix is giving Banacek the history of the Book of Hours, he tells the sleuth about the book's first owner, Galeazzo Sfrorza, and his widow, Bona of Savoy. Gian Galeazzo Sfrorza was the son of Galeazzo Sforza, and Bona of Savoy. Gian Galeazzo's daughter, Bona Sforza, later became Queen of Poland.

#2: Felix says Walter Tyson's childhood was like something out of *Oliver Twist*, one of many famous novels written by Charles Dickens. In nineteenth-century Poland, Dickens was the most widely read and published foreign novelist.

#3: After Banacek talks about Walter Tyson being unique, Glassman replies, "So was Genghis Khan." In the year 1240, Genghis Khan's Mongol Hordes invaded Hungary and Poland, winning victory over the European knights at Mohi in Hungary and Liegnitz in Poland.

#4: Jay's joke about the Polish Olympic star who's so proud he wants to have his gold bronzed references the medals won by Irena Szewińska and Witold Woyda in the 1968 and 1972 Summer Olympics. In 1968, sprinter Szewińska won the Gold in the Women's 200 meter; in 1972, she won Bronze in the same event. Woyda won the Bronze in Fencing on the Men's Team in 1968, in 1972, he won Gold in the same sport.

#5: When Glassman tells Banacek that Tyson was planning to build ten more museums over the next five years, Banacek remarks, "Even King Cheops only needed one pyramid." This line refers to the only remaining Seventh Wonder of the World: the Great Pyramid of Giza, which most Egyptologists believe was built as the tomb of fourth dynasty Egyptian Pharaoh Cheops – a.k.a. Khufu. Over the years, numerous scientists and scholars made different estimates as to the number of men required to build the pyramids. Among these individuals was Polish architect Wieslaw Kozinski. Kozinski believed the workforce might have been 300,000 men on the construction site, with an additional sixty thousand off-site.

Notes:

Written by *Banacek* story editor Paul Playdon, what sets this episode apart from the series' preceding entries is, the story is based on real-life. About 1490, Bona Sforza, widow of Galeazzo Sforza, Duke of Milan, commissioned illuminator Giovanni Pietro Birago to do a Book of Hours. A Book of Hours was the most popular type of religious book in medieval Europe. Intended for individual use at home, a Book of Hours was a collection of Christian prayers for recitation at different times (hours) of the day. The prayers were simplified versions of the eight periods of daily prayer observed by monks and nuns, from matins in the morning to compline at night. The prayers were written in Latin, the language of the medieval Church. A masterpiece of the Renaissance, the Sforza Hours took some thirty years to put together; finishing the task was a second artist, Gerard Horenbout, who was commissioned to complete the Hours by the Book's second owner, Margaret of Austria, Regent of the Netherlands, in 1517. It took Horenbout three years to complete the work. In 1894, the year it was discovered that Bona of Savoy and Margaret of Austria were the original owners of the Sforza Hours, also found was a letter written in 1490 from the original artist Birago to an unnamed correspondent referred to as "your Excellency," who possessed a stolen portion of the manuscript. In the letter, Birago claimed that a friar, Fra Johanne Jacopo, had stolen the incomplete Book, which he stated was worth more than 500 ducats, a great deal of money at that time. Based on the present-day condition of the Book, it has been determined that the pages taken included: the entire calendar, Folios from the Gospel lessons, the Hours of the Cross, the Hours of the Holy Spirit, the Hours of the Virgin, the Passion according to Saint Luke, three prayers to the Virgin, and the Suffrages of the Saints: eight portions in all. Birago's letter makes the theft of the Sforza Hours one of the earliest recorded examples of art theft.

David Wayne, Stella Stevens, George Peppard and George Lindsey in the "recovery" sequence from the NBC/Universal *Banacek* episode, "Ten Thousand Dollars a Page."

By writing a story about the Sforza Hours, *Banacek*'s Paul Playdon accomplished three things: first, the object which Banacek sought to retrieve existed in real-life; it was not a fictional creation; second, the theft of the object stolen in "Ten Thousand Dollars a Page" had actually taken place, centuries earlier. Third, the real-life object and its theft created a match: of the number eight. The prayers in the Sforza Hours were for the eight periods of daily prayer; the number of portions determined to have been stolen from the Book was eight. What with its Contents, its theft, and the portions stolen in the theft, the Book of Hours, and its history was tailor-made for *Banacek*. Through Felix Mulholland's mention of both Galeazzo Sforza, and his widow, Bona of Savoy, Playdon also works in a Polish connection to the stolen object.

Additional note: Those wishing to look at the real Sforza Hours may do so at the British Library Online Gallery: http://www.bl.uk/onlinegallery/sacredtexts/sforza.html.

Reviews and Publicity:
January 13, 1973: *TV Guide*, Vol 21, No. 2– Issue#533 – "TV Crossword" - 1 Across: Answer: Banacek

BANACEK Challenges: "Ten Thousand Dollars a Page"

#1. In the guest credits, excluding that their last names begin with S, there are two connections between Stella Stevens and Richard Schaal. Can you identify both?

#2. During the course of this episode, Jill Hammond speaks a sentence to Banacek which: one: creates a match to the episode title; two: contains a match to the name of her portrayer, Stella Stevens; and three: possesses a clue which identifies the mastermind behind the theft. Can you detect this sentence?

#3: This sixth-aired episode contains six "elevens," beginning with the writer of the show: the eleven-letter Paul Playdon. Can you identify the other five? Hint: You'll find two of them in the teaser.

#4: There are two connections between actors David Doyle and Ted Cassidy when it comes to their characters in this episode. Can you identify both; the first connection is pretty obvious, the second less so.

#5. Banacek's introduction to Walter Tyson and his employees creates a numerical progression of five. Can you detect it? Note: this progression is not presented in order.

#6. At one point in the story, Walter Tyson says to Banacek, "As you can see, the ravages of time have done their ravaging." In this line, there are a total of three twelves. Can you find them?

#7. At another time, Art Woodward and Walter Tyson have the following conversation:

> *Woodward*: "It can't be done."
>
> *Tyson*: "I tell you it can be done, and it will be done if I have to do it."

This conversation contains six sixes. Can you find them?

Episode #7: "The Greatest Collection of Them All," January 24, 1973

"*There's an old Polish proverb that says, 'A wise man never tries to warm himself in front of a painting of a fire.'*" —Banacek to Gloria Hamilton

Exteriors/Filming Locations: Boston Museum of the Arts

W: Theodore J. Flicker
D: George McCowan
Guest Stars
Penny Fuller — Gloria Hamilton
Mike Farrell — Jason Trotter
Also starring
Lloyd Gough — Allen Trotter
Arch Johnson — Larry Casey
Co-starring
Barbara Stuart — Sailor
David Spielberg — Church
George Murdock — Cavanaugh
John Hoyt — Dr. Shelby
Eugene Troobnick — Norm Katz
With
Garry Walberg — Lt. Warsaw
Gene Dynarski — Wheeler
Robert DoQui — Sgt. Flynn
Penny Marshall — Receptionist
John Gilgreen — Jim
George Brenlin — Davis

SECTION ONE: MATCHES

Matches in series credits:

Opening credits:

*The billing for guest star Lloyd Gough immediately follows that for series regular Ralph Manza. Like Manza, Gough has the same number of letters in both his first and last name: five.

*The fourth and last-billed guest is Arch Johnson. The four letters in his first name: Arch, match his guest billing. His character name Larry Casey yields another match: there are five letters in the first name Larry, five letters in the last name Casey.

Closing Credits:

*In the co-starring credits, the fifth, and last-billed, is Eugene Troobnick. The fifth-billed Troobnick's first name begins with the fifth letter of the alphabet; in the "with" credits, sixth, and last-billed is George Brenlin. His first name is a total of six letters.

*Fourth-billed in the co-starring credits is the four letters in his first name/four letters in his last name John Hoyt.

Opening and closing credits:

*There are two women named "Penny" in the guest credits: Penny Fuller and Penny Marshall; two men named "George" in the guest credits: George Murdock and George Brenlin; two men named "John": John Hoyt and John Gilgreen.

*The first two guests in the opening credits have last names that begin with "F": Fuller and Farrell; the first two guests in the co-starring credits have last names that begin with "S": Stuart and Spielberg.

*The first two guests in the "With" credits have first names that begin with "G": Garry and Gene; the last names of the characters played by these guests have last names that begin with a "W": Warsaw and Wheeler.

Matches through physical production and editing:

*In the sequence in the two-word Sailor's Bar, there are two men: Banacek and Wheeler who go outside to fight; in the bar are Wheeler's two friends; both of them are wearing checked sport-coats, and both are standing. Also in the bar are two Black men sitting at a table, and two White men; one of them: Jay is sitting at the bar; the other man is sitting at a table.

*In the bar is a two-word sign: "Bottled Beer"; both of these words begin with B: the second letter of the alphabet.

*Outside the bar, in the alley where Banacek and Wheeler fight, there is a sign saying DELIVERY ENTRANCE. The second word: ENTRANCE, is placed under the word DELIVERY. As a result there are two DE's (one reading horizontally and one reading vertically), and two EN's (again, one reading horizontally and one reading vertically).

*The fight itself involves two blows: one punch from Wheeler to Banacek, and one knock on the head, with a block of wood, from Banacek to Wheeler. The knock leaves Wheeler unconscious. Note that both men involved in the fight: Banacek and Wheeler, have seven-letter last names.

*Among those betting on the fight, in favor of Wheeler, is Jay. Losing to Sailor, Jay drops two bills on the counter.

*The three-named Trotter Van Lines is the name of the trucking company that is handling the transportation of the paintings from New York to Boston. The Trotter truck is part of a three-vehicle convoy: a police car drives in front of the truck, another police car follows the truck.

*Church and Cavanaugh (whose last names begin with C: the third letter of the alphabet) work for the three-named Boston Casualty Company. They are shown walking in front of a sign that says Cook & Cobb Company. There are three words in this sign, each word begins with the third letter of the alphabet.

*When Banacek says "The three of them modified the truck . . . ." he is addressing three men: Lt. Warsaw, Dr. Shelby, and Wendell Church.

*In the teaser, in the opening scene at the New York art museum, there are two signs that identify the location, and the exhibit. The exhibit is the seven-word "The World's Greatest Collection of French Impressionists." Its current location is the six-word "New York Museum of Contemporary Art." Six words describe the purpose of the exhibit: "All Profits Benefit Heart Disease Alliance." The six-letter Boston is the next city to which the exhibit will travel. Note that, as the story opens the exhibit is located in the seven-letter city, New York.

*Five paintings are shown in the close-up tracking shot as the story begins. The fifth painting is the first shown being packed in the crate by the museum workers. Five crates are shown when they arrive at the Boston Museum of Art.

*Five people accompany the truck from New York to Boston: two police cars: each car contains two officers, and the exhibit's director: Gloria Hamilton; Gloria rides in the second police car: the "follow" car.

*Altogether, the weight of the collection amounts to five-tons; as we have just noted, a total of five people accompany this five-ton load from New York to Boston; the trip lasts approximately five hours.

*Gloria Hamilton: one of the above five people has a (five-letter) lunch with Banacek at the (five-letter by five-letter) STEAK JOINT restaurant.

*The six word sign BOSTON MUSEUM OF ART RECEIVING ROOM begins with the six-letter word BOSTON.

Matching through numbers:
TWOS:

*Sailor gives Banacek and Jay two choices of Beer: Domestic or Imported.

*Wheeler tells Banacek he's the second insurance man who's come in Sailor's Bar asking about the stolen paintings. When Wheeler tells Banacek he ran the insurance representative out of the bar, one of his two friends adds, "Fast. Fast."

THREES:

*When Gloria Hamilton says "The Renoir completes crate three, gentlemen," she is in an alignment of three women: one woman is to Gloria's left, at that woman's left is another woman.

*After Wendell Church tells Banacek, "See Banacek, I tried everything . . . ." the sleuth completes his rival's thought, pointing out that Church tried to keep him off the missing paintings case, because he considers the sleuth to be "overrated, overdressed, overpaid, and under-qualified." Although Banacek lists four negatives, three of these four begin with the same four-letter word, "over."

*There are over 3,000 drivers working for the three-named Trotter Van Lines.

*Allen Trotter, the founder of the three-named Trotter Van Lines, reassures Dr. Shelby with the repeated three words, "They'll be here."

*Banacek tells Gloria Hamilton about a former Chicago gangster named "No Nose Calvelli." The third name Calvelli has three syllables and begins with the third letter of the alphabet.

*Lt. Warsaw tells Banacek the police have already solved the case with the exception of three things: one: who took the collection; two: how it was stolen; three: where it is now.

*Allen Trotter spends his money on three separate branches of the arts: one: the art museum; two: the symphony orchestra; three: the local ballet company.

*Banacek speaks of a three inch space in the truck; the truck was part of a three-vehicle convoy.

*During the course of this story we meet three named employees of the three-named Trotter Van Lines: Larry Casey, Norm Katz and Davis.

*At one point, we see three men who are in the same Trotter Van Lines truck.

FIVES:

*In the teaser, Wheeler says to Gloria Hamilton, "I figure almost five hours to Boston" when telling her the traveling time from New York to

Boston. The five-letter word "hours" follows the number five. "Hours" is the fifth word in the sentence.

*When Allen Trotter hears the sound of the truck approaching, he says to Dr. Shelby, "I think our little five-ton mother is about to deliver." "Five-ton" is the fifth word in the line; it is followed by five words: "mother is about to deliver."

*Wendell Church whom we met in the fifth episode, "To Steal a King" tells Cavanaugh that he has been on about five cases with Banacek.

*When Banacek asks Gloria Hamilton how many dinners it took with (the five letters in his first name) Jason Trotter to get what she wanted, she replies, "Five. Every night for a week." Beginning with the five-letter word, "Every" which begins with E: the fifth letter of the alphabet, five words follow the number five.

SIXES:

*Shelby is the six-letter last name of the curator at the Boston Museum of Art (Six letters in Boston, six letters in Museum.) Lionel Havens is the name of the assistant curator. There are six letters in the first name, Lionel; ditto in the last name Havens.

SEVENS:

*Gloria Hamilton names six French Impressionists represented in the collection she is shepherding in the teaser. Including the unmentioned Braque, this makes for a total of seven French Impressionists in the collection. This is the seventh-aired episode.

*Jason Trotter (seven letters in the last name Trotter) has to be in his office at seven every morning.

Alliteration:
A: acid ate; answering any; all absolutely; anything at all; Aramic? Aramaic; as arrogant and
B: Back Bay; Banacheek. Banacek; begged, borrowed; Big boss; Bottled Beer

C: Casualty Company; Church, Chief; complete cooperation; completes Crate; confused, Church; corporation, controlled
D: difference does; dinner date; drop dead
E: emptied each; entire exhibit; everything, Even; everything, Everything; everything except
F: fast four; father for
H: Harvard. Harvard?; have happened; he has his; Hello, Hamilton; Hello. Hi.; his hang-up
I: I'll, I'll . . . .; I'm, I'm, I'm . . . .; I'm investigating; I'm involved; If it is; indirectly insulted; I've identified
L: look like
M: masterminded; Maurice. My; meet Mr.; meet Mrs.; Montrachet. Montrachet; much more; my meditation; my men; my mind; my music
N: nickname; No. Never; No, no, no; No No. Not; No. Not; no naked; No Nose; No Nothing; not necessarily
O: Oh-oh; only once; overrated, overdressed, overpaid
P: Piano Player; pre-rigged panels
R: Receiving Room; Right? Right.
S: same serial; saw, straight; Say, Say that; say something; says she; Sea Scroll; seal still; shoestring; shrink said; small space; solution. So; some Sherry; some silly; someone stole; Soon? Soon; stop signal
T: take twenty; take thirty that; talk to the; That's,that's; their trick; they take the; they took them; three thousand; to talk to these; today that's; too too; translate that; translates to; Trotter truck; Trotter's trucks; truck traveling time; twenty-two
W: welcome. Well. Well what? Well; Well, where; witnesses watched

Double alliteration:
G&T: gonna go talk to
I&T: I'm investigating the theft; I'm involved in the theft
O&T: out of the truck
W&S: wild what she says
W&T: What was the truck traveling time?

Matches to previous episodes:

*In the pilot episode, "Detour to Nowhere," a two-punch fight between Banacek and the character played by Gene Dynarski occurs in the bar where Banacek is having a beer. In this episode, ordering a beer in a bar, Banacek is challenged to, and accepts, a fight from the character played by Gene Dynarski. Just as was the case with the pilot film, the second punch, from Banacek, knocks Dynarski's character unconscious.

*In "Detour to Nowhere," the armored truck that disappears has Texas plates. In this episode, the truck carrying the paintings which are stolen has been in Texas. The truck's being in Texas proves an important clue in Banacek's solution of the mystery.

*In "A Million the Hard Way," Banacek collects $100,000 as his fee for solving the disappearance of the $1 million from the casino exhibit. In "To Steal a King," Sharon Clark tells Banacek she placed a $100,000 bet on him. In this episode, Banacek tells Lt. Warsaw that the Braque, which the thieves left behind, is worth $100,000.

*In "Ten Thousand Dollars a Page," Felix tells Banacek the Book of Hours changed ownership more than twenty-three times. In this episode Gloria Hamilton tells the policemen that the French Impressionist collection they are escorting to Boston has an insured value of twenty-three million dollars.

*In "Ten Thousand Dollars a Page," insurance man Elliott tells Banacek he is an "overrated, overpaid showboat." In this episode, Banacek tells insurance man Church that Church considers Banacek "overrated, overdressed, overpaid, and under-qualified." Two of the same words beginning with "over" are repeated, and a third word beginning with "over" is added.

*In "Ten Thousand Dollars a Page," after discounting doors and windows as a possible means of entry for the thief, Elliott then discounts the third possibility: the ventilator openings, which are three by three inches. In this episode, a three-inch space in a truck that is part of a three-vehicle convoy proves an important element in Banacek's summation of the case at story's end.

Future Matches:
  *Gloria Hamilton's telling Banacek she's an Aquarius.
  *Banacek's fight with Gene Dynarski.
  *The three-inch space in the truck.
  *Leo, the first name of Banacek's late father.

SECTION TWO

Behind the scenes:
Executive producer George Eckstein:
"This is probably telling tales out of school, but I'll do it anyway, since I don't see him anymore. Anyway ... Ted Flicker. Ted did a movie of the week for me, and he started directing this film, this *Banacek*, and by the end of the first day, or second day, he was like two days over schedule, and he was blaming (director of photography) Sam Leavitt for being too slow. So finally, Teddy came to George, and said, 'Listen, I can't do this with Sam Leavitt. Either he goes, or I go,' and that was the end of Teddy Flicker, because George was very dependent on Sam Leavitt. So George completed the rest of the show. That was a very awkward situation at the time. I don't remember George McCowan working on it. I have no recollection of him."[11]

George Peppard discussing the series' production:
"We use a lot of illusions and special effects in the (*Banacek*) scripts. We've got a permit to set off dynamite. Once I got to tear a bedroom apart with a sword to ward off someone who was trying to get me [episode#3 'No Sign of the Cross']. On another occasion we got to shoot hell out of a garage with a machine gun [this episode, "The Greatest Collection of them All"]. It's wonderful. We're like kids gathering around a wrecking operation!"[12]

The Polish connection:

1, 2, 3, and 4: Among the paintings stolen are works by Toulousse-Lautrec, and Renoir. Polish-born pianist Misia Sert was one of the models for Lautrec's poster for *La Revue Blanche* in 1895. Renoir painted her portrait. Born Maria Zofia Olga Zenajda Godebska, Misia Sert ran a literary and artistic salon in Paris. Musician Claude DeBussy was among the guests at the salon; Pablo Picasso was one of her confidantes. Both DeBussy and Picasso are mentioned later in this episode.

#5: Son of the painter, Auguste Renoir, was director Jean Renoir. In 1956, Jean Renoir directed the movie, *Elena and her Men*. The movie starred Ingrid Bergman as a beautiful but poor Polish princess who drove men of all ranks and stations to fits of desperate love.

#6: Banacek mentions the names Peron and Bormann during one of his visits to Felix' book shop. Poland being one of the countries overrun by the Nazis, Martin Bormann's connection to the Polish is evident; Bormann was private secretary to Adolf Hitler. As for Eva Peron, the wife of Argentinian president Juan Peron, early in her life, she worked as an actress. Eva specialized in dramatizations of historical figures for Radio Belgrano. One of her best known voice portrayals was that of Polish Countess Maria Walewska (1786-1817), mistress of Napoleon Bonaparte.

#7: In addition to Pablo Picasso, Georges Braque is another artist mentioned in this episode. The painting by Braque is the one not stolen by the art thieves. Given the brief biography that follows of Braques' association with the Polish, it's easy to understand why he is the one artist singled out in this story: Louis Marcoussis (born Lodwicz Casimir Ladislas Markus in Warsaw, Poland) and his companion Marcelle Humbert (the pseudonym of Polish-born Eva Gouzel) had met Guillaume Apollinaire (a fellow Pole) and Georges Braque in 1910. (Thus Braque was acquainted with three Poles.) Apollinaire persuaded Markus to adopt a French surname; Lodwicz Markus became Louis Marcoussis. Picasso and Braque encouraged Marcoussis to take up painting again; he'd stopped for a while. Marcoussis quickly adopted cubism; Braque and Picasso were in the analytical phase of their cubism.

#8: During one of Banacek's visits to Felix's bookshop, Felix talks about Palestine. In 1942, when the (Wladyslaw) Anders Army reached Palestine, most of the Polish Jews deserted the regiment to join their fellow Jews living in the settlement there. Menachem Begin, the sixth prime minister of Israel, was one of the members of Anders' Army.

#9: Felix and his friend from the University of Jerusalem are trying to translate the Dead Sea Scrolls. Consisting of about nine hundred documents, including texts from the Hebrew Bible, the Dead Sea Scrolls were discovered between 1947 and 1956. They were found in eleven caves on the northwest shore of the Dead Sea. Cave #4 was discovered in August, 1952; it was excavated from September 22 to September 29, 1952 by Gerald Lankester Harding, Roland de Vaux and Polish Biblical scholar and former Catholic priest Josef Milik. Cave #4 produced 90% of the Dead Sea Scrolls and Scroll fragments. Milik published more texts of the Dead Sea Scrolls than any other original team member—unfortunately, since he did not complete all the work on his portion, he received a good part of the blame for (all of) the Scrolls not being published until almost forty years had passed.

#10: When Banacek and Jay pay a visit to truck-driver Norman Katz, he is playing Bach on his violin. Johann Sebastian Bach was nominated as court composer to the king of Poland and the Elector of Saxony in 1736.

#11: Banacek tells Katz his playing reminds him of David Oistrakh. One of the great Russian violinists of the twentieth century, David Oistrakh took second prize in the first Henryk Wieniawski Violin Competition in 1935 in Warsaw. A violinist of genius, Wieniawski wrote some of the most important works in the violin repertoire, including two very difficult violin concertos.

#12: Claude Monet is another French Impressionist artist mentioned in this story. In 1889, Polish illustrator Wladyslaw Podkowinski journeyed to Paris. Though Podkowinski had done watercolor and oil paintings a few years earlier, after he made the trip, he decided to try painting as a profession. The French Impressionist painters Podkowinski encountered in Paris influenced him considerably, none more so than Claude Monet. Podkowinski later received credit for bringing the Impressionist movement to Poland.

#13: The character Garry Walberg plays is Lt. Warsaw. Warsaw is the capital and largest city in Poland.

Notes:

Like the preceding episode, this entry has Banacek looking for something that is not a fictional creation: in this case, paintings by such real French artists as Degas, Renoir, and Lautrec. Having the total number of artists featured in the stolen collection match the number of the episode, and tying these artists to Polish people and places is another carryover from the previous outing. Foreshadowing the tone of the second season is the un-credited direction by George Peppard, the use of authentic Boston locations, and the return of the two insurance company men: Cavanaugh and Church. As can best be determined, the twelfth century Polish King Stanislaus whom Felix's friend from the University of Jerusalem references, never existed.

BANACEK Challenges:
"The Greatest Collection of Them All"

#1: In the teaser, riding in the "follow car," Gloria Hamilton and one of the police officers say something that results in a match of a certain number. Can you identify the number?

#2: In the teaser, the policemen stop the truck that had been carrying the crates near something that contains a match of three to one of the regular *Banacek* talents. What is that something, and to which talent does it match? Hint: "The play's the thing."

#3: After Gloria Hamilton overhears Banacek telling Dr. Shelby that she would have been involved in the theft if such and such theory was correct, she tells the sleuth she wouldn't have lunch with him if he was the last man on earth. As Gloria makes this statement, Banacek echoes her, speaking her last few words at exactly the same time. How many words spoken by Gloria does Banacek echo, and why?

#4. In this episode, we learn that the first name of Banacek's father is Leo. Why is the sleuth's father's name given in this episode, and why is his name Leo?

#5. At one point, Gloria Hamilton tells Banacek three personal things about herself. The third thing establishes a connection between Gloria and the sleuth's father. How?

#6. Towards the end of the story, Banacek finds Gloria in a bus station. This scene and the subsequent walk-and-talk sequence between the two creates a match of threes. Can you identify this match?

#7. As noted earlier, in the teaser, upon hearing the sound of the approaching truck, Lloyd Gough's Allen Trotter says to John Hoyt's Dr. Shelby, "I think our little five-ton mother is about to deliver." How is the fifth word in the line: "five-ton" an important clue to the location of the missing Impressionist paintings?

Episode #8: "The Two Million Clams of Cap'n Jack," February 7, 1973

"There's an old Polish proverb that says, 'When an owl comes to a mouse picnic, it's not there for the sack races.'" –Banacek to Felix

"There's an old Polish proverb that says, 'Even a thousand Zloty note can't tap dance.'" –Banacek to Erica and Leo Osborn

Teleplay by Stanley Ralph Ross
Story by Shirl Hendryx and Pat Fielder and Richard Bluel
D: Richard T. Heffron

Guest Stars
Jessica Walter — Erica Osburn
Andrew Duggan — Cap'n Jack Osburn
Linden Chiles — Penniman
Also starring
David White — W. Crawford Morgan
Jason Evers — Roger Sloan
And
William Schallert as — Leo Osburn
Co-starring
Wally Taylor — Ed Spencer
Fredd Wayne — Stein
And
Gregory Sierra as — Esposito
With
Liam Dunn — Hanrahan
Joan Pringle — Ann Spencer
Michael DeLano — Simson

Selette Cole   Lucille Sloan
Fredericka Myers   Nora

SECTION ONE: MATCHES

Matches in series credits:

On screen the title is presented as:

THE TWO
MILLION CLAMS
OF CAP'N JACK

*There are three lines in this title. In the first line, there are two three-letter words ("The" and "Two"). In the next line, following the third word in the title, "Million," is the word, "Clams" which begins with C: the third letter of the alphabet. The third line has three words ("Of," "Cap'n" and "Jack"). C is the third letter in the third and last word, "Jack." Altogether, there are a total of three Cs in the episode title.

*Following the episode title, there are three actors billed under the "Guest Stars" credit: Jessica Walter, Andrew Duggan, and Linden Chiles. Chiles, the last name of the third-billed "Guest Star" begins with the third letter of the alphabet.

*After these three "Guest Stars" three more actors: David White, Jason Evers and William Schallert are billed. The third actor, Schallert, is billed under the three-letter word, "And." His character's first name, "Leo," is a total of three letters.

*The billing of the episode's writers and director continue the pattern of the three. Writer of the three-syllable "teleplay" is the three-named Stanley Ralph Ross; his teleplay is based on a story by three writers: Shirl Hendryx, Pat Fielder and Richard Bluel.

*Directing his third *Banacek* is the three-named Richard T. Heffron.

*The threes of the opening credits continue into the closing credits; there are three actors billed before the "With" credits: Wally Taylor, Fredd Wayne, and Gregory Sierra. Sierra is billed under the three-letter word, "And." There are three syllables in his first name, three syllables in his last. As for the third three possessed by Sierra, like Wally Taylor, and Fredd Wayne, Gregory Sierra has a pair of side by side consonants in his performer name: in this case, two "r"s in the last name. In the case of Wally Taylor, there are two "l"s in the first name "Wally"; in regards to Fredd Wayne, there are two "d"s in the first name "Fredd."

Matches through physical production and editing

*This episode features two brothers: Leo and Jack Osburn.

*This is the second episode to feature the two-word restaurant STEAK JOINT. There are five letters in the first word of the restaurant, five letters in the second word as well.

*The teaser features two Black security guards, and two White security guards.

*The sign on the outside of the building where the theft takes place identifies the structure as the BARRON BANKNOTE BUILDING. Each of these three words begins with B: the second letter of the alphabet. Each of these three words is two syllables. Each word contains two of the same letter: two (side by side) Rs in BARRON, two Ns in BANKNOTE, two Is in BUILDING.

*Complimenting the horizontal Rs in BARRON are two vertically placed As (the second word BANKNOTE is placed under BARRON).

*Later in the story, Banacek and Erica pay a visit to the underground newspaper, *Open Secret*. The sign on the outside is a total of four words: "OPEN SECRET, A WEEKLY.' The first two words "OPEN SECRET" are of the same style. The last two words, "A WEEKLY" are of a smaller size. Note that the first two words on the sign "OPEN SECRET" are both two syllables.

*In the OPEN SECRET newspaper office, there is a poster showing the Astrological sign, Gemini. In the Zodiac, Gemini is the sign of the twins.

*In addition to the two-word (five letters in each word) restaurant, STEAK JOINT, this episode also features the two-word (five letters in each word) ATLAS HOTEL. The latter is shown in the background when Banacek and Jay pay a visit to the home of suspect Ed Spencer.

*After the three-word sign BARRON BANKNOTE BUILDING is shown on the exterior of the building, we are taken inside the building and to the vault where the plates are stored. There we see three men: Penniman, Spencer, and the engraver.

*The opening credits feature three new scenes.

*The pictures of three people are shown during Felix's slideshow presentation: Roger Sloan, Captain Jack Osburn and Erica Osburn.

*Three people, including Banacek, feature in the sequence where the crooks are apprehended. At one point, Banacek hits the switch on a fuse-box which plunges the room into darkness. On the box is a large 3.

*Three people: Banacek, (the three-syllable) Penniman, and the three-named W. Crawford Morgan appear in the explanation scene at Banacek's home.

*Three people: Banacek, Erica Osburn, and her uncle Leo appear in the conclusion at Leo's home.

*Three pencils are seen on Esposito's desk: two are in a cup, one is lying near the crossword puzzle page in the newspaper.

*Following the credits, we see Banacek and his friends playing football. There are five men on each team.

*As noted earlier, the ATLAS HOTEL faces the street on which Ed Spencer lives. On Spencer's street, we see five cars. On the side of the street where Spencer lives are five people. When Banacek visits Spencer, we meet five members of the Spencer family: Ed, his wife, Ann, their two children, and Ed's brother, Tim.

*Inside the *Open Secret* newspaper office, there is a seven-word sign saying, "THERE ARE NO SECRETS IN PUBLIC LIFE." The six-letter word, "PUBLIC" is the sixth word in the sign. In the first scene in the office, there are a total of seven people, including Banacek.

*During the Banacek plays football with his friends sequence, we see the (six letters in his first name, seven letters in his last name) Thomas Banacek standing next to a man in a number 67 football jersey.

Matching through numbers:
TWOS:

*During the football game between Banacek and his friends, there are two two-word expressions said twice: "Watch him" and "I gotcha."

*The special security elevator is programmed to stop at just two floors: the 1st and 8th. The term, "Special security elevator" contains two side by side "S" words, and two side by side eight-letter words: "security" and "elevator."

*The (two letters in his first name) Security Guard Ed Spencer is found unconscious two miles from the BARRON BANKNOTE BUILDING.

*Prior to starting the Cap'n Jack's chain, the two brothers Jack and Leo Osburn had been in and out of twenty different businesses.

*Three side by side twos can be found in the six-word company name: "Cap'n Jack's Down East Clam Bakery." The first two words: "Cap'n Jack's" identifies who heads the company; the second two words: "Down East" tells where the company is located: the last two words: "Clam Bakery" identifies the company's product. Note that with every one of these two words, there is a match. In the first two words, both words have an apostrophe. In the second combination, each word is four letters long; in the third combination, the first word, Clam, begins with the third letter of the alphabet and the second word, Bakery, contains three syllables.

*Banacek usually tips the waiter at the two-word STEAK JOINT twenty percent.

*Felix tells Banacek that the two Osburn brothers spent more time in court than the fictional lawyer Perry Mason. Two syllables in both Perry and Mason; each name has the same number of letters.

*Felix lists four businesses among the twenty in which the two Osburn brothers worked: "used cars," "window washing," "industrial supplies," and "shoe repairs." Each of these businesses is described in two words. The "two" also surfaces in the first two businesses listed: "used cars," and "window washing." In the first business, each word: "used" and "cars" is four letters long; in the second business, window washing, each word starts with a "W."

*Jack Osburn loves every second of being a national celebrity; his brother Leo retained twenty percent of the business.

*There are just two Osburns living in the same home: Jack, and his daughter Erica.

A dramatic scene from the NBC/Universal *Banacek* "The Two Million Clams of Cap'n Jack" with (left to right) George Peppard, Jessica Walter, and Andrew Duggan.

*Erica mentions two "Doctors" she's read: Dr. Seuss and Dr. Rubin-both last names are five letters long.

*Erica Osburn has been romantically involved with two men: Skip Garland of the Boston Red Sox who was an All Star for two years, and Roger Sloan; Erica broke up with Sloan two years ago.

*On the day of the robbery, Esposito was two blocks away at Clara's Coffee Shop, having his usual breakfast of two eggs over easy.

THREES:

*Setting up the next play in the football game, Banacek tells his team he will: (One) "Come down the left side-line," (Two) "then through the center," (Three) "on a slant pattern on three."

*The three syllable Penniman works for the three-named W. Crawford Morgan. The three-named Morgan's Montauk Insurance insures Roger Sloan's three-named United Foods Company.

*The three-word "Special Security Elevator" cannot reach the basement because there are three-inch steel bars built in to prevent the elevator from slipping through.

*Just three men have a (three-letter) key to the basement. They are, in order of mention: One: head of security Stein; Two: the owner of the building; Three: the custodial engineer Norman Esposito.

*Erica Osborn was told three things about Banacek: One: He was tall; Two: He was blond; Three: He was handsome.

*Erica dated the three-syllable Skip Garland of the three-named Boston Red Sox. But when his average dipped below .300, she stopped seeing him. Later Banacek talks to Garland. He informs Erica that Garland was hitting .310, not below .300.

*Banacek tells Esposito that three DOWN in the crossword puzzle he is working is ITER.

*(The three-letters in his first name) Tim Spencer's bail is $3,000. Note that three 0s follow the number 3 in 3,000.

*Esposito says he needs three cups of coffee before he goes to work (at the three-named Barron Banknote Building.)

FOURS:

*Penniman's question, "What do you want to talk to them for," and Banacek's reply, "Oh, I don't know. I thought they just might be fun to talk to" produces a clever use of fours. Penniman's last word "for" comes after he has spoken four four-letter words: "What," "want," "talk" and "them," and four alliterative (side-by-side) words: "to talk to them." The first sentence in Banacek's two-sentence reply is a total of four words; the four-letter word, "know" is the last word in the sentence, "Oh, I don't know." In the sleuth's second sentence, the four-letter word "just" is the fourth word; there are a total of four words between "just" and the last four-letter word, "talk."

FIVES:

*The five-letter Erica whose first name begins with the fifth letter of the alphabet, tells Banacek she met "Crawfish" Morgan when she was doing an article on pornography for the (five-letter) Globe (The Boston Globe.) The radio station announcer refers to Erica as (the five-word) "Our Lady of the Clouds." Erica tells Banacek she is on the protein diet; she lists five food types she can eat: meat, fish, eggs, cottage cheese, and poultry.

*Like Banacek, Erica Osborn is attempting to recover the plates: Morgan made a deal with her—she'll get five percent if she succeeds. Erica tells Banacek that her father and her uncle have not gotten along well for five years. Felix remarks to Banacek that the sleuth might describe Erica as (five words) "a bit of a flake." At one time, Erica was going with the five letter-by-five-letter Roger Sloan.

*After Penniman tells the man at the *Open Secret* that they're the fifth paper he's contacted, and that they have the information he's been seeking, he then asks the man if he's the editor. "Right," the man replies. Following this one-word, five-letter reply, the man lists five more positions/jobs he holds at the paper: publisher, advertising director, columnist, reporter, and occasionally, newsboy.

*On Friday, the day of the theft (the fifth day of the work-week), Esposito was at Clara's (five letters in Clara) Coffee Shop having his usual (five-word) breakfast: Two eggs over easy, tomatoes.

*Felix mentions five people/groups who own part of Captain Jack's stock: One: Roger Sloan, Two: Erica Osburn, Three: Leo Osburn, Four: Various long-time employees and investors, Five: Captain Jack Osburn.

SIXES:

*After noting to Banacek that it's six-thirty in the morning, a few moments later, Esposito tells the sleuth that he hasn't had a vacation in six years.

EIGHTS:

*In this, the eighth-aired episode, the payoff (from Montauk to the thief who has the plates) is scheduled for eight o'clock Monday morning.

TENS:

*The ten-letter Jack Osburn's name begins with J, the tenth letter of the alphabet. Jack and his brother Leo started their seafood business ten years ago. Jack's daughter Erica owns ten percent of the above business.

*The ten-letter Roger Sloan is taking over the ten-year old "Cap'n Jack's Down East Clam Bakery."

*The person who puts the ad in the (ten-letter) underground newspaper, *Open Secret*, about the plates tells Montauk he'll call them at ten p.m. There are a total of ten words in the ad.

FIFTEENS:

*Banacek will meet the fifteen-letter W. Crawford Morgan in fifteen minutes.

Alliteration:

A: about an ad; ad application; anything at all about; appraise antiques as

B: Barron Banknote Building; baseball; beeping, bumpers banging; been better, Banacek; big Boston; brother's bail

C: car couldn't; carrying case; certificate ceremony; check, Crawfish; clam chowder; Clara's Coffee; classier circles

D: daughter did

E: emergency exit; ever engraved

F: first floor

G: game going; Generation Gap; good, good; great girl

H: Howard Hanrahan

I: I imagine; I'm in it; insurance investigator

L: little lunch

M: male motorists; merchandise myself; Monday morning

O: over old

P: particularly praised; passport; Penniman's people; protest period

R: real reason; right. Roger

S: see Spencer; Sloan staking; sound sexy; special security; Spencer stepped; success story; sufficient sleep

T: terribly tall; They tend to; to talk to; to talk to them

W: were well worth; What? What? What?; Why? Why?; work. Work, work, work

Y: Yeah, yeah

Double alliteration:

A&T: are all that type

O&T: out of the trunk

T&A: to take an ad

Matches to previous episodes:

*In the *Banacek* pilot, "Detour to Nowhere," Banacek asks the *Vantage Sentinel's* Earl Lewis if he's the editor of the paper. "Yes sir," Lewis replies.

"Also the writer, printer, maintenance man, and delivery boy." In this episode, Penniman asks the man at the underground newspaper, *Open Secret* if he's the editor. "Right," the man replies. "And the publisher, and advertising director and columnist and reporter and every now and then, newsboy." In both episodes, the list of jobs begins with editor and ends with delivery boy/newsboy.

*In the first episode of the season, "Let's Hear It For A Living Legend," Banacek is introduced watching a football game. In this episode (the last original aired episode of the season), Banacek is introduced playing a football game.

*In "Legend," Felix and his Russian friend are playing a long-distance chess game (by mail); in this episode, two friends are playing a chess game (by phone.)

*In "Project Phoenix," Jay tells Banacek that he needs three cups of coffee with three teaspoons of sugar in each cup every day because he has low blood sugar. In this episode, Norman Esposito informs the sleuth that he needs three cups of coffee before he goes to work.

*In episode#4, the title of the episode is "A Million the Hard Way." This is the second episode with "Million" in the episode title. This time, the amount is two million.

*In "A Million the Hard Way," Banacek romances a woman who flies her own plane. In this episode, Banacek romances a woman who flies a helicopter.

*The Asian man who was an extra in the casino scenes of "A Million the Hard Way" returns in this episode; this time he's one of the party guests at Roger Sloan's home.

*In episode#5: "To Steal a King," Banacek meets feminist Sharon Clark; in this episode, feminist helicopter traffic scout Erica Osburn tells Banacek that she is a friend of Sharon Clark.

*In episode #6, "Ten Thousand Dollars a Page," Banacek tells Glassman that "King Cheops only needed one pyramid." In this episode, when Banacek enters Felix's book shop, he finds Felix and his female companion working with a Styrofoam pyramid.

*In the previous episode, "The Greatest Collection of them All," Banacek and his love interest Gloria Hamilton have lunch at the STEAK JOINT. In this episode, Banacek and his love interest Erica Osburn have lunch at the STEAK JOINT.

*In "Greatest Collection," Ben Wheeler calls Banacek a "Polack." In this episode, Tim Spencer calls Banacek "Mr. Polack." Both Ben Wheeler and Tim Spencer have ten-letter names. Each character's first name is three letters, his last name seven.

*This is the third episode to use the words, "three-inch." In episode#6, "Ten Thousand Dollars a Page," Elliott told Banacek the ventilator openings were three-by-three inches; in episode#7, "The Greatest Collection of them All," Banacek talked about a three-inch space in a truck; in this, the eighth episode, Banacek learns that the elevator cannot reach the basement because there are three-inch steel bars built in to prevent it from slipping through.

*In the previous episode, we learn that the first name of Banacek's father is Leo. In this episode, the first name of William Schallert's character is Leo.

*In the previous episode, Gloria Hamilton tells Banacek she's an Aquarius, one of the signs in the Zodiac. This episode features two signs of the Zodiac: the aforementioned Leo, through the William Schallert character, and Gemini: the name on the poster in the *Open Secret* office.

Future Matches:

*The name Leo.

*The word "Million" as part of the episode title.

*The word "picnic" being part of Banacek's old Polish proverb.

*Linden Chiles as an insurance representative who's opposed to Banacek being hired.

*The amount of time Banacek is given to recover the stolen item—forty-eight hours (two days).

*Banacek getting a Sunday newspaper.

*Erica keeping track of Banacek by helicopter.

*Felix making a "pyramid."

*Elevators possibly figuring in the theft

*A period of ten years

*A woman competing against Banacek to retrieve the missing item

*The words, "Success story."

*Norman Esposito working a crossword puzzle.

*Erica Osborn's three-word greeting on Banacek's mobile phone: "Mr. Banacek's car."

SECTION TWO

Behind the scenes:
Executive producer George Eckstein: "She (Eckstein's actress-wife Selette Cole) was in it. Yeah, that was all right. (But) it was not one of my favorite episodes."[13]

The Polish connection:
#1, 2&3 Penniman asks Banacek how he is able to convince others that he's a combination of Sherlock Holmes, the Scarlet Pimpernel, and Humphrey Bogart. All three references connect to something Polish. In regards to Bogart, in the 1937 Warner Bros. picture, *Black Legion*, the actor plays a workman who gets passed over for a promotion; the job goes to a Polish-American (Henry Brandon). Furious, Bogart joins the "Black Legion," a group that hates newly, or recently-arrived immigrants. *The Scarlet Pimpernel* is the title of a famous novel by Baroness Elizabeth Orczy. During the course of her life, Orczy wrote a number of detective stories and novels. One such collection of stories, entitled "Skin O'My Tooth" featured an Irish detective-lawyer named Patrick Mulligan. Among the stories in this collection: "The Case of the Polish Prince." The story was later reworked and presented under the new title, "The Case of the Sicilian Prince." As for the Sherlock Holmes reference, as previously noted in this book, the "Brigadier Gerard" stories of Holmes' creator Sir Arthur Conan Doyle featured Polish characters.

#4: Erica talks about Banacek putting on a Ravel tape. Maurice Ravel had a close-friendship with the Godebskis: a Polish family living in Paris; they were friends of Ravel's father. The family was artistic and held Sunday evenings at home for many musicians and painters. After the death of Ravel's father, the Godebskis became something like his second family. Polish-born pianist Misia Sert was the sister of the head of the family, Cipa Godebski.

Notes:

Despite George Eckstein's misgivings, "The Two Million Clams of Cap'n Jack" is a very watchable episode, thanks to Jessica Walter's amusing performance as the flaky Erica Osburn, and Linden Chiles' funny portrayal of the easily fooled Penniman. Also providing fun moments are Andrew Duggan, William Schallert, and Gregory Sierra. Making this episode even more watchable are the many matches it presents to previous episodes. The "three-inch" bit of business is particularly clever; this is the third episode in a row to use the words "three-inch." Foreshadowing the return of Christine Belford's Carlie Kirkland in the following season is Jessica Walter as the wisecracking, competitive Erica Osburn. With the return of Belford, the addition of Linden Chiles as the fussy and easily fooled Henry Dewitt, plus a new story editor more adept at comic situations, the best of *Banacek* was on its way.

BANACEK Challenges:
"The Two Million Clams of Cap'n Jack"

#1: What is there about supporting guest Michael DeLano's billing that connects to his name?

#2: In the closing credits, what three things do supporting guests Joan Pringle and Selette Cole have in common?

#3: Besides each actor's last name beginning with a W, and each having the same number of letters in his first name as in his last, what other two things do this episode's supporting guest David White and the premiere episode's lead guest Robert Webber have in common?

#4: In this episode, Banacek delivers two "old Polish proverbs," rather than his customary one. In what two ways does this departure from typical series procedure connect to this episode?

#5: How does the poster in the stairway outside the *Open Secret* office connect to the character played by Claire Brennen in episode#4: "A Million the Hard Way?"

#6. During his conversation with Stein, Banacek learns that eighteen seconds is all it takes for the elevator to travel from the first to the eighth floor. Besides the word "eight" being present in both "eighteen" and "eighth," what other eight match is there between the eighteen second traveling time and the eighth floor?

#7. The ad placed in the underground newspaper *Open Secret* contains two clues which identify the mastermind behind the theft. What are they?

Reviews and Publicity from February through July 1973:

February 12, 13, 14, 15, 16, 1973 - Peppard appears on *Password* with Linda Kaye Henning.

February 17, 1973: *TV Guide* – Vol. 21, No. 7 — Issue#538 TV Crossword – 8 Down – Banacek (2 words)

February 24, 1973: *TV Guide* – Vol. 21, No. 8 — Issue#539 TV Crossword – 8 Down – answer: George Peppard

March, 1973, *TV Picture Life*, Vol. 18, No. 3, , "Peppard: Woman Around," pg. 24. George tells *TV Picture Life*'s Betty Samuelson, "We've got to make these women's libbers stop trying to diminish women's roles as sex symbols."

Later he tells Samuelson, "Right or wrong, I think it's part of the feminine personality to want to please her man in whatever way she can. Being sexy is part of that. A woman likes to know people are looking at her favorably—that they find her pleasing."

March 10, 1973: *TV Guide* – Vol. 21, No. 10 — Issue#541 – "The Doan Report" – Richard K. Doan reports that among the series NBC is likely to cancel: *Banacek* and *Cool Million*

March 17, 1973: *TV Guide* – Vol. 21, No. 11,- Issue#542 – "TV Crossword" – 9 Down – Star of *Banacek* (2 words)

March 24, 1973: *TV Guide* – Vol. 21, No. 12,- Issue#543 – "TV Crossword" – 9 Down – answer: George Peppard.

March 31, 1973: *TV Guide* – Vol. 21, No. 13– Issue#544 – "TV Crossword" – 5 Down – Banacek. In "TV Teletype: Hollywood," Joseph Finnigan reports that *Banacek* has finished production for the year, and that George Peppard has signed up for the movie, *Newman*

April 7, 1973: *TV Guide* – Vol. 21, No. 14– Issue#545 – "TV Crossword" – 5 Down – Answer: Peppard

April 14, 1973: *TV Guide* – Vol. 21, No. 15– Issue#546 – "The Doan Report" – Richard K. Doan reports that *Banacek* will NOT be dropped from *The NBC Wednesday Mystery Movie*, but *Cool Million* and *Madigan* will.

April 28, 1973: *TV Guide* – Vol. 21, No. 17– Issue#548 – *Banacek* mentioned in two-page profile of Christine Belford, "Off Came the White Gloves" Pg. 35. Christine Belford was a Monique James "discovery."

May 5, 1973: *TV Guide* – Vol. 21, No. 18– Issue#549 – "TV Crossword" – 33 Down – *Banacek* star abbreviation

May 6, 1973: The *Philadelphia Sunday Bulletin* – *TV Time* — "Private Eye Peppard – Give George Dynamite . . . And Look Out!" By Rex Polier – Bulletin TV Writer/Associate Editor – TV Time – pg 3.

May 12, 1973: *TV Guide* – Vol. 21, No. 19– Issue#550 – "The Doan Report" – Richard K. Doan reports that in the upcoming season, *Banacek* will be rotating with *Tenafly*, starring James McEachin, *The Snoop Sisters* with Helen

Hayes and Mildred Natwick, and *Faraday & Co.* starring Dan Dailey; "TV Crossword" – 33 Down – answer: Geo

May 26, 1973: *TV Guide* – Vol. 21, No. 21– Issue#552 – "TV Crossword" – 65 Across – Banacek

June 2, 1973: *TV Guide* – Vol. 21, No. 22– Issue#553 – "TV Crossword" – 65 Across – Answer: Peppard; in "Second Thoughts," Cleveland Amory explains how he was taken to task for his review of *Banacek*; he admits his critics had a point—*Banacek* is better than he thought.

June 9, 1973: *Tonight Show* (rerun, George Peppard is guest, along with Suzanne Pleshette)

June 14, 1973: *Password* – ABC –George Eckstein guests in episode with future *Banacek* guest Dick Gautier. *Password* host Allen Ludden will also be a future *Banacek* guest.

June 30, 1973: *TV Guide* – Vol 21, No. 26,– Issue#557 – *Banacek* mentioned in tongue-in-cheek article, "It's Murder," pg. 28 in article on writing for TV crime dramas by George Tolliver. On page 30, it's mentioned again. Seems the writer has done a script for the show in which the entire state of Florida disappears. The story is turned down because the show has an episode in the works where the entire state of Michigan vanishes. Banacek discovers that the culprit there is a man who's a great bit like Ralph Nader. In the *Banacek* pilot, "Detour to Nowhere," Carlie made a crack about Banacek driving her back to her hotel in a "Ralph Nader" nightmare of a truck.

July 7, 1973: *TV Guide* – Vol 21, No. 27– Issue#558 – "TV Crossword" – 15 Across – He's Banacek – 2 words

July 14, 1973: *TV Guide* – Vol. 21, No. 28– Issue#559 – "TV Crossword of July 7" – 15 Across – Answer: George Peppard; "TV Crossword of July 14" – 28 Down – Belonging to a Polish detective

July 21, 1973: *TV Guide* – Vol. 21, No. 29– Issue#560 – "TV Crossword of July 14" – 28 Down -Answer: Banacek's

September 8, 1973: *TV Guide* – Vol. 21, No. 36 — Issue#567 – In *Changes*, pg. 9, it is revealed that Banacek will have a steady girlfriend—insurance investigator Christine Belford; on page 50, it's revealed that *The NBC Wednesday*

Mystery Movie will premiere October 3. On page 54, in *Kojak* blurb, *Banacek* is mentioned (Polish-American detective)

September 24: *NBC Monday Night at the Movies* premieres *The Groundstar Conspiracy* starring George Peppard and Christine Belford.

September 29, 1973: *TV Guide* – Vol. 21, No. 39 — Issue#570 – NBC 73 – Come And See! BANACEK 8:30 p.m/Premiere George Peppard, as the polished Polish investigator, returns to "NBC Wednesday Mystery Movie." And now, he's got a girl! Pg. 78.

George Peppard's Banacek in the recovery scene from the second season NBC/Universal premiere, "No Stone Unturned."

Season Two

Episode #9: "No Stone Unturned" – October 3, 1973

"There's an old Polish proverb that says, 'Only the centipede can hear all the hundred footsteps of his uncle.'" –Banacek to Jay

Teleplay by George Sheldon Smith and Lee Santley and Robert Van Scoyk, story by Stephen Lord
D: Richard T. Heffron

Guest Stars
Gary Lockwood   Owen Russell
Don Stroud   Chief Vince O'Hara
Scott Brady   Collier
Candace Clark   Gretel
Co-starring
Joe Maross   Lieutenant Nash
Linden Chiles   Henry DeWitt
Co-starring
Larry Pennell   Pete Biesecker
Peggy Walton   Jennifer Nesborne

SECTION ONE: MATCHES

Matches in series credits:
Opening credits:
   *The episode was written by a total of four people: George Sheldon Smith, Lee Santley, Robert Van Scoyk and Stephen Lord. There are four letters in

the last name of the fourth writer listed: Stephen Lord. The last letter in his last name: d, is the fourth letter of the alphabet.

*There are a total of four actors receiving "Guest Stars" billing in the opening credits: Gary Lockwood, Don Stroud, Scott Brady, and Candace Clark. In addition to each having a "D" in their first or last name (they also have an "R"), each performer name creates a match of some kind. For example, the top-billed Gary Lockwood is a match of fours; his first name, Gary, is four letters; his last name, Lockwood, is a combination of two four-letter words: "lock," and "wood." The second billed Don Stroud is a reverse match of D. D is the first letter in the first name Don; d is the last letter in the last name, Stroud. The third-billed Scott Brady is a five-by-five match. His first name, Scott, is five letters; ditto his last name Brady. As for the fourth-billed Candace Clark, her first and last name begins with the same letter: C. The fact that she is billed on this occasion as Candace, rather than her usual billing of Candy, is another sign from the makers of *Banacek* that they were doing a match show; the name Candace Clark yields three Cs; the billing Candy Clark would of course only yield two. Like the "D" in the last name Brady, the "D" in "Candace" is the fourth letter in the name.

*Sixth-billed in the opening credits is the six letters in his first name/six letters in his last name, Linden Chiles.

*There are two "Co-starring" guests in the opening credits: Joe Maross and Linden Chiles; there are two "Co-starring" guests in the closing credits: Larry Pennell and Peggy Walton. In the opening credits, the last names of both "Co-starring" guests are six letters apiece; in the closing credits, the first names of both "Co-starring" guests are a total of five letters. Each of these first names ends in a "y."

Matches through physical production and editing:

*There are two scenes featuring Felix and his female companion. In the first scene, Felix is on the left, and the girl at the right; in the second, Felix is on the right, and the girl is on the left.

*In the exterior scene of Boston Memorial Hospital, director Richard T. Heffron presents a number of twos in the same scene. There are two nurses walking towards the hospital. Above them and to the right, are two people on the balcony of the first floor. To the left of the two walking nurses is a sign saying BOSTON MEMORIAL HOSPITAL. On the first line are the two words BOSTON MEMORIAL. The eight-letter word MEMORIAL is followed by the eight-letter word HOSPITAL. The eight-letter HOSPITAL is followed by the eight-letter word, ENTRANCE, but the type/print size of ENTRANCE is smaller than the preceding word HOSPITAL. In front of the two walking nurses is a car with a license plate that reads 228 850. The first two numbers on the plate are the same: 2. These two 2s are followed by two 8s.

*In the scene where Carlie explains the disappearance of Man in Harmony, Heffron presents another batch of twos. Standing against the same wall of the Collier Center are two trios of security guards. One trio is on the ground floor of the Center; the second trio is above them, standing near the windows. Below Carlie, and to the left, are two people: Banacek and Lt. Nash; below Carlie, and to the right, are two people: Collier and Jennifer Nesborne. In front of Collier and Jennifer Nesborne, are two security guards. One guard is to the right of Carlie, the other is to her left.

*Three men on the back of the truck transporting the three-named statue, Man in Harmony.

*Three pieces of stone outside Russell's art studio when Banacek arrives.

*Three shots fired back-to-back by Lt. Nash in the capture of the crooks sequence.

*Collier pokes Banacek in the chest three times.

*At the fruit market, we see three people: a mother, a father, and their daughter; behind the little girl is a campaign sign with three words: "Select Serra Senator."

*The Biesecker Crane Co. is right next to the PACIFIC METAL PRODUCTS Co. The fourth word, Co. is of smaller size, so this gives us three words: PACIFIC, METAL, and PRODUCTS, of the same size.

*Five people at the statue base as the teaser fades out; five spotlights in the room housing the statue.

*There are seven people at the loading of the statue. They are: Owen Rusell, Pete Biesecker, Gretel, two of Bisecker's men; two policemen on motorcycles. There are seven people inside the gallery where the statue is unloaded. They are: Owen Russell, Pete Biesecker, Gretel, two of Bisecker's men, Jennifer Nesborne, Chief Vince O'Hara.

Matching through numbers:
THREES:

*The three-word statue, Man in Harmony, is insured by the three-word Boston Insurance Company for $3 million. (Note that in the three-word name, "Man in Harmony," the first word, "Man," is three letters, and the last word, "Harmony" is three syllables.)

*The word "Thanks" is spoken three times in a row.

*Collier obtained the rights to the three-word "Man in Harmony" three months ago.

*The truck from the liquor store delivers three cases of champagne to the reception for the opening of "Man in Harmony."

*Gretel tells Banacek that her film concerning "Man in Harmony" will be ready by around three o'clock that afternoon.

*When Carlie tells Banacek she would like to see the movies Gretel took, he asks his rival to come to his house at three-thirty.

*Carlie has a witness who will testify she saw a truck leaving the Collier building about a half-hour (or thirty minutes) before the theft.

*Henry DeWitt will pay Banacek sixty percent of the recovery of the $500,000 ransom for the statue, but only if Banacek has the money on DeWitt's desk by three o'clock. Sixty percent of half a million is $300,000.

*When Banacek finds the statue for DeWitt, it is three hours and eighteen minutes past two days.

*After speaking the three four-letter words, "Stop. Okay. Slow," Gretel repeats them in reverse: "Slow. Okay. Stop."

FOURS:

*Davy Collier's four-word question "What does that mean?" contains four four-letter words.

FIVES:

*In their ransom note to the Boston Insurance Company, the thieves who took the statue ask for $500,000 in old $20 bills. Divided by 20, 500,000 is the five-digit 20,500.

EIGHTS:

*The eight-letter Jennifer says to Owen Russell "He wants you at the unveiling ceremony at eight." Eight words precede the last word "eight" in this sentence.

*Banacek's first encounter with Carlie Kirkland (eight letters in her full first name Caroline, eight letters in her last name, Kirkland) takes place in the (eight-letter) basement.

*When chauffeur Jay (full name Jay Drury-eight letters in the full name) sees his passenger Carlie (full name Caroline Kirkland-eight letters in the first name, eight letters in the last) exploring the interior of Banacek's car with her hands as they make their way to the ransom drop, he asks her what she's doing. "I'm just making sure I'm not riding in an eight-cylinder Watergate," she replies. The number eight is followed by the eight-letter word, "cylinder." An automobile running on an eight-cylinder engine is nothing unusual, thus the cleverness of this line is missed, unless one is aware of the other "eights" that have been worked into the scene.

FIFTEENS:

*It takes Biesecker one hour and fifteen minutes to get from Russell's studio to the Collier building. When Banacek arrives at the Collier lobby to begin his investigation, Jennifer Nesborne tells him that DeWitt called them fifteen minutes ago to alert them to his arrival.

Alliteration:

A: about artistic; along, and all; anything? Anything

B: Banasek. Banacek; be beaten; bright, Banacek; building back

C: certainly check; cheap champagne; Collier Compound; couple collectors; Crane cab; Crane Co.

D: dedication dates

E: early Egyptians; entire empire; exchange ethnic

F: father fixation; film from; five-foot

G: gonna get; gonna give; granite gray; guy's got

H: half-hour; happened here; hit him; hot-heads; How'd he

I: if it's in; if it isn't, I; internal injuries

L: least let; love life

M: makes me; masterpiece, Man; mean, Man; mean Mr.; means more; missing masterpiece; my men

N: No. Not; No new; Nothing new

O: O'Hara. Oh ho; Oodles, oodles; on occasion; on Owen; only owns

P: Pants. Promises, promises; Polish proverb; public place

R: Rapture. Rapture; reception room; Removal? Relevant; Right, right

S: sculptor's studio; Select Serra Senator; service. Surely; shoulda seen; sniper strikes; so sleepy; solid steel; some security; sorry, Sir; start sniping; Statue. Sure; statue, stop; switched sometime

T: Thanks, Thanks, Thanks; Tony. Thanks; that than three tons; that thought; Then they transferred the; three-thirty; to the trouble; touch that

W: way windows; Well, what? What?; what, when; what we were; Wicked Witch; window washers; won't wash; won't. Why?

Y: Yeah, yeah; Yeah, yeah, yeah

Double alliteration:

A&H: approximately a half-hour

L&I: looks like I'm in

T&S: testify that she saw

W&I: Well, what if I; Well, what's in it?

Triple alliteration:

W,A&Y: Who was asking about your young

Matches to previous episodes:

*In the pilot, *Detour to Nowhere*, Banacek's name is twice mispronounced as "Banasek"—newspaperman Earl Lewis does it the first time, television reporter Mario Machado does it the second time. In episode#2, "Project Phoenix," Banacek's rival, Thaddenhurst mispronounces the name as "Banasek" three times. In this episode, Banacek's rival, Carlie Kirkland mispronounces the name as "Banasek" two times. This gives us a total of three episodes where the name Banacek is mispronounced as "Banasek." Total number of times the name is mispronounced as "Banasek": seven.

*In the premiere episode: "Let's Hear it For a Living Legend," top-billing goes to the Polish-American Stefanie Powers; in "No Stone Unturned," top-billing goes to Powers' former husband: the Polish-American Gary Lockwood; Gary Lockwood was born John Gary Yurosek.

*In episode two, "Project Phoenix," the character Collier is played by the five-letter by five-letter Bruce Kirby. In this episode, the character Collier is played by the five-letter by five-letter Scott Brady. Note that in "Phoenix," the first name of the guest star playing the Collier character begins with a B, and that in this episode, the last name of the guest star playing the Collier character starts with a B.

*In "Project Phoenix," director Richard T. Heffron's first *Banacek* of the first season, Banacek retraces the route of the missing Phoenix by helicopter; this sequence takes place in the daytime. In "No Stone Unturned," director Richard T. Heffron's first *Banacek* of the second season, Banacek follows the route Carlie is taking to the ransom drop for the missing "Man in Harmony" by helicopter; this scene takes place at night.

*In "Ten Thousand Dollars a Page," Banacek talks to Glassman about King Cheops and the Pyramids; in the previous episode, "The Two Million Clams of Cap'n Jack," Banacek finds Felix and his girlfriend working with a Styrofoam pyramid; in this episode, Banacek, Lt. Nash, and Carlie all talk about pyramids. This gives us three episodes in which the three-syllable word "pyramid" is mentioned. In this, the third such episode, we have a total of three people speaking the word.

*In the previous episode, Linden Chiles plays an insurance company representative named Penniman; in this episode, Linden Chiles plays an insurance company representative named DeWitt.

*In the previous episode, Banacek gets a Sunday newspaper out of a vending machine; in this episode, Jay brings Banacek a Sunday newspaper.

*In the previous episode, Erica Osburn states that Banacek is afraid of being shown up by a "mere woman." In this episode Carlie believes the sleuth convinced DeWitt "that a mere woman (Carlie) couldn't possibly compete with the great Polish wonder."

*In the previous episode, ten years have passed since Cap'n Jack and his brother Leo had their falling out; in "No Stone Unturned," Davy Collier has a ten-year option on Owen Russell's work; he exercises that option on Russell's "Man in Harmony."

*In "The Two Million Clams of Cap'n Jack," the theft occurred while security guard Spencer was riding down in the elevator. In this episode, an elevator is used in the theft.

Future Matches:
　*Carlie and DeWitt working for the same company
　*The large red dollar sign on the top of Banacek's limousine.
　*Carlie's description of herself as a "wicked witch"
　*The ten year option Davy Collier has on "Man in Harmony."

SECTION TWO

Behind the scenes:
Executive producer George Eckstein:
　"Paul Playdon was very good at developing these complicated stories; he

George Peppard, guest Jennifer Walton, and bit player Vickie Grant in the second season Universal/NBC *Banacek* opener, "No Stone Unturned." This scene was among those filmed at Harold Lloyd's Hollywood estate, "Greenacres."

was very involved in working out the *Banacek* plots. We all were. I don't remember why he left, how the change was made. (Whatever the reason, Playdon went on to produce the 1973-1974 NBC/Bill Bixby series, *The Magician*) It would have been very hard (for Playdon) to do both shows. Paul was a very good constructionist. He was not a great dialogue writer if I remember in terms of the comedic overtones that we were trying to inject. Bob (new story editor Robert Van Scoyk) was basically a comedy writer. He was a very good guy, a wonderful man.

"Christine (Belford) was fine. There was no specific reason why we didn't use her again right away (after the series got the green light following the pilot) so I don't know what the answer to that was. She was a good girl, and under contract to the studio. So she was always there, and always available, and it was good. She had good chemistry with George and he liked working with her. When she wasn't available, we used, usually, David Spielberg or somebody to play that role: the competing investigator."[14]

Behind the scenes: A piece of old Hollywood preserved on film: the film location for the Collier Compound.

For a series whose protagonist made his living "restoring" costly stolen objects to their rightful owners; for a show whose title character generally preferred the "old" to the "new," no better locale could have been selected for the "Collier Compound" than silent film comedian Harold Lloyd's fabulous Hollywood estate, Greenacres. Located in the Benedict Canyon section of Beverly Hills, California, this fifteen-acre estate included: a forty-four room mansion designed in the Italian Renaissance Mediterranean Revival style, numerous gardens, a twenty-eight-foot Italian fountain in the front court, huge iron gates at the front entrance, and, an Olympic-sized swimming pool. The pool measured 50 feet by 150 feet*; it held 250 gallons.

Built in the late 1920s by Lloyd (the star of such comedies as "Safety Last"), Greenacres was his home until his death in 1971. The comedian's will left his estate to the "benefit of the public at large" (it was Lloyd's hope that the estate would serve "as an educational facility and museum for research into the history of the motion picture in the United States.") Greenacres was opened to public tours soon after his passing. Unfortunately, financial and legal reasons soon put an end to such tours, and, because maintaining the original estate was too much of a financial burden for any one person (even Lloyd had experienced difficulties), in 1975, Greenacres was sold at auction. Retired Iranian businessman Nasrolla Afshani purchased the property for $1.6 million, $400,000 less than Lloyd had spent to build the estate. Afshani subdivided the estate into fifteen lots, in addition to the mansion. Individual lots sold for as much as $1.2 million.

As a result, it was only between the beginning of the public tours in the early 1970s and the auction in 1975 when Greenacres could be seen in its original state. It was during this time that the *Banacek* production team shot on the estate. Among the portions of Greenacres seen in "No Stone Unturned": the front gates, the twenty-eight foot Italian fountain in the front courtyard of the estate; the main house and surrounding gardens, and the Olympic-sized swimming pool. The episode also contains something of a tribute to the late Harold Lloyd; when Banacek visits documentary filmmaker Gretel at her work-place, that workplace is the Collier Compound!

*Some sources say 85 feet by 40 feet.

The Polish connection:

#1: As noted in the "Matches to Previous Episodes" section, guest star Gary Lockwood is a Polish-American.

#2: During the phone conversation between Banacek and DeWitt, the sleuth remarks that not even a Rodin is insured for $3,000,000. Auguste Rodin (the sculptor of The Thinker among other works) was a great sculptor of women. The Polish-born Sophie Postolska was one of his models. She also was one of his students, and, mistresses. Along with Joanny Peytel and Albert Kahn, Sophie's brother-in-law, Louis Dorizon, chairman of the bank, Societe Generale, financed Rodin's exhibition at the Pavillon de'l Alma in 1900.

#3: At the seafood restaurant, Banacek and Carlie's humorous banter includes such Benjamin Franklin quotes as "Honesty is the best policy," and "Early to bed ...." Named for the famous eighteenth century inventor, statesman, and Founding Father, the Benjamin Franklin Bridge is a suspension bridge across the Delaware River connecting Philadelphia, Pennsylvania, and Camden, New Jersey. Construction of the bridge was completed July 1, 1926. Chief engineer on the project was the Polish-born Ralph Modjeski.

#4: As noted earlier, when Jay asks Carlie why she's exploring the interior of Banacek's car, she references the 1972 Watergate burglary in her reply. Leon Jaworski, the son of a Polish father, and an Austrian mother who immigrated to Waco, Texas, was appointed Special Prosecutor in the Watergate case in late 1973. This episode first aired on October 3, 1973.

#5: When Banacek tells Carlie the girl who's just left his house is named Gretel, Carlie jokes that Banacek is Hansel, and she's the Wicked Witch of the West. (Carlie is referencing the classic fairy tale, "Hansel and Gretel," which is the story of two children captured by an evil witch who plans to make a meal of them.) Set in the northwestern corner of the Rynek* in Wroclaw, Poland, are two townhouses called Hansel and Gretel. They are linked together by a Baroque archway from 1728; the archway once led to the church cemetery of St. Elizabeth's. Built in the sixteenth and eighteenth centuries respectively, Hansel and Gretel are all that remain of the line of townhouses that once circled the cemetery. These two townhouses are called Hansel and Gretel because the archway that connects them is symbolic of a couple holding hands.

*i.e. Main Market Square; most towns in Poland have a Rynek.

Notes:

With the return of Christine Belford, and the replacement of Paul Playdon by Robert Van Scoyk, the series' level of humor increases considerably. For one thing, while Banacek's encounters with his rivals had almost always yielded moments of levity, until the return of Carlie Kirkland, the sleuth was never matched against a rival who, when it came to wisecracks, could give as good as he, or she got. The fact that Carlie and Banacek are sometimes a couple provides another new dimension to the series. Adding further humor is Linden Chiles reprising the role of the so-easily-manipulated-by-Banacek insurance executive, now named Henry DeWitt. The episode also tops the previous *Banacek*s in terms of pulchritude; when Banacek and Jay pay a visit to the Collier Compound, they encounter one scantily-clad or topless female after another. The topless women are shown only from the back, though. This, after all, was prime-time television.

Of further interest are two potential bloopers. The first: on their way to the Biesecker Crane Company, Banacek and Jay pass the Pacific Metal Products company. In fact, Pacific Metal Products is right next door to the Boston-based Biesecker Crane Company. Why would there be a Pacific Metal Products in Boston? A much more serious error though is Banacek's solution to the disappearance of Man in Harmony. Though the solution is cleverly thought out, and explains a number of things, it fails to take into account the sounds heard in the teaser as the statue is lowered onto the truck. If Banacek's solution concerning the disappearance of the statue is correct, such sounds could never have been produced.

BANACEK Challenges: "No Stone Unturned"

#1: Besides the fact he is operating it, what is the other connection between Pete Biesecker and his crane?

#2. During the course of the story, we are told that the statue. "Man in Harmony" weighs 6,000 pounds. If the statue's weight was given in tons, why would that make for a match to the object?

#3: At one point, Jay references Banacek's solution to the disappearance of the Book of Hours: the object stolen in the first-season episode, "Ten Thousand

Dollars a Page," written by former story editor Paul Playdon. This mention is not this episode's only reference to Playdon. Can you identify the others?

#4: Other than the obvious, how else does the ransom note from which Carlie reads, connect to the stolen "Man in Harmony?"

#5: Besides her guest-starring in both *Banacek* season premieres, what is the other connection between supporting guest Peggy Walton's two appearances?

#6: In his solution to the disappearance of the Man in Harmony statue, Banacek references Thanksgiving Day. How does the sleuth's mention of this holiday connect to this episode's original air-date, and, the "biography" Banacek gives Stefanie Powers' Angie Ives at the end of the first-season premiere episode, "Let's Hear it For a Living Legend." Note: To answer this one, a good knowledge of American history helps.

#7: In the previous episode, "The Two Million Clams of Cap'n Jack," and in this episode, Banacek's first sequence has him interacting with rival insurance investigator Linden Chiles. Besides the presence of Banacek and rival Chiles, there is another element in these first sequences that produces a match between both of these episodes. Can you identify it?

Reviews and Publicity:

October 20, 1973: *TV Guide*– Vol. 21, No. 42 — Issue#1073 –Special Feature: "The House that Laughs Built" – *Banacek* crew mentioned in this three-page (pg. 12, 13, 14) feature on the Harold Lloyd estate, Greenacres.

Episode #10: "If Max is So Smart, Why Doesn't He Tell Us Where He Is?," November 7, 1973

"There's an old Polish proverb that says, 'No matter how warm the smile on the face of the sun, the cat still has her kittens under the porch.'" –Banacek to Ed McKay

W: Robert Van Scoyk
D: Bernard Kowalski

Guest Stars
Anne Baxter
Richard Jordan
Jim Davis
Paul Richards
Co-starring
Sabrina Scharf
Alan Fudge
George Murdock
Julie Rogers
And
William Sylvester as
With
Poupee Bocar
John Zaremba
Nancy Bonniwell
And
The St. William's Boston CYO Band

Lesley Lyle
Chris Bailey
Ed McKay
Dr. Kanter

Wyn
Logan Howard
Cavanaugh
Lois

Dr. Stahl

Wanda
Dr. Wickham
Girl

Exteriors/Filming Locations: Boston: The Esplanade (on the East side of the Charles River), the Hatch Shell, Old Statehouse seen in background; Los Angeles/Hollywood: The California Institute of the Arts.

SECTION ONE: MATCHES

Matches in series credits:

Opening and closing credits:

*There are a total of thirteen words in the episode title; including the Boston St. Williams CYO Band, there are a total of thirteen credited guests.

*The five-letter word, "Smart" is the fifth word in the title: in between this word and the next five-letter word "Where" are a total of five words (Why, Doesn't, He, Tell, and Us).

*Preceding the third word, "Is," is the three-letter word, "Max."

*There are two two-letter Is's' and two two-letter He's in the title.

*In the guest cast, the first name Anne begins with the first letter of the alphabet, the second name Baxter begins with the second letter of the alphabet. Baxter's character name Lesley Lyle is a reverse match of the actress' four-by-six name: there are six letters in the first name, Lesley, four in the last name Lyle.

*Baxter plays the alliteratively named Lesley Lyle; the alliteratively named Sabrina Scharf plays her nurse.

*There are a total of three actresses who are top-billed in three guest star categories: Anne Baxter is the first name in the opening guest star credits; Sabrina Scharf is the first name in the co-starring credits; Poupee Bocar is the first name in the "with" credits.

*Third-billed in the guest cast is Jim Davis; the first name Jim is three letters.

*Fourth-billed is Paul Richards, four letters in the first name Paul.

*Sixth-billed in the cast is Alan Fudge. The last name Fudge begins with the sixth letter of the alphabet.

*The seven-by-seven George Murdock is the seventh-billed; the actor's first name begins with the seventh letter of the alphabet; there are seven letters in the last name Murdock.

*Ninth-billed in the cast is William Sylvester; there are nine letters in the last name Sylvester.

Anne Baxter's Lesley Lyle was one of the many highpoints in second season story editor Robert Van Scoyk's unforgettably titled episode, "If Max is So Smart, Why Doesn't He Tell Us Where He Is?" NBC/Universal.

Matches through physical production and editing:

*Two visits to Max by Lesley Lyle, et al in the teaser.

*Banacek uses two rubber mats as part of his solution to the crime; two women wink at Banacek: nurse Wyn Reiver and Felix's girlfriend; two six-letter words side by side: NURSE'S LOUNGE; two nurses whose first names begin with W: Wyn Reiver, and Wanda.

*Two screwdrivers: one is the alcoholic drink of orange juice and vodka; the other is the actual tool.

*Each ring of the phone in the car consists of three beeps on the horn; it is on the third such ring that Banacek calls to his chauffeur Jay to answer the phone; after answering the phone and talking to the person on the other end, Jay points three times, twice at the phone; once at Carlie. Three people point at Carlie: Jay, Banacek, and Carlie; in the scene where Banacek and Carlie are pointing at her, there is a third person: Jay's nurse-girlfriend. Jay is off-camera in this particular scene.

*Three people wink at others in this episode: Christopher Bailey (whose first name begins with the third letter of the alphabet) winks at (the three-letter) Wyn with his right eye; Wyn winks at (the three-syllable Banacek) with her left eye; the third person is Felix's girlfriend. She winks at Banacek with her right eye.

*There are three pieces of barbed wire at the top of the electric fence; on the fence is a three-word sign: Danger: Electric Fence. (The sign is an alphabetical and numerical progression of three; in the alphabet, the fourth letter: D is followed by the fifth letter: E which is followed by the sixth letter: F; at one point there are three people standing in front of this fence: Banacek, Ed McKay and Carlie.

*Three sets of legs in one shot, one pair are Banacek's; the other two are nurses.

*Three nurses in the background in the explanation sequence.

*On the four-word Lyle Pavilion Medical Center stationery, below the four-word name is a line of four words: in order: Doctor, Case No, Days. The four-letter word Days is the fourth and last word.

*Seven people outside the electric fence in the first visit to Max in the teaser. The seventh is the seven-letter Ed McKay. Seven people inside the building that houses MAX in the first visit to the computer. (McKay does not enter the building; the seventh person inside the building is MAX creator Logan Howard.) Seven people outside the building that houses Max in the second visit to Max in the teaser. Seven people at Banacek's right when he's at the top of the electric fence in the explanation sequence.

*Seven nurses in the nurse's lounge in the first shot.

*Thirteen letters in the words MEDICAL CENTER on the second line of the sign: LYLE PAVILION MEDICAL CENTER

*Thirteen letters in the side-by-side words, ELECTRIC FENCE. (These words are shown on the warning sign, DANGER: ELECTRIC FENCE)

Matching through numbers:
THREES:

*The three-letter Jay's first line is three words, "Mr. Banacek's car."

*MAX is short for Maximum Data Coordinator. The alarm at the door behind which sits the three-word computer "MAX" is set off by three things: light, body heat, and movement.

*Logan Howard tells Carlie that MAX filled three quarters of the room. Prior to his employment at the Lyle Pavilion Medical Center, Logan Howard worked with computers at three places: MIT, Cal Tech, and private industry.

*Lesley Lyle lists three female relatives who all died before the age of fifty-one: her mother, her grandmother, and her aunt. Lesley knows that her obituaries will describe her as a "madcap heiress of the 1930s."

*When Chris Bailey asks Wyn Reiver, "Then why the thanks?" she replies, "Why the third degree?" (Note that in Chris Bailey's question, there are three words that begin with a "t": "then," "the," and "thanks.") In her first encounter with Christopher Bailey, Carlie Kirkland repeats three of his three-word phrases/questions. These are, in order: "Why don't I?" "You're sort of," and "type for me."

*Dr. Kanter describes Dr. Stahl as a "pill pushing parasite." This triple alliteration is also a numerical progression of three in terms of syllables. The first word "pill" is one syllable; the second word "pushing" two; the third word "parasite" contains three syllables. Banacek finds three types of pills in Dr. Stahl's bag: "uppers, downers, and far-outers."

*When nurse Lois exclaims she should be reading *Peter Rabbit* to the children in the children's ward, Carlie replies, "Would you settle for Flopsy (one), Mopsy (two), and Cottontail?" (three). Cottontail is a three-syllable character whose name begins with the third letter of the alphabet.

FOURS:

*At the end of the story, Banacek is walking and talking with four adoring nurses. During this chat, he mentions four fictional characters from children's stories: Winnie the Pooh and Eeyore from the A.A. Milne *Winnie the Pooh* tales, and the rabbits Flopsy and Mopsy from Beatrix Potter's *Peter Rabbit* stories.

FIVES:

*In the two-sentence line, "I don't want that thing stuck in my mouth. I don't want it stuck anywhere," the five-letter word "stuck" is repeated. Preceding the first "stuck" are five words: "I don't want that thing"; in the second sentence, the second "stuck" is the fifth word.

SIXES AND TWOS:

*"Why are you nurses always telling me to assume positions I do not wish to assume?" an angry Lesley Lyle says to her nurse Wyn Reiver at one point. In the question, the words "to" and "assume" are repeated. "To" is a two-letter word, thus it is said twice. Total number of letters in the word "assume" is six. In between the first "assume" and the second "assume" are a total of six words.

TENS:

*After telling Banacek she wouldn't trust Dr. Kanter within ten feet of her, Lesley Lyle then wonders what might have happened had she met Banacek ten years ago.

Anne Baxter's Lesley Lyle begins displaying romantic interest in George Peppard's Banacek in another amusing scene from "If Max . . . ." NBC/Universal.

THIRTEENS:
　*There are a total of thirteen letters in Jay's first line, "Mr. Banacek's car."
　*Lesley Lyle's aunt died of a heart disease she contracted when she was thirteen years old.

Alliteration:
B: been. Burt; being buried; big booby-trap; black bag
C: can't come; Cavanaugh can; certainly came; Cinderella cop; computer components; computer could; computer count; computer counts; computers confirmed; conned Cavanaugh; could cooperate
D: dangerous drugs; department, didn't; Dr. Davidson; doing dressed
E: everybody else's; everyone especially; exhausting experiments
F: for fun
G: gonna give; gotta go
H: have heard; he has his
L: Lesley Lyle; limitless; Lois, look
M: matter, Ma'am?; Max. Maximum; misguided medical; modern medicine; morning, Max
P: pill pushing parasite
R: Rabbit, right; remotely resembled
S: settlement should; she'll see; sleeper, sure; so scared; so seriously; so smart; so sorry; somewhere sulking; sorry she; Sorry. So; speak, swallow; still say
T: tell them to; test tube; that. That's; to the teeth; two telephone
V: very vividly; vice versa
W: wire will; wouldn't want
Y: you years
Double alliteration:
A&T: after all this time
W&G: what we've got going; with what we've got going

Matches to previous episodes:
　*In the pilot, the sheriff's deputy is reading the classic fairytale, "Puss

N'Boots." In this episode, Banacek reveals that the newspapers described Ed McKay as the "Cinderella cop." Both "Puss N'Boots" and "Cinderella" were among the fairytales written by seventeenth century French author Charles Perrault.

*In "Let's Hear it For a Living Legend," Angie Ives says she was once told that the only difference between a man and a computer is a man doesn't count. In this episode, when Felix asks Banacek if stealing a computer would count as grand larceny, Banacek smart-cracks, "Of course a computer counts."

*In episode#3, "No Sign of the Cross," in the small cemetery on the Gomez farm, there is a cross with the saying, "Duarme en los Brazos **de Jesus**." Music for this episode, "If Max is so Smart, Why Doesn't He Tell Us Where He is?" was composed by Luchi **de Jesus**.

*In "No Sign of the Cross," Maria Gomez died in the year 1951. In this episode, Lesley Lyle lists three female relatives who died before the age of fifty-one.

*In his first episode, "A Million the Hard Way" (episode#4), director Bernard Kowalski presents three pairs of legs as his first live-action shot. Two pairs are female; the other male; the two women are walking; the man sitting. In this episode, Kowalski presents three pairs of legs during the nurses playing volleyball sequence. The legs belong to two women and one man reclining on chaise lounges a short distance from the volleyball game. The male pair of legs belongs to Banacek.

*In the last episode of the first season, "The Two Million Clams of Cap'n Jack," when the mobile phone in Banacek's Packard Darrin rings, Erica Osborn picks up the receiver and says, "Mr. Banacek's car." In this episode, when Jay answers the mobile phone, he also says "Mr. Banacek's car."

*In the previous episode, "No Stone Unturned," Carlie describes herself to Banacek as "the Wicked Witch of the West." In this episode, when Lesley Lyle is describing herself to Banacek, she says she has a "reputation of being something of a witch."

*In the previous episode, Carlie makes a reference to "Hansel and Gretel," the well-known fairytale by the Brothers Grimm; in this episode, Banacek makes a reference to the fairytale "Cinderella." Though this story was written by the aforementioned Charles Perrault, it was later re-told by the Brothers Grimm.

*In the previous episode, Banacek scales a fence which has barbed wire at the top; in this episode, Banacek scales an electric fence (the power is off, of course) which has barbed wire at the top.

Future Matches:
*The name Max.
*Felix and his girlfriend feeling one another's earlobes.
*A woman winking at Banacek.
*Nurse Lois' "big black dog."
*Banacek whistling.
*Banacek squatting and using a tape measure.
*Lesley Lyle's word "Hippopotami."
Lesley Lyle's "Blast the insurance company, and blast you for having a full life ahead of you."

SECTION TWO

Behind the scenes:

George Eckstein on the show's depiction of attractive women: "I don't remember anybody objecting. The show was no more chauvinistic than James Bond would be. It was the same kind of treatment. It was so blatantly obvious what we were doing. (The female characters were) there to work as foils for our romantic leading man. That was the purpose they served most of the time. The actresses enjoyed that. (Plus) George was always very gracious, and he was a total gentleman."[15]

The Polish connection:

#1: Polish-American director Bernard Kowalski directs this episode.

#2: After Banacek jokes about a computer counting, Felix tells the sleuth he is not going to play Bud Abbott to Banacek's "Frank Costello." "You mean Lou (Costello)," Banacek replies. Famous gangster Frank Costello's two best friends were fellow gangsters Lucky Luciano and Meyer Lansky. A Jew from Grodno, Poland, born Maier Suchowljansky, Meyer Lansky was the Godfather of the National Crime Syndicate, the parent organization of what eventually would become the American Mafia.

#3: As noted in the 'Matches to Previous Episodes," during the course of its run, *Banacek* referenced two classic fairytales: "PussN'Boots" and "Cinderella." On March 15, 1968, the country of Poland issued a series of eight commemorative stamps; each one illustrating a classic children's fairytale. Among those fairytales commemorated on the stamps: "PussN'Boots" and "Cinderella."

#4: At the end of the episode, Banacek is talking about children's books and tales; he mentions A.A. Milne's *Winnie the Pooh*. In Poland, *Winnie the Pooh* is such a popular character that a street in Warsaw is named after him: "Ulica Kubusia Puchatka" (translation: "Winnie the Pooh Street with Piglet")

Notes:

Having played characters who employed disguises and masquerades in order to achieve their objectives in such motion-pictures as *Operation: Crossbow*, George Peppard was certainly capable of playing similar scenarios on television were such opportunities handed him. Thanks to new story editor Robert Van Scoyk, he was given this chance with Van Scoyk's first solo *Banacek*: "If Max is so Smart, Why Doesn't He Tell Us Where He Is?" Up to this point, the Banacek investigations had been pretty much cut-and-dried as the sleuth collected information from various parties and persons, then put together the clues, and explained to his on (and off) screen audiences how the object (or person) in question had disappeared. From time to time, Banacek's solution of the mystery had required some violent action on his part. While such moments added a bit more variety to the character, they really weren't anything uncommon for Peppard. With "If Max is So Smart . . . ." all of this changed. For the first time, Banacek found it necessary to resort to a disguise: posing as a hospital attendant, in order to gain access to the room of Lesley Lyle: the wealthy woman who'd financed the building and operation of the stolen computer, MAX. Also for the first time, Banacek's explanation/recreation of the theft required him to don an unusual costume—a wetsuit—in order to explain how the thief was able to get past the obstacle which denied him access to the object he wished to steal. The first sight of Banacek in this wetsuit, smoking one of his trademark cigars, is priceless. "He just had to make an entrance," Carlie cracks. Another change Van Scoyk brought to the series was giving more obvious hints to the audience as to how he, George Eckstein, et al were working matches into the show. Banacek's telling Jay to buy two rubber door mats, then commenting how it would be nice if both could say, "Welcome, Max" (Mats, Max) was an example of matching through pronunciation. The alliteratively named Lesley Lyle sarcastically complimenting Dr. Kanter on his alliterative description of Dr. Stahl as a "pill pushing parasite" was also a case of matching—through alliteration. As for the lengthy episode title, "If Max is so Smart, Why Doesn't He Tell Us Where He Is?" this was matching by numbers. The title was a total of thirteen words: the same number of letters in the name of the series star and the character he played, the same number of letters in the name of the series creator: Anthony Wilson. Thus it was rather appropriate that this episode marked the on-screen directorial debut of George Peppard as the series' second-unit director. The authentic Boston locales Peppard presented in his directorial debut, the number of activities he depicted going on behind Banacek, Carlie, and Jay, and, the showcasing of the Boston CYO St Williams Band as they rehearsed a medley of songs, gave the series a realism and quality it had rarely had before. With its star now having a greater input on the finished product, the second season of *Banacek* looked to be even better than the first.

BANACEK Challenges:
"If Max is So Smart, Why Doesn't He Tell Us Where He Is?"

#1: In the teaser, writer Robert Van Scoyk drops two references to himself. Can you identify them?

#2: In the first sequence featuring Banacek, how many times does the phone ring in the sleuth's car and why?

#3: Entering Lesley Lyle's hospital room with a bouquet of flowers, Banacek does something that matches and builds onto something that occurred in his first scene. Can you identify it?

#4: When Banacek enters Lesley Lyle's hospital room, there are three people present: Lesley, Dr. Kanter and Dr. Stahl. During the interchange between the aforementioned three people, writer Robert Van Scoyk drops a reference to George Peppard. What is it?

#5: In his first sequence, Banacek does something which simultaneously creates a numerical match of three and thirteen to his character. What does he do?

#6: As noted in the episode guide, there are three characters in this episode who wink at others: Christopher Bailey, Wyn Reiver, and Felix's girlfriend. Why three characters?

#7: At the end of the story, Banacek references three children's books, *The Wind in the Willows*, *Winnie the Pooh*, and *Peter Rabbit*. Other than his mentioning these books, what is Banacek's second connection to them?

Reviews and Publicity:

November 10, 1973: "TV Guide" – Vol 21., No. 45 — Issue #1076 – 15 across – Banacek star (abbr) – 3 squares

Episode #11: "The Three Million Dollar Piracy," November 21, 1973

"There's an old Polish proverb that says, 'Even though a man anoint himself with fragrant oils, he can still wind up with a broken face.'" –Banacek to Mario Fratelli

Teleplay by Stanley Ralph Ross and Robert Van Scoyk; story by Jack Turley
D: Andrew V. McLaglen

Guest Stars
Linden Chiles	Henry DeWitt
Don Knight	Porter
Dick Gautier	Mario Fratelli

Co-starring
Arlene Martell	Diana Maitland
Hal Buckley	Sanborn
Titos Vandis	Captain Larkos
Martin Kosleck	Bruno
Susan Damante	Leona Sanborn

With
Rudy Challenger	Lt. Trask
Lada Edmund, Jr	Lila
Jean Manson	Wilda
Byron Morrow	Max Benson
Hal Baylor	Foreman

Exteriors: Court of Miracles (at Universal Studios), Little Europe (also Universal)

SECTION ONE: MATCHES

Matches in series credits:
Opening and closing credits:

*This is the third aired episode of the season, and the third (and last) of the "Million" titles. This "Three"-named title aired on the 21st: the third Wednesday in November, 1973. As noted earlier, Wednesday is the third day of the work-week.

*A total of three threes can be found in the episode title, "The Three Million Dollar Piracy." The first word in the title is the three-letter word, "The." The second three is the word "Three." The fifth and last word, "Piracy" is the third three. There are a total of three syllables in the word "Piracy."

*A total of three writers (Robert Van Scoyk, Stanley Ralph Ross, and Jack Turley) wrote this "three"-named episode.

*The three-named director Andrew V. McLaglen directed "The Three Million Dollar Piracy."

*There are a total of three guest stars in the opening credits. Each of these guest stars has a "three" in his performer name. The first-billed Linden Chiles' last name begins with C: the third letter of the alphabet. The next guest, Don Knight, has a three-letter first name. The third-billed Dick Gautier has a three-syllable last name.

*There are a total of three credit blocks concerning the episode's guest stars. The first credit block is the opening credits; the second: Co-starrring, the third: With.

*In the monetary figure presented in the title: THREE MILLION DOLLAR, there are a total of three side-by-side letters (EE), (LL) and (LL) in three consecutive words: THREE, MILLION, and DOLLAR.

Matches through physical production and editing:

*Two women who will be getting married in this episode: Carlie Kirkland and Diana Maitland.

(Note that both women have eight letter last names, and that the last four letters in each last name is "land.")

*Two women named Leona: Diana Maitland's maid, and Doug Sanborn's wife.

*Two Sanborns: Doug and Leona.

*Two home addresses for Zach Porter; Porter has two wives; Lila and Wilda; they're both blonde and pretty.

*Two chauffeurs: Jay and Felix's sexy blonde driver. Both Jay and the girl are shown working crossword puzzles.

*Three investigators working on the case of the missing wedding coach, Banacek, Carlie, and Henry DeWitt.

*Three blue cars at the right in the aerial shot that opens the teaser.

*Three people in Fratelli's: Fratelli, Gloria and a guard, when Banacek enters.

*Three chains in front of Banacek and Jay when they get out of the limousine at the shipyard.

*A shot of three people in black uniforms (a policeman, Captain Larkos, Lt. Trask) is followed by a shot featuring just three people: (Benson, Elliott, and Carlie). This shot is followed by another three-people shot showing Elliott facing Benson; behind Benson is Captain Larkos, who is facing the same direction as Elliott.

*Three chairs behind Banacek at the three-word Bruno's Cabinet Shop.

*In the conclusion when Banacek is explaining how the coach disappeared, he is talking to a group of seven people.

Matching through numbers:
TWOS:

*After Diana mentions there are things she'll miss after she moves to

Baraga, Banacek wonders if she's referring to things such as two daytime TV programs: *Edge of Night* and *Hollywood Squares.*

*Jay has two theories as to how the coach disappeared: 1. It was taken off the ship by helicopter; 2. The thieves used a submarine to slip under the boat, then they cut a hole in the bottom of the ship, took the coach out, and whisked away.

*Zach Porter was arrested for D&D: Drunk & Disorderly.

*There are two ways Carlie and DeWitt could reach the Bahamas: by boat, or by airplane.

*Henry makes a joke referencing the (two) Wright Brothers: Wilbur and Orville.

*Henry plays two sports at the country club on the weekends: golf on Saturday, tennis on Sunday.

THREES:

*The Shah of Baraga, who was allowed two or three wives at the same time, married one of his wives three different times.

*Described by Banacek as one: "solid," two: "upstanding" and three: "predictable," Henry DeWitt follows a certain pattern at the end of each week: first, on Fridays, he has dinner with his family, then on Saturdays, he plays golf at the country club, third, and last, he plays tennis at the country club on Sunday.

*There are three people in this story who dine at the same places for lunch and dinner: Banacek, Carlie, and Henry DeWitt.

*Banacek is called into the case by the three-syllable Cavanaugh; Cavanaugh's last name starts with the third letter of the alphabet.

*Felix shows Banacek pictures of three objects which wedding coach designer Bruno Aufterheide has made: one: a beautifully carved chair for a millionaire; two: a figurehead for a private yacht; three: a chess set for a king in exile.

*Felix is a fan of three directors: Alfred Hitchcock, Francois Truffaut, and Federico Fellini.

*The three-letter Jay wonders why the $3 million wedding coach wasn't transported by a three-digit 747.

*At one point, Carlie says to Banacek the three-sentence line , "Blast you Banacek. Do you know what you are? Do you?"

THIRTEENS:

*Captain of the ship on which the coach is being transported is the thirteen-letter Captain Larkos.

Alliteration:
A: almost anything
B: better believe
C: Cavanaugh call; country club
D: do deny
E: esteemed employer
F: faithful fan
G: great granddaughter
H: had his hands; haven't heard; Hush Henry
L: love letters
N: not needed; not now
O: off of one of
S: say something; sea shanty; see something; shipshape; signed, sealed; sound snide; steamship
T: tell the truth
V: very valuable
W: we're working; what's wrong with; white what; wonderful woman; wonderful working with

Matches to previous episodes:

*In the pilot film, "Detour to Nowhere," Carlie gets angry and storms out of Banacek's home after he lets her know that he's seen through her ruse. In this episode, after learning that Banacek and Diana Maitland spent the night together at his place, Carlie, who's dropped by to talk with the sleuth about the case, gets angry, smashes an ashtray, and storms out of Banacek's house.

*In the fourth-aired episode of the first season, the title of the episode is "A Million the Hard Way." In the eighth and last-aired episode of the first season, the amount of the million stolen is doubled, as made clear by the episode title, "The Two Million Clams of Cap'n Jack." In this episode, another million has been added to the previous $2 million: thus we have "The Three Million Dollar Piracy." As noted earlier, "Piracy" is the third-aired episode of the second season.

*In the first season's "The Two Million Clams of Cap'n Jack," one person: Norman Esposito is working a crossword puzzle. This is the second episode where a character is working a crossword puzzle; this time there are two people working crossword puzzles: Banacek's chauffeur Jay, and Felix's sexy blonde chauffeur.

*In the two first-season episodes, "To Steal a King," and "Ten Thousand Dollars a Page," when Banacek enters the scene of the crime, and sees a policeman he knows, he greets him with the one-word, "Sullivan." "Mr. Banacek," the officer replies. This same three-word greeting between the two men occurs in this episode moments after the sleuth enters the case, and, the scene of the crime.

*In the third-aired episode of the first season, "No Sign of the Cross," part of Banacek's investigation has him talking to a woodworker named Anselmo Gomez. In this episode, the third-aired episode of the second season, part of Banacek's investigation has him talking to woodcarver Bruno Aufterheide. Though the words "woodworker" and "woodcarver" are somewhat different, both the Mexican Anselmo and the German Bruno are in essence men who fashion objects from wood.

*In the first *Banacek* with the word "million" in its episode title, the second-billed guest is Don Porter; in the third *Banacek* with the word "million" in its episode title, the first name of the second-billed guest is also Don (Don Knight). The last name of the character he plays is Porter.

*In the previous episode, "If Max is so Smart, Why Doesn't He Tell Us

Where He Is?" Banacek tells Felix that "they're called earlobes" when he comes upon the bookseller and his girlfriend touching one another's earlobes as part of their Sensitivity Awareness Sessions; in this episode, after the sleuth introduces himself to Captain Larkos, the Captain remarks that he sailed with a Banacek at one time, and that this Banacek was missing his right earlobe.

*In the previous episode, Banacek was looking for the computer Max. In this episode, the wedding coach is put inside a crate on which we see the words, MAX GROSS (referring to the amount the crate can hold). Moreover, at one point, Banacek is served by a waitress whom he knows; her first name is Maxine.

*In the second-season premiere episode, "No Stone Unturned," Carlie theorizes that the sculpture, "Man in Harmony" was taken away by truck; in the episode that follows, Jay offers the idea that the building, which housed the enormous computer, "Max" was taken off the hospital grounds by truck; in this episode, the teaser which concludes with the discovery that the wedding coach has disappeared, begins with a wide-angle shot of trucks.

*In "No Stone Unturned," expecting a kiss on the lips from Banacek for the information she gives him, Gretel is disappointed when he kisses her on the cheek; in this episode, expecting a kiss on the lips from her fiancée, Henry DeWitt, Carlie is disappointed when he kisses her on the forehead.

*In "No Stone Unturned," Banacek and the police are able to follow his limousine carrying Carlie to the ransom drop thanks to the huge red dollar sign painted on the roof of the limousine. In this episode, after Banacek restores the stolen golden wedding coach to Diana Matiland, Carlie recognizes his triumph by chalking a giant dollar sign on the crate containing the coach.

*In "If Max is So Smart . . . ." an infuriated Lesley Lyle tells insurance company representative Carlie Kirkland, "Blast the insurance company, and blast you for having a full life ahead of you." In this episode, infuriated insurance company representative Carlie unloads on her competitor with a "Blast you, Banacek. Do you know what you are? Do you?"

*In "If Max is so Smart . . . ." Banacek is shown squatting and using a tape measure near the building that housed the stolen super-computer, Max. In this episode, Banacek is shown squatting and using a tape measure near the spot where the wedding coach disappeared.

Future Matches:
　*Jay's theory that the coach was taken away by submarine.
　*Zach Porter's asking Banacek if there is "some bone" the sleuth can "throw" to the captain.
　*Banacek's reference to *Hollywood Squares*.
　*Henry DeWitt kissing Carlie on the forehead.
　*The first name Leona.
　*Carlie's repetition of "Cavanaugh call."
　*The name of the ship on which the coach is being loaded: Molly Pitcher.

SECTION TWO

Behind the scenes:
Executive producer George Eckstein:
　"Stanley (Ralph Ross) did a bunch of shows for us—he did three of them, as I remember, and, unfortunately, they went downhill. They got silly . . . they didn't . . . one by one, they got a little less credible."[16]

Guest star Dick Gautier:
　"I did that role . . . barely a cameo (see BIT PART) for George Eckstein as a favor. I was there maybe an hour or two."[17]

Guest commentary:
　Future *Banacek* guest Harry Carey, Jr. on "The Three Million Dollar Piracy" director Andrew McLaglen:
　"One thing about Universal . . . some of the directors were not pleasant to work with, but when Andy was there, it was a cinch. But the rest of em… some of those other shows… were real tough."[18]

George Eckstein on the Universal Studios Glam Trams*:

"The tram was a pain in the ass, but, it wasn't a major problem. There was very little shooting (in the series) done in the areas that they were coming around. I mean, if we were on a sound stage it wouldn't really be a problem."[19]

*(Glam Trams were the vehicles that took visitors on a tour through the Universal lot. The tours made it possible for visitors to see famous sets such as the house in Alfred Hitchcock's *Psycho*, as well as Universal productions in the making.)

The Polish Connection:

#1: When Banacek asks Aufterheide for a photograph of the wedding coach, the woodcarver replies, "Photograph. That's like only listening to Marlene Dietrich." In 1967, Marlene Dietrich's young lover, a Polish actor, came to see her off at a train station. He tripped and fell onto the tracks and was crushed by a train.

#2, #3, and #4 – Felix admits to being a fan of Alfred Hitchcock, Francois Truffaut, and Federico Fellini. Charles Deiner was a French actor of Polish descent who worked with Truffaut. Polish director Wojciech Has (director of such films as *The Saragossa Manuscript* and *The Hour-Glass Sanatorium*) has been compared to Fellini for his visual style. Alfred Hitchcock made *Bon Voyage*, a short movie (about 27 minutes long) in 1944. The movie was about an RAF Man, who was being escorted out of France through the Resistance Channels. His escort is a Polish officer, but the man is actually a Gestapo agent.

Inside jokes and references:

*After Carlie expresses the desire to travel to their honeymoon destination: the Bahamas, by boat rather than airplane, her fiancée, Henry DeWitt, tells her, "If God had wanted us to travel by steamship, he would not have invented the Wright Brothers." Working in their hometown of Dayton, Ohio, Wilbur and Orville Wright's experiments in powered flight earned for the city the designation, "The Birthplace of Aviation." Robert Van Scoyk, co-writer on "The Three Million Dollar Piracy" was a native of Dayton, Ohio.

*The name of Diana Maitland's maid is "Leona." This is also the first name of Doug Sanborn's wife. The first name of co-writer Van Scoyk's wife was Leona.

*When Carlie comments on DeWitt's thoroughness and care in supervising the loading of the wedding coach, he replies, "Well, darling, for a security chief, thoroughness is the name of the game." As noted earlier, Banacek executive producer George Eckstein produced episodes of the series, *The Name of the Game*.

Notes:

Taking a cue from its episode title, "The Three Million Dollar Piracy" is an episode overflowing in more "threes" than usual. Besides those "threes" already noted, in the teaser, after Carlie speaks the three-word question, "What is that?" DeWitt then speaks a total of three lines prior to the discovery of the missing coach. His first line is the three-word command "Open that case," his second: a repeat of the first line, his third, the two-word, three-syllable order, "Open it!" As a result, beginning with Carlie's "What is that?" there are three three-word sentences in a row. The fact that DeWitt also begins each line with the word "Open" creates another three. The writers continue to have Carlie and DeWitt do threes after Banacek enters the case. With Carlie, this is through her repetition of the same three back-to-back-words: "Cavanaugh" "call" and "you." (The second sentence helps direct attention away from the repetition by adding an "ed" to the word "call.") In her third last sentence/question, "Why did Cavanaugh call you," the writers drop a hint as to what they are doing by working in a total of three three-letter words: "Why," "did," and "you." But, because of the way Christine Belford delivers the line, it is the humor of the poetry/repetition which registers with the viewer, not the writers' playing with words, and numbers. The played-for-laughs exchange between Banacek and DeWitt is another example of the humor hiding the clever word/number game writing. During this exchange, the words, "know" "what" and "deny" are spoken three times, while the three-word phrase "you and Carlie" is twice preceded by a total of three words; the first time by DeWitt's, "I know about," the second, by the three four-letter words: "know," "what" and "that." Banacek speaks the first two words, DeWitt, the last.

Christine Belford's comedic talents were showcased in "The Three Million Dollar Piracy."

Linden Chiles receiving top guest billing in this episode, and his Henry DeWitt's becoming the fiancée of Carlie Kirkland, reveals the new direction in which the series is going; clearly, in Season Two, more layers are being added to the Banacek character, particularly through his relationship with his now regular competition, Carlie Kirkland. The next episode, "The Vanishing Chalice" was to take full advantage of this.

BANACEK Challenges:
"The Three Million Dollar Piracy"

#1: As noted in the Matching in Series Credits section, this third-aired episode of the season aired on the third Wednesday in November, and Wednesday is the third day of the work week. What is the other three connected to this episode's airdate?

#2. In the teaser, Carlie performs a number match before her fiancée Henry DeWitt. What is it?

#3: After Mario Fratelli boasts to Banacek of his seductive power over women, Banacek replies with a Polish proverb which references Diana Maitland's earlier comment to the sleuth about breaking Fratelli's face. Why is Diana the inspiration for this proverb, and Fratelli its' recipient?

#4: During the course of this episode, Felix admits to being a fan of directors Alfred Hitchcock, Francois Truffaut and Federico Fellini. As noted in the Polish Connection section, all three of these directors are related to things or people Polish. What is the other reason Felix mentions these directors?

#5: According to Banacek, Henry DeWitt, whom the sleuth characterizes as "solid," "upstanding," and "predictable," follows a certain pattern at the end of each week; on Fridays, he dines with his family, on Saturdays, he plays golf at the country club, on Sundays, he plays tennis at this same club. Besides the three descriptions from Banacek, the three activities, and the three days on which Henry DeWitt performs these activities, what other three can be found in the above information?

#6: When Banacek visits the two homes of bigamist Zach Porter, we see a photo of Porter in each home. In the home Porter shares with Lila, his picture is at the left, in the home he shares with Wilda, the picture is at the right. Why is Porter's photo at the left at Lila's and at the right at Wilda's.

#7: At the end of this episode, Carlie draws a giant dollar sign on the crate containing the Golden Wedding Coach as a way of recognizing Banacek's triumph. In the second season premiere, "No Stone Unturned," there is a giant dollar sign painted on the roof of Banacek's limousine which allows the sleuth and the police to track the vehicle and its occupant (Carlie) to the ransom drop for the stolen item. Why do giant dollar signs connected to both Banacek and Carlie appear in both of these episodes?

A scene from the opening credits of "The Vanishing Chalice."

Episode #12: "The Vanishing Chalice," January 15, 1974

"Though the hippopotamus has no stinger in his tail, the wise man would rather be sat on by the bee." – A Polish proverb delivered by Banacek to Felix and his girlfriend

"A duck with three wings and a loaf of bread is brother to the turkey." – Another Polish proverb spoken to Felix and the same girlfriend

Exteriors: Government Center, the Charles River, Boston Skyline, Boston Art Museum

W: Mort Fine
D: Bernard Kowalski

Guest Stars
Cesar Romero	Marius
Eric Braeden	Paul Belitho
Sue Ane Langdon	Sybil Payson
Special Guest Star: John Saxon	Harry Harlan

Co-starring
Robert Wolders	Tommy Forrest
Don Collier	Jimmy Scarne
Lester Rawlins	John Sharmon
George Murdock	Cavanaugh
Paul Picerni	Det. Ed Winslow
Nedra Deen	Cee Cee

With

Ruth Price	Bonnie Gray
Carle Bensen	Captain
Little Egypt	Belly Dancer
Elizabeth Talbot-Martin	Mrs. Glynn
Dorrie Thomson	Young Woman

SECTION ONE: MATCHES

Matches in series credits:

Opening and closing credits:

*There are three performers given "Guest Star" billing in the opening credits: Cesar Romero, Eric Braeden, and Sue Ane Langdon. The first, Romero, has a first name that begins with the third letter of the alphabet; his last name Romero is three syllables. The next performer, Eric Braeden, has a first name where the last letter: the third letter of the alphabet, C, is preceded by three letters. The third performer: Sue Ane Langdon has a three-part name. Preceding the third name: Langdon, are two three-letter names: Sue, and Ane.

*The fourth actor billed in the opening credits (under the three-word billing "Special Guest Star") is John Saxon. His first name is the four-letter "John."

*In the "off-screen talent" off-screen opening credits, the fourth talent listed is the episode writer, Mort Fine. His first name Mort is four letters; his surname Fine is four letters.

*There are six guests listed in the "Co-starring" credits: The sixth: Nedra Deen portrays the six-letter character Cee Cee.

Matches through physical production and editing:

*In the teaser, the third shot is of an easel holding a sign saying (in bold print): PRIVATE MUSEUM SHOWING. Below these words are the words

(BY INVITATION ONLY) which are not in bold print. Below these three words is the time of the event: 8:30 p.m. Thus, on this sign there are three bold print words followed by three regular type words, followed by three numbers.

*At the Boston Art Museum, there are three people (the three syllable Banacek, the three-letter Jay and Carlie, whose first name begins with the third letter of the alphabet) looking at the three-word painting, "Dog with Bone."

*Three people: John Sharman, Paul Belitho, and Carlie facing Banacek in the museum's Grecian lounge.

*Three vehicles shown in one shot during the sequence where Sybil gets a ride from Banacek: Sybil's car, Banacek's limousine, a delivery truck behind Sybil's car.

Matching through numbers:
TWOS:

*Banacek quotes two Polish proverbs. Neither one is preceded by the familiar phrase: "There's an old Polish proverb that says . . . ."

*During the course of this episode, Banacek deliberately mispronounces Carlie's two-syllable last name Kirkland in two different ways: on one occasion, he calls her "Kirkwood," on another, "Kirkside."

THREES:

*Early in the show, Banacek tells Carlie she wouldn't like being his assistant because of the different types of people he has to deal with. He lists three types: redheaded types, blonde types, ash-blonde types.

*After telling Banacek she'll pick him up at three p.m., Sybil speaks the three-word sentence, "You'll love Marius."

*At Marius' party, Banacek sets in motion a bit of repeated dialogue when he asks Sybil the two-word question, "Which one?" "Which one what?" she replies, answering a question with a question. "Which one of your friends wanted to meet me?" Banacek responds, answering her question with another question; he then follows this question with a third question, "Marius, Harry, or the gentleman listening behind the statue?" Thanks to this dialogue, Banacek not only speaks three questions, he also speaks the third "Which," the third "one," and in his third question, refers to three of Sybil's friends: Marius, Harry Harlan, and Tommy Forrest. As for Sybil, each of the words in her three-word question, "Which one what" is pronounced with the same "w" sound.

(left to right) George Peppard, Sue Ane Langdon, and Cesar Romero in the NBC/Universal *Banacek* "The Vanishing Chalice."

FOURS:

*In episode four, Banacek states that Jimmy Scarne called him four times yesterday.

*At one point Sybil tells Banacek about her wealthy friends. Both of these words are repeated in the conversation between Sybil and Banacek. The word "wealthy" is spoken a total of four times.

"Friends" is spoken just twice. The first "friends" is the fourth word in the sentence; the second "friends" is the fourth word after the first "friends."

*Sybil lists four women who've been companions of Marius: one is a woman whose name she doesn't know; two is Cynthia; three is Melina; fourth, and most recent is Sybil herself. When Marius spots Sybil, and Banacek, at his party, he greets her by speaking her name four times.

FIVES:

*When Banacek and Carlie are discussing her becoming his assistant, he tells her, "You're out of your gourd." Within this five-word sentence, the writers do five pairs, or five matches. The first is the words "You're" and "your." Both are pronounced the same way. The second pair/match is the alliterative words "out" and "of". The third pair/match is the rhyming words "you're," "your" and "gourd." The fourth pair/match plays with numbers: the four-letter "your" is the fourth word in the sentence. The fifth pair/match also plays with numbers: the five-letter "gourd" is the fifth word in the sentence.

SEVENS:

*Towards the end of the episode, Carlie says to Banacek, "I was supposed to be your apprentice, and you wouldn't even let me . . . apprent." This seven-letter made-up word, "apprent" is the writers' way of telling the audience they have just done a match of seven with the word, "apprentice"; in Carlie's line, "apprentice" is the seventh word in the sentence.

ELEVENS:

*The eleven-letter Paul Belitho has been at the museum for about eleven years.

THIRTEENS:

*The object for which Banacek is searching is the "Darien Chalice." There are thirteen letters in the name "Darien Chalice."

*Moments after meeting Banacek's "assistant" Carlie, Sybil says to the sleuth, "She, uh, seems a perfect jewel. Where on earth did you find her?" "In the yellow pages, under 'jewels perfect'," he replies. "Jewels," the plural of "jewel" is the thirteenth word after "jewel." Total number of letters in Banacek's two-word description of Carlie: "jewels perfect" is thirteen.

*At the nightclub Banacek hears his friend Bonnie Gray performing a song. Within this song, there are thirteen lines of repetition, including rhyming ("ground" "found") and alliteration ("big brass bands.")

Alliteration:
A: and, as an added; assistant ask; Associate. Assistant; Athens apartment.
B: before Banacek; Bye-bye
C: came calling; chalice case; clever copy; crazy calling
D: Date doctor
E: evil eye
F: fifty-five; Furniture? Faces?
G: game goes; good grief; Grecian gallery; Greek government
H: Harrison Harlan; Hello, Harry;
M: money markets; my my
O: One's opinion of oneself; Only one of
P: Paul, perhaps; police photos; posh party
R: recent rediscovery; rushed right
S: Saloon singers; Scollay Square; seen something; somebody stole; Special Security; somehow snatch; stop smirking; Sumerian script
T: they thought that; time to time
U: Uh, upstairs
W: Where were we?

Double alliteration:
W & T: What would the thief

Matches to previous episodes:

*In the pilot episode, "Detour to Nowhere," after the athletic pursuit of sculling on the Charles River, Banacek enters his home, and begins sorting his mail; a scarf is around his neck. In this episode, after the athletic pursuit of jogging in the park, Banacek enters his home, with Sybil Payson accompanying, and begins sorting his mail; a towel is around his neck.

*In the first season's "Project Phoenix," the five-letter-by-five-letter supporting guest Bruce Kirby plays a character whose last name is Collier. In the second season's premiere episode, "No Stone Unturned," the five-letter-by-five-letter opening credits guest Scott Brady plays a character whose last name is Collier. In this episode, supporting guest Don Collier plays a character whose first name is (the five-letter) Jimmy.

*In the first season's "A Million the Hard Way" (the first *Banacek* directed by Bernard Kowalski), the director's first live-action shot is a shot of three pairs of legs: one male, two female. In this episode, Kowalski does another unusual leg shot; one pair of legs is that of a table's; Banacek is shown crawling between these. The other pair belongs to supporting guest Dorrie Thomson; Felix is shown crawling between these; he's looking for the last piece of the jigsaw puzzle he and Thomson are doing. The look on Thomson's face as she senses Felix crawling between her legs is priceless.

*In the second season's second-aired episode, "If Max is So Smart, Why Doesn't He Tell Us Where He Is?" Lesley Lyle compares her male companion Chris Bailey to "hippopotami" (the plural of hippopotamus.) In this episode, Banacek's first Polish proverb has to do with the hippopotamus.

*In the previous episode, Jay's theory as to how the wedding coach was stolen involves a submarine. In this episode, when Banacek tells Sybil another way she can solve her car's flat-tire problem is by catching the next limousine, she quips, "How 'bout the next submarine?"

*In "Max," nurse Lois tells Banacek she saw a big black dog at the electric fence protecting the computer Max the night Max disappeared. In the next episode, "The Three Million Dollar Piracy" first mate Zach Porter asks Banacek for some "bone" to throw to his captain. In this episode, Banacek,

Jay and Carlie come upon a painting in the art museum entitled "Dog with Bone."

*In the previous episode, Molly Pitcher is the ship on which the golden wedding coach is being loaded. In this episode, as Banacek sculls his way to shore, Carlie calls him the Polish John Paul Jones. Both General John Paul Jones and Molly Pitcher were historical figures that played key roles in the American Revolution.

*In the first season's "To Steal a King," there are three top-billed guest star names (Brenda Vaccaro, Kevin McCarthy, Roger C. Carmel) with side by side Cs in their names. Total number of Cs in this top-billed guest cast is six. In the previous episode, Carlie Kirkland speaks the alliterative "Cavanaugh call" three times. Total number of C words spoken in this alliteration is of course six. In this episode, supporting guest Nedra Deen plays a six-letter character named "Cee Cee."

Future Matches:
*The last name Plotkin.
*Banacek's quoting two Polish proverbs.
*The 8:30 p.m. time of the private showing of the Darien Chalice.

SECTION TWO

Behind the scenes:
Executive producer George Eckstein:

"The (surface of the) show was elaborate plots. "That's what it was all about. Everybody knew what they were doing, which was sort of fairytale kind of storylines, which, if you really got down to it, were sometimes a bit bordering on the silly. But it was what it was. You had to suspend your disbelief. There was no real expert working on the show. We would manufacture tiny brains, make it seem that you could pull something like that off."[20]

Guest commentary: *Banacek* guest star Harry Carey, Jr. on episode guest John Saxon:

"He's a very very quiet guy. You never know what's going on in his head, but there were no problems. He was very easy to work with. He just seemed like he was . . . .he had sort of a style all his own—off the screen, as well as on."[21]

Inside jokes and references:
*The private museum showing of the Darien Chalice is at 8:30 p.m. *Banacek* aired at 8:30 p.m. Wednesdays and later Tuesdays.
*Artist of the painting, "Dog with Bone" is L. Plotkin. Plotkin is the maiden name of story editor Robert Van Scoyk's wife, Leona.

The Polish Connection:
#1. Early in the episode, Carlie calls Banacek "Silas Marner." According to some critics, author George Eliot based her novel, *Silas Marner,* on the plot of the Polish novel, *Jermola the Polter. Jermola the Polter* is the story of a lonely old man who adopts a deserted infant. Taking care of the child brings the old man into contact with his own kind.

#2. When the wax dummy in the museum loses her head, Sybil Payson picks up the head and compares it to "Marie Antoinette." (France's queen, Marie Antoinette was beheaded during the French Revolution.) Polish cultural anthropologist Maria Czaplicka is sometimes referred to as "Marie Antoinette Czaplicka." The reason is because Czaplicka was born into a poor Polish noble family.

#3. Marie Antoinette was the wife of French king Louis XVI, the grandson of Poland's Marie Leszcynska. Leszcynska married King Louis XV of France.

#4. When Felix talks to Banacek about tennis player Bobby Riggs, he frets that the mention of Riggs will remind Banacek of some old Polish proverb, which it does. Riggs played against American tennis player Frank Parker many times. Born on January 31, 1916 to Polish immigrant parents,

Frank Parker's birth name was Franciszek Andrzej Pajkowski. Riggs wrote about Frank Parker in his autobiography, "Tennis is My Racket."

#5. Carlie tells Banacek to look at her as his Dr. Watson. Watson is the faithful companion of Sherlock Holmes in the classic mysteries written by Arthur Conan Doyle. As previously noted, Doyle's "Exploits of Brigadier Gerard" featured Polish characters.

#6. Arriving at Harry Harlan's home, Jay comments on the look of the place. "Even Dracula lived in a castle," Banacek replies. A year or so before the airing of this episode, Polish actress Ingrid Pitt portrayed real life Hungarian countess Elizabeth Bathory in the Hammer horror classic, *Countess Dracula*. Countess Bathory believed she could stay young by bathing in the blood of young virgins.

#7. Among the paintings in Harry Harlan's home are originals by French painter Maurice Utrillo. The first art dealer for Maurice Utrillo was Polish poet, and writer Leopold Zborowski.

Notes:

Banacek, having always gotten the better of his competitors in the past and frequently tricking them along the way, this episode gets off to a great start with the sleuth getting a taste of his own medicine thanks to Carlie Kirkland and her boss Cavanaugh. Carlie becoming Banacek's assistant, her eagerness to learn his methods and her desire to become as successful as the sleuth, makes for a lot of great moments in the show. As does the sleuth giving Carlie a taste of HER own medicine by deliberately mispronouncing her last name. Making the episode further notable is director Bernard Kowalski's previously discussed leg shot, second-unit director Peppard's brand-new footage for the opening credits, and George Eckstein's musical number (performed by Ruth Price's 'Bonnie Gray.') This was Eckstein's third known song for a television series. His previous efforts came on *The Fugitive*.

George Peppard and exotic dancer Little Egypt in the second season's "The Vanishing Chalice."

BANACEK Challenges: "The Vanishing Chalice"

#1: When director Bernard Kowalski receives his credit in this episode, it is the third trio connected with the director. All three trios result from Kowalski's participation in this episode. Can you identify all three of them?

#2: Early in the episode, Banacek and Carlie have the following exchange:

> *Carlie:* "I'm part of the package. Like the toy in a box of Cracker Jacks."
>
> *Banacek*: "Or the weevil in a bag of noodles."

Besides referencing Carlie, how else does this exchange connect to her?

#3: When Carlie and Cavanaugh see Banacek at the beginning of this episode, she calls the sleuth "the Polish John Paul Jones." Other than Carlie calling Banacek by this name, how else does the name connect to the sleuth?

#4: By describing Banacek as "the Polish John Paul Jones," Carlie establishes two name connections between this show (the fourth-aired episode of the second season) and "A Million the Hard Way" (the fourth-aired show of the first season). What are these name connections?

#5: At the party thrown by Marius, Harry Harlan tells Sybil and Cee Cee that he and the other kids who grew up in Scollay Square referred to Banacek as the "neighborhood jock" since there were a number of sports at which the sleuth excelled. How many sports does Harlan name, and why these in particular?

#6: During this episode, Banacek delivers two Polish proverbs. Besides their being Polish proverbs, what is the other match between the two sayings?

#7: Towards the end of the story, Banacek asks some of the people who were present at the scene of the crime to return to that same location at 1:00 p.m. on the day he will give them the solution to that crime. Why does Banacek make the appointment at 1:00 p.m.?

George Peppard's Banacek is about to solve the mystery of the disappearing race horse in executive producer George Eckstein's favorite *Banacek* episode, "Horse of a Slightly Different Color," NBC/Universal.

Episode #13: "Horse of a Slightly Different Color," January 22, 1974

"There's an old Polish proverb that says, 'The chicken that clucks the loudest is the one most likely to go to the steamfitter's picnic.'" –Banacek to John Hargroves

"There's an old Polish proverb that says, 'Only someone with nothing to be sorry about smiles back at the rear of an elephant.'" –Banacek to Sally James

Exteriors: Santa Anita park and racetrack; the park in Boston Commons

240

Teleplay by Jimmy Sangster; story by Harold Livingston
D: Herschel Daugherty

Guest Stars
Anne Francis   Katherine Wells
Tim O'Connor   Howard James
Lane Bradbury   Sally James
Ramon Bieri   John Hargroves
John Crawford   Owen Summers
And Linden Chiles   Henry DeWitt
Co-starring
Harry Carey, Jr   Dean Barrett
And
Allen Ludden as   The Interviewer
With
Willard Sage   Anthony
William Harmatz   Tim Diamond
Terry Wilson   Chuck Smith
Robert Swan   Track Official
Rocky Frier   Tommy
Pamela Hensley   Mandy

SECTION ONE: MATCHES

Matches in series credits:
Opening and closing credits:
　*In this, the fifth-aired episode of the second season, the first word in the episode title, "Horse," is five letters; the last word, "color," is five letters. In other words, five words (Of, A, Slightly, Different, Color) follow the five-letter "Horse"; five words (Horse, Of, A, Slightly, Different) precede the five-letter last word "color."

　*In the fifth-aired episode, there are five one-time guests in the opening credits: Anne Francis, Tim O'Connor, Lane Bradbury, Ramon Bieri, and John Crawford.

*In between the five-letter by five-letter supporting guest Harry Carey, Jr. and the five-letter by five-letter supporting guest Rocky Frier are five supporting guest names: Allen Ludden, Willard Sage, William Harmatz, Terry Wilson, and Robert Swan.

*Terry Wilson, who plays the five-letter by five-letter Chuck Smith is the fifth guest listed in the closing credits.

*The five-letter by five-letter actor Rocky Frier is the fifth guest billed under the "With" credit.

*Under the "With' credit, there are three actors: Willard Sage, William Harmatz, and Terry Wilson, who share the same three letters (W,i,l) in common.

*The thirteen-letter name Pamela Hensley is preceded by the names of thirteen guests.

Matches through physical production and editing:

*The walk-and-talk scene featuring Banacek and Felix presents numerous pairs of both things and people. Among the more striking:

*Two little boys wearing football team winter caps and playing in the leaf piles.

*A man walking his dog.

*Two bicyclists in the same scene: as the second bicyclist enters the scene behind Banacek's left, the first cyclist is moving from behind Felix at the right.

*Banacek and Felix walk past two old men who are sitting on park benches and talking.

*Banacek and Felix walk past a couple on the grass; when the couple is seen at Banacek's left, a policeman pushing forward a crook enters the scene at Felix's right.

*Banacek receives seven pieces of mail. His girlfriend Mandy sorts through, and identifies six. The seventh: a newspaper showing the front-page headline of Oxford Don's kidnapping, is handled by the seven-letter Banacek.

*In this, the fifth-aired episode of the season, there are a total of five people listening to Banacek's explanation at the end.

Matching through numbers:
THREES:

*Felix mentions three members of the Wells family to Banacek: Katherine, her mother Margaret, and her father Donald.

*In response to Sally's three-word question, "What's the matter?" her father Howard states that the three-syllable Oxford Don (three letters in Don) is three seconds off what he should be doing.

*When Diamond returns from the morning workout, James asks him, "What went wrong, Tim?" Preceding the three-letter first name Tim are three words, all of which begin with the same letter: W.

*The three-syllable Tim Diamond has been barred from the track for three years.

*The horse Banacek bets on, Polish Pride, comes in third.

*After Sally tells Banacek she spent three hours fixing herself up for their date, Banacek tells her in three words, "You look wonderful." His three-word compliment begins with the three-letter pronoun, "You," and concludes with the three-syllable adjective "wonderful." Note that there are three letters in each syllable of the third word, "wonderful."

*In the scene in DeWitt's office, there are three characters speaking: Banacek, DeWitt, and Hargroves. The scene concludes with each character speaking the same three words: "working for me." Banacek is the third and last character to speak.

FIVES:

*After seeing the $5 million horse, Oxford Don, perform his mathematical trick, interviewer Allen Ludden tells Katherine Wells that his five-year-old son couldn't do that.

*In interviewer Ludden's six-word comment, "That's a great deal of money," five words follow the five-letter word "That's," and of course, five words precede the five-letter last word, "money."

*During the run around the track, the $5 million Oxford Don is out of sight, behind the tote board, for about five seconds.

*Jockey Tim Diamond, who is the jockey aboard Oxford Don, has been working for Howard James for about five years.

*In this, the fifth-aired episode of the second season, the $5 million Oxford Don is kept in the stall numbered 50.

SEVENS:
*The seven-letter Banacek tells Sally he will come to her place at seven.

Alliteration:
A: as an adjunct
B: big boss
C: cockamamie chauffeur; convicted crook
D: dinner drink
E: every effort
F: father first; field falls; fractious filly
H: hand here; handicapped horse; Hargroves' horse; hired hand; horse here
J: James just
M: mentioning marriage
O: own Oxford
P: Polish Pride
S: said some stupid; sideshow; simply switched; Sorry, Sally; straight salary
T: the traveling type; trainer's time
W: What went wrong; word weird

Double Alliteration:
H&A: He has an appointment
N&A: No. Not at all

Matches to previous episodes:

*In the pilot episode, "Detour to Nowhere," Banacek finds his newest case in the out of town newspaper, *The Vantage Sentinel*. In this episode, Banacek finds his newest case in the local newspaper, *The Boston Sentinel*.

*In the pilot episode, we learn that when Banacek's father was let go from his company, he was given a watch. In the first-season's seventh-aired episode, we learn that the first name of Banacek's father is Leo. In this episode, in the teaser, we see a number of close-ups of Howard James' stopwatch. The brand name on the stopwatch is Leo.

*In the first-season's last episode, Banacek's first Polish proverb mentions a specific bird (an owl) at a "mouse picnic." In this episode, Banacek's first Polish proverb mentions a specific bird (a chicken) at a "steamfitter's picnic."

*In the previous episode, "The Vanishing Chalice," Banacek delivers two Polish proverbs. In this episode, Banacek delivers two Polish proverbs.

Future Matches:

*Chuck Smith's mention of the old TV series, *Frontier Circus*.

SECTION TWO

Behind the scenes: Executive producer George Eckstein:

"I really liked the episode with the missing racehorse. I thought that was one of the better concepts. I thought that the story was very ingenious and very clever. Anne Francis was fine to work with; we never had a problem with her."[22]

Guest star Harry Carey, Jr. on making the episode: "They just called up and asked for me. I was with Lou Shaw. They said 'Can we get Harry Carey?' and made the deal, that's all. Everybody on the show was fine. There wasn't anybody was giving any problems. The show I did was with a stupid horse, and not much stunt stuff. I think I was a trainer. Usually I have a lot of horse stuff, but I didn't in this one. We were at Santa Anita (racetrack) I believe. It was closed then, so it was perfect. I think we worked two days out there and probably around the barn. It seemed to be a pretty tight schedule. All the TVs (TV series) had a schedule, and they were pretty tight. It wasn't unpleasant, but they don't want to take any time. It's just 'Hurry up, hurry up, hurry up,' and try to get ahead of schedule, instead of behind. It's how fast they get the thing done and get it in the can and saving the studio money. That's what it was all about, especially at Universal. They had more money than anybody, but they were tight."

Guest star Harry Carey, Jr. on...

*George Peppard: "I didn't have any problems with him. He seemed like he was overworked, but he wasn't unpleasant to work with. He was fine. I didn't get to visit or talk with him much. There wasn't much camaraderie connected with it at all. He told me later on that he was blacked out in a lot of those shows—he'd been drinking so much, and when I saw him later on, at a gathering with (director) Andy McLaglen, he said he didn't remember a lot of the *Banacek*s. I remember Richard Burton said the same thing about movies that he did ... (where Burton had) alcoholic blackouts. But Burton remembered all those lines. And George was the same way. He knew his lines. He never missed any dialogue (on *Banacek*). Later on when I worked on that feature with George (*One More Train to Rob*), he was very different. He was much more down to earth and sociable. He was much easier to get along with."

*Viewing the episode: "Yes, I saw it. I wanted to see it because of George Peppard. He was a very, very good actor. I saw him ... he played this Irish revolutionary (Dennis Walsh) during the Irish Rebellion ... Oh, he was marvelous. He had a great brogue, and it was one of those big theatrical programs—a special showing (*Hallmark Hall of Fame* "The Little Moon of Alban," March 24, 1958, NBC), and a very dramatic thing. He was excellent."

*George Peppard's stunt double: "George liked to do his own fights and stuff. He was pretty active, pretty well coordinated, but Alan Gibbs doubled George in *Banacek*. He was a blond guy, doubled Steve McQueen too. He was a very handsome guy. Looked like an actor. He rode the horse when he was stealing him or whatever." (Gibbs, who, according to sources, also doubled for Jack Nicholson, Burt Reynolds, Dustin Hoffman, and Charles Bronson, did a good bit of television and movies pre-*Banacek*. Among the latter: John Wayne's *The Green Berets* and *Hellfighters*; among the former: *Star Trek, The Immortal, Mission: Impossible*.)

*Fellow guest star John Crawford: "I remember John very well. He was very actorish, you know, not hard to work with, but very strong, very stylized, took his job very seriously, and seemed to (approach it) almost like we were doing *Hamlet* on Broadway. He was a decent guy. I remember he was trying to lose weight at the time."

*Episode director Herschel Daugherty: "He was very nice. He was a neat guy. Herschel was very well liked. I think he was the most well-liked director in the television world. Everybody just loved him. I think he'd be a good guy to work for (if you were a just beginning actor or actress), yeah, very much so, cuz some of the other guys just wouldn't be good at all. They were just too much in a hurry. Herschel had a much calmer attitude. He was just flexible. If you wanted to discuss characterization with him, he didn't mind that. And he worked fast too. I wish I had worked for him more."

*Assistant director Reuben Watt: "I worked with him on other shows. He was okay. As long as you're on time, and know your lines. Otherwise, you're miserable."[23]

The Polish Connection:

#1: When Banacek's girlfriend Mandy discovers that he's received a perfumed letter, she jokes: "I thought perfumed letters went out with the Coolidge Administration." In 1926, to thank the U.S. for its help in restoring statehood to their country following World War I, the people of Poland presented to U.S President Calvin Coolidge a unique gift to mark the 150th anniversary of America's independence: the 111-volume, *Polish Declarations of Admiration and Friendship for the United States*. Signed over an eight-month period by nearly one-sixth of Poland's population as it existed in 1926, these richly illustrated volumes (which included greetings, poems, messages, etc.) contained some 5,500,000 signatures; many came from villages so small they were not even listed in Filip Sulimierski's 15-volume *Geographic Dictionary of the Polish Kingdom and Other Slavic Lands*. Along with the signatures of Poland's national, regional, and local officials, religious dignitaries, and people of prominence in the various professions, the massive 111-volume work also collected the signatures of Poland's school children, and their teachers. Volumes 7 through 13 contained the signatures of the students and faculty of 1,170 mostly secondary schools; Volumes 14 through 110 contained signatures from the students and faculty of some 20,000 elementary schools representing 235 school districts. President Coolidge was so moved by this gift, he asked for it to be transferred to the Library of Congress.

Inside jokes and references:

*The name of the studio where Chuck Smith works is Globe. The Globe trademark includes a globe of the earth. The Universal Studios' trademark also features a globe of the earth.

*Chuck Smith was a very successful performer at Globe when the studio was making Westerns. Playing Chuck Smith is Terry Wilson. Wilson was a regular in one of Universal Studios' most successful TV Westerns, *Wagon Train*. Along with fellow regular Frank McGrath, he appeared in all eight seasons of the series.

*During one of the horse races, one of the entrants that is mentioned is Hallie J. Hallie is the first name of one of George Eckstein's daughters.

Notes:

Like the first season's premiere episode, "Let's Hear it for a Living Legend," and the later first-season entry, "Ten Thousand Dollars a Page," this episode is one of the series' most realistic thanks to the presence of 1959 Triple Crown racer William Harmatz. One of America's leading jockeys for nearly twenty years, Harmatz began racing professionally at the Caliente Track in Tijuana in 1953. By the time he retired in 1971, he had some 1,770 wins to his credit. These wins included a first-place finish in the 1959 Preakness (at age twenty-eight), aboard Royal Orbit.

Following his retirement, William Harmatz began a brief acting career. He made his debut as IMF team member/jockey Nick Pressy in the December 11, 1971 sixth-season *Mission: Impossible* episode, "Run for the Money" (the series' one and only horse-racing-themed episode). *Banacek*-Horse of a Slightly Different Color" was Harmatz's second (and as can best be determined) last dramatic role. The fact that there is just one historical reference in this episode which results in a "Polish connection" lends credence to the view that it was indeed George that provided each episode's "Polish connections." Having become the series' second-unit director for the Boston locales, and his previously mentioned walk-and-talk scene in the park sequence being such a complex piece of work, it's more than likely this sequence occupied most of his time during production.

To appreciate George's skill and artistry in directing this walk-and-talk, it is best to freeze the picture on one's DVD or media player and advance it frame by frame. In closing, just as the Polish proverb "Just because a dress is red satin, doesn't mean it comes off easily" is distinguished from the series' other Polish proverbs by being the one proverb specifically mentioned by George Eckstein, so too is "Horse of a Slightly Different Color" separated from the other *Banacek*s because it is the episode singled out by the producer. Both proverb and episode are thirteens: " . . . red satin . . . . " is thirteen words, "Horse" is the thirteenth-aired ninety-minute *Banacek*.

BANACEK Challenges:
"Horse of a Slightly Different Color"

#1: In this episode, guest stars John Crawford and Harry Carey, Jr. respectively play a racehorse owner, and his employee. Besides this relationship and the fact that both of these guest stars' last names begin with the letter C, what are the two other connections between both performers?

#2: Name the five "fives" directly connected to Katherine Wells.

#3: In the teaser, the writers give the audience a match clue that points the way to Banacek's solution. What is it?

#4: In the walk-and-talk sequence in the park, Felix mentions three races Oxford Don won to Banacek. The third race Felix mentions is the Belmont (Belmont Stakes). What three "threes" are connected to the Belmont Stakes?

#5: Another reason for referencing the Belmont Stakes is that the race produces three *Banacek* numbers that connect to the series, as well as this episode. What are these three numbers?

#6: Can you identify the five "fives" associated with guest star Terry Wilson's character?

#7: Like the previous episode, "The Vanishing Chalice," this episode features two Polish proverbs, but there are two more connections between this episode's proverbs and the previous episode's proverbs. What are they?

Reviews and Publicity:
  January 26, 1974: *TV Guide* – Vol. 22, No. 4 — Issue#1087 – *Banacek* referenced in Cleveland Amory's review of *Tenafly*
  February 9, 1974: *TV Guide* – Vol. 22, No. 6 — Issue#1089 – *Banacek* referenced in Cleveland Amory's review of *Faraday and Company*

250 There's an Old Polish Proverb That Says, "Banacek"

Episode #14: "Rocket to Oblivion," February 12, 1974

"There's an old Polish proverb that says, 'If the butterfly had teeth like the tiger, it would never make it out of the hangar.'" –Banacek to Tom Wardlow

"There's an old Polish proverb that says, 'It is harder for the spider to catch the fly than it is for the fly to catch a horse.'" –Banacek to Jay

W: Robert Van Scoyk
D: Andrew V. McLaglen

Guest Stars
Linda Evans   Cherry Saint-Saens
Andrew Prine   Tom Wardlow
Don Gordon   Buck Powell
Tom Drake   Roger Fanchon
Philip Carey   Art Gallagher
Co-starring
Roy Poole as   Det. Garrett
George Murdock as   Cavanaugh
And
Dick Van Patten as   Donald Morgan
With
Polly Middleton   Beautiful Girl
Robert Rothwell   Officer Lonigan
Jayne Kennedy   Girl Demonstrator
Jimmy Joyce   Eddie

SECTION ONE: MATCHES
Matches in series credits:

Opening and closing credits:

*There are three talents in this episode who have three-part names: writer Robert Van Scoyk, director Andrew V. McLaglen, and supporting guest star Dick Van Patten.

*There are three talents in this episode who have the three-letter "van" in their names: Robert Van Scoyk, lead guest Linda Evans, and Dick Van Patten.

*Third-billed in the guest cast is Don Gordon, whose first name is the three-letter Don. Don Gordon is the third Don to be billed in the opening guest credits in the series' second season. (The other Dons were Don Stroud in the second-season premiere, "No Stone Unturned," and Don Porter in "The Three Million Dollar Piracy.")

*The top-billed guest in the opening credits: Linda Evans, has a five-letter by five-letter name; the last billed guest in the closing credits: Jimmy Joyce, has a five-letter by five-letter name.

*The second-billed guest in the opening credits: Andrew Prine, has a five-letter last name; the guest billed above the last guest in the closing credits: Jayne Kennedy, has a five-letter first name.

*The third guest in the opening credits: Don Gordon, has a three-letter first name; the third guest in the closing credits: Dick Van Patten, has a three-part full name.

Matches through physical production and editing:

*The attendant at the country club stops at three tables on the tennis court; each time he asks the man at the table if he is Mr. Banacek. There are three people (two women and one man) at the first table; ditto at the second table. At the third table is just one man: Banacek's chauffeur, Jay Drury; at the tennis court, we see three people in one shot: Jay, Banacek, and Banacek's female tennis partner.

*The sign on the building is the four-word "Science and Industry Expo." The fourth word is the four-letter Expo.

*Inside the building is Tom Wardlow's rocket engine exhibit. The sign at Wardlow's exhibit is four words, "The Wardlow Rocket Engine"; four men put a cylinder over the rocket engine prior to the test.

*Later in the story, Banacek visits Art Gallager at (the four-word) "Boston Businessmen's Athletic Club." Once again there is a sign with four words, and the fourth and last word is a four-letter word, in this instance, Club.

*Four people in Cherry's office: Cherry, Wardlow, Lt. Garrett, and, Buck Powell. After Cherry sits down, and the scene becomes a shot of four people, a shot of Cherry alone then follows; there are four pictures behind her in this shot.

*Donald Morgan's is the fourth exhibit Cherry shows to Banacek. There are four people in the scene: Cherry, Banacek, Morgan, and Jayne, Morgan's demonstrator.

*Seven people sitting at the tables on the tennis court; Jay is the seventh person shown.

*The newspaper *The Boston Chronicle* features three sevens. First, as the notice on the front page indicates, the edition of the paper is the "Seven-Star." Second, on the front page of the *Chronicle* is a seven-word headline, "THEFT OF ROCKET ENGINE CALLED PUBLICITY STUNT." Third, there are a total of seven columns on the front page.

*Seven TV sets showing Banacek at the Expo's video exhibit ; the brand name on the TV sets is the seven-letter "Concord."

*Seven people involved in the physical theft of the engine.

*After the culprits are nabbed, there are just seven people left in the scene.

*Banacek and Cherry stop at the Jacuzzi Whirlpool Bath exhibit. The brand name Jacuzzi is seven letters. The product description, Whirlpool Bath, is thirteen.

*After seven passes of the medicine ball, Gallagher throws it to Banacek, who throws it back to him. Altogether there are thirteen throws of the ball. Banacek is the last person to throw the ball.

*In the explanation sequence, there are thirteen people in the shot. Only one: Banacek, is shown facing the camera.

Matching through numbers:
THREES:

*When the scene switches to the interior of the Exposition, and rocket engine inventor Tom Wardlow, Wardlow is speaking to his audience about the third stage of the Saturn V rocket. In the teaser, The Wardlow Rocket Engine is the third exhibit which the three-named Cherry Saint-Saens visits.

*In his (and the) final line of dialogue in the teaser, Tom Wardlow repeats three two-word phrases/sentences: "It's gone," "Help me," and "Lift it."

*Cherry tells Banacek of three separate show/exposition types she's worked: home shows, antique shows, and a boat show.

*Banacek tells Buck Powell that he has about three pounds of Polish links in his refrigerator. When Banacek speaks this line, "three" is the third word in the line.

*At one point, there are three consecutive sentences of three words apiece: "Key to what?" "Try them where?" and "Lead the way." Note that the last word in each sentence begins with a W.

*Banacek calls Felix at three in the morning.

*In his solution to the mystery, Banacek references a three-dimensional holographic picture.

SIXES:

*In this, the sixth-aired episode, in promoting his Wardlow Rocket Engine, inventor Tom Wardlow references the real-life Saturn V rocket, and notes that it is 600 pounds. The Saturn V rocket was of course named after the (six-letter) planet Saturn: the sixth planet from the Sun.

SIXES and SEVENS:

*According to Tom Wardlow, the third stage of the Saturn V carries 67,000 gallons of liquid hydrogen. (In reality, the figure is closer to 63,000 gallons.)

"She's not thirteen anymore, Mr. Banacek." Linda Evans and George Peppard in story editor Robert Van Scoyk's highly enjoyable "Rocket to Oblivion."

SEVENS:

*Instead of charging Cavanaugh's Boston Insurance Company a ten percent fee for the recovery of the stolen rocket, Banacek's partner, Jay, will only charge them seven percent. As noted earlier, Jay is the seventh person shown sitting at the tables on the tennis court. It is at the tennis court where Jay takes Cavanaugh's phone call.

TWELVES:

*Cherry's maiden name is (the twelve-letter) Charity Kelly; Cherry has been working on the Science and Industry Exposition for twelve months; it is 12:10 a.m. when Cherry arrives at Banacek's home.

THIRTEENS:

*The last time Banacek saw Cherry, she was thirteen years old.

TWENTIES:

*In the teaser, Cherry comments to Tom Wardlow that he must have checked the "turntable twenty times." The first name Tom begins with the letter T: the twentieth letter in the alphabet; in the teaser, Wardlow tells his audience that his Wardlow Rocket Engine has the "thrust and the sustained power capability of an engine twenty times its size.

Alliteration:
A: About an assignment; almost anywhere
B: back booth. Bingo; been burned; better believe; Boston Businessmen's
C: Cape Canaveral; cleaning crew
D: display! Dammit!; dollar deal
E: everyone else
F: fall flat; football fan
G: great gift
H: heaven help
I: Insurance investigator

M: middle man; misplaced missile motor; more money
P: paranoid personality; photographic plate; police people; pre-planned; proper place
S: Saint-Saens said; season seats; small share; Space Shuttle; Spruce St.; supposedly searching
T: Tom turned; trying to take; trying to tell; turntable twenty times
W: Wardlow. Wait!
M&S: Morning, Miss Saint-Saens
Y&P: Yeah, yeah. Pretty. Pretty?

Matches to previous episodes:

*In the pilot episode, "Detour to Nowhere," Banacek turns to the back page of the out-of-town newspaper, the *Vantage Sentinel*. In the fourth column is a story with the six-word headline, "Cries for Vote Reform in Congress." In this episode, Banacek is reading the front page of the *Boston Chronicle*. In the third column is a story with the six-word headline, "Cries for Vote Reform in Congress."

*In the premiere episode, "Let's Hear it for a Living Legend," football player Jerry Mulligan has a "glass knee." In this episode, former football player Art Gallagher has a "trick knee."

*In the second-aired episode, "Project Phoenix," the thirteen-letter Concord Motors is the company interested in buying the Experimental Safety Vehicle, the Phoenix. In this episode, Banacek sees himself displayed on television sets made by Concord.

*In the third-aired episode, "No Sign of the Cross," third-billed in the opening credits is Gordon Pinsent. In this episode, third-billed in the opening credits is Don Gordon. Thus the first name Gordon receives third-billing in one episode, and the last name Gordon receives third-billing in another episode.

*In the fourth-aired episode, "A Million the Hard Way," Banacek is looking for $1,000,000 that vanished from a revolving turntable covered by a glass dome. In this episode, he attempts to retrieve an invaluable rocket engine which vanished from a revolving turntable protected by an outer shield.

*In second-season story editor Robert Van Scoyk's first solo-written *Banacek*, "If Max is So Smart, Why Doesn't He Tell Us Where He Is?," two women: nurse Wyn Reiver, and Felix's girlfriend both wink at Banacek, on separate occasions. In this episode, Van Scoyk's second solo-written *Banacek*, the girl brushing her hair in the mirror winks at Banacek.

*In the second-season, fourth-aired episode, "The Vanishing Chalice," the museum painting "Dog with Bone," which attracts the attention of Banacek, Jay, and Carlie, was painted by one L. Plotkin. In this episode, an orthodontist named Dr. Plotkin gives Banacek an invaluable piece of information.

SECTION TWO

Behind the scenes:
Executive producer George Eckstein: "Andy McLaglen was okay. He was basically an action director, and unfortunately, or fortunately, we weren't really an action show. I mean we had to recreate these moments, but it was, basically, not an action show."[24]

Guest commentary:
Banacek guest star Harry Carey, Jr. on episode guest Andrew Prine: "Andy Prine... he's an old friend. I've known Andy for so long; I knew him when he first came out from New York. He's more temperamental than most. I mean, not with me, but he would be with directors and producers. He could be a little controversial at times."

On director McLaglen: "I worked for Andy. He was easy. He'd stand on your feet—stepped on your feet; he loved to do that, and—great big guy—he's six-seven. We always had a kind of a club. He had the same bunch of guys a lot of the time. Me and Denver Pyle, and Ken Curtis. It was always fun to work on Andy's shows. And he didn't waste any time either. He shot very fast. That's why he worked a lot."[25]

The Polish Connection:

#1: In the teaser, inventor Tom Wardlow is discussing the Saturn V, and how it is powered by a combination of liquid hydrogen and liquid oxygen. On April 5, 1883, the first measurable quantity of liquid oxygen was produced by Polish professors Zygmunt Wroblewski and Karol Olszewski at Jagiellonian University. The two men were the first to liquefy oxygen, nitrogen and carbon dioxide from the atmosphere in a stable state. Until then, these elements could only be produced in the dynamic state in the transitional form as vapor.

#2: One year later, in 1884, working in his laboratory in Krakow, Olszewski was the first to liquefy hydrogen in a dynamic state; he achieved a record low temperature of -225°centigrade.

#3: During the course of this episode, Felix tells Banacek he's finally dug out his copy of the classic novel, *Little Women*, so he can finally read it. While vacationing in Europe, author Louisa May Alcott met a Polish freedom fighter named Ladislas Wisneiwski in Switzerland. The two later enjoyed a brief romance in Paris. When Alcott later wrote *Little Women*, she used Wisneiwski as the inspiration for her male character, Laurie.

#4: Louisa May Alcott also wrote short stories and novels, such as *The Baron's Gloves*. The fourth chapter of the book was entitled, "A Polish Exile."

#5: When Art Gallagher calls him a "Polack," Banacek gently corrects him with the response, "Polish. So was Copernicus."

Inside jokes and references:

*In the teaser, Cherry says that the morning she received the note threatening the Wardlow Rocket Engine, she arrived about 8:30 a.m. (EST). 8:30 p.m. (EST) was the time *Banacek* aired.

*Later when discussing his upcoming date with Cherry, Banacek expresses the wish that the date not consist of his being treated to a *Beach Party* double feature. Lead guest Linda Evans appeared in *Beach Blanket Bingo* (1965).

*In the explanation scene, one of the culprits' alibis is destroyed thanks to the information Banacek obtains from the orthodontist Dr. Plotkin. Again,

Plotkin is the maiden name of (episode writer, and second season story editor) Robert Van Scoyk's wife, Leona.

Notes:

Like the previous episode, "Rocket to Oblivion" is one of the more realistic *Banacek*s, thanks to the stolen item, the Wardlow Rocket Engine that is running on liquid hydrogen and liquid oxygen, the same fuel as NASA's real-life Saturn V. As noted above in the Polish connections, Polish professors Zygmunt Wroblewski and Karol Olszewski were the first to liquefy these elements. Tying the stolen object to real Polish scientists was clever writing on second season story editor Robert Van Scoyk's part.

The fact that Banacek is also hunting an item modeled after the real-life Saturn V rocket engine makes for additional connections; the name Saturn V possesses seven characters; the last name Banacek is of course seven letters; Saturn is the sixth planet from the Sun; there are a total of six letters in Banacek's first name, Thomas. Note too that the inventor of the rocket engine in this episode has the same first name as the sleuth, although he goes by the shorter name, Tom. Moreover, because of Tom Wardlow's reference to the Saturn V, Van Scoyk establishes yet another connection: this one to the full thirteen-letter name, Thomas Banacek. By the time this episode aired, NASA had successfully launched a total of thirteen Saturn V rockets from the Kennedy Space Center in Florida; in the case of each launch, there was no loss of crew or payload. Another Banacekian number connection results from the name, Jacuzzi; the Jacuzzi Whirlpool Bath is one of the exhibits Cherry shows to Banacek early in the story. Jacuzzi was the last name of seven brothers who immigrated to the United States from Pordenone, Friuli, Italy, around 1900. In 1915, they founded the company which in time invented the whirlpool bathtub. The names of the seven brothers: Francesco, Rachele, Valeriano, Galindo, Candido, Giocondo, and Gisueppe. Plotkin being the maiden name of Van Scoyk's wife, Leona, the writer's having the unseen orthodontist Dr. Plotkin present Banacek with some valuable information which helps the sleuth identify the culprits, is another clever touch. Ditto the casting of Linda

Evans as villainess Cherry Saint-Saens. Seeing Evans playing a woman who is catty, clinging and possessive, not to mention the brains behind the crime is surprising to say the least. She makes the most of this rare opportunity. Also good is Andrew Prine, who, as evidenced by the above commentary from *Banacek* guest Harry Carey, Jr., is perfectly cast as the hot-headed (and humorous) Tom Wardlow. Philip Carey has a funny bit as well. Unfortunately, for Carlie Kirkland fans, this is Christine Belford's last appearance as Carlie.

Is George Peppard's 'Banacek' arresting Linda Evans' 'Cherry Saint-Saens?'

BANACEK Challenges: "Rocket to Oblivion"

#1: In her first meeting with Banacek, Cherry reveals a biographical detail that matches a biographical detail Banacek discloses about her at the end of the story. What is that match?

#2: Why does Cherry say "twelve months" rather than a year?

#3: Why is Donald Morgan using a laser to dry-clean?

#4: In the teaser, other than the fact she is standing right behind him, a second connection is established between Carlie Kirkland and Art Gallagher. What is it?

#5: In the teaser, after the lights go out thanks to the unexpected accident, we hear the word lights" in the following three lines:

> "Turn on the emergency lights!"
> "Get those lights on."
> "Lights, please."

Can you detect the numerical progression in these lines?

#6: In the credits, there is a match of five "fives." Can you spot it?

#7: Banacek's identification of the culprits in this episode creates a perfect match between this: the sixth-aired episode of the second season, and "Ten Thousand Dollars a Page," the sixth-aired episode of the first season. Can you identify this match?

Reviews and Publicity:

February 16, 1974: *TV Guide* – Vol. 22, No. 7 — Issue#1090 – *Banacek* revealed to be in danger of cancellation in article, "Forecast for Fall: Warm and Human" by Bill Davidson, pg. 8.

Episode#15: "Fly Me If You Can Find Me," February 19, 1974

"There's an old Polish proverb that says, 'When the wolf is chasing your sleigh, throw him a raisin cookie, but don't stop to bake a cake.'" –Banacek to Jay

Banacek: "There's an old Polish proverb that says . . . ."
Girlfriend: "Better safe than sorry?"
Banacek: "Well, that's close, but the Polish version is, 'A truly wise man never plays leapfrog with a unicorn.'"

W: Harold Livingston
D: Bernard Kowalski

Guest Stars
Sterling Hayden
Victoria Principal
Jack Kelly
And
Pat Quinn as
Co-starring
James Daris
Charles H. Gray
Carlos Romero
Richard Roat
Paul Cavonis

Anthony Fowler
Brooke Collins
Lou Wayne

Charlotte

Roy Gilbert
Capt. Roberts
Sheriff Ortega
Stan Price
Andy Hall

With

Beverly Gill	Gina
Laurence Haddon	Joe Daley
Larry Ward	Len Malloy
Don Hanmer	Charlie Tyson
Byron Mabe	Walt Kinsdale

SECTION ONE: MATCHES

Matches in series credits:
Opening and closing credits:

*There are three three-letter words in the episode title: "Fly," "You," and "Can."

*There are three three-letter words: "Fly," "You," and "Can," and three two-letter words: "If," and two "Me"s.

*Two side-by-side two-letter words: "Me," and "If" are followed by two side-by-side three-letter words: "You," and "Can."

*Because the title is presented on screen as:

FLY ME

IF YOU CAN

FIND ME

The third word in the second line is the three-letter Can. Note that this three-letter word begins with the third letter in the alphabet.

*In the closing credits, there are five guest stars billed under the co-starring label and five guests billed under the "With" label.

*In the closing credits, the five-letter by five-letter James Daris is the first of five one-time guests billed under the co-starring credits.

Sterling Hayden as Tony Fowler in one of the more outrageous "stolen object" *Banacek* entries, "Fly Me If You Can Find Me," NBC/Universal.

Matches through physical production and editing:

*In the teaser, at the Hangston Airport, we see a total of three signs: Malloy Flying School, Hall Aviation Service, and Fowler Industries. Each of the signs is a three of some kind. In the case of the first two: Malloy Flying School, and Hall Aviation Service, each sign is a total of three words; in the third, Fowler Industries, the second and last word, Industries, is a total of three syllables; as the plane lands in the teaser, we hear the sound of three tire blow-outs.

*Banacek's arrival in Hangston is the character's third location scene. The first is the toy store in Boston, featuring both inside and outside the store. The second: the entrance to Boston Logan International Airport. When Banacek arrives in the third location: Hangston, we're shown the three-word sign, Malloy Flying School.

*There are three signs: Malloy Flying School, Hall Aviation Service, and Desert Sands Motel, which identify the structure/building/location; Banacek goes to each one of these. Each of these signs has a total of three words.

*After we see three women, including Brooke Collins, walking down the hallway, in the background, at Fowler's home, we then see three men: Banacek, Fowler, and Gilbert, in the foreground; three swords on the wall in the guest room at Fowler's.

*In the courthouse scene, a shot of three men (the sheriff, Dave and Stan) is followed by another shot of three men (Wayne, Banacek, and FAA investigator Joe Daley).

*On the ground outside the Quonset hut, a three-shot of the sheriff, the pilot, and the co-pilot is followed by a shot of the two stewardesses, which is followed by a shot of Jay and FAA investigator Joe Daley. Note that this third shot features characters whose first names (Jay and Joe) are a total of three letters.

*As the plane taxis to a stop, three men wheel the exit ramp towards the door.

*Seven people in the (seven-letter) Quonset hut at Hangston waiting for the plane carrying Banacek, Fowler, and Wayne.

*When Jay enters the Quonset hut, this makes the number of people eight. These eight people match the eight-letter sign, Hangston, on top of the hut. The eight-letter Hangston begins with H: the eighth letter of the alphabet.

Matching through numbers:
THREES:
*The three-letter first-named Lou Wayne owns three planes: Wayne Charter I, Wayne Charter II and Wayne Charter III. The last is never depicted.

*Along with working for the same airline, the pilot, co-pilot, and flight engineer have another thing in common. All three men have four-letter first names: Dave, Stan, and Walt.

*Felix gives Banacek three measurements concerning the missing DC-8 plane: length, height, wingspan.

*Besides the three-syllable Banacek, also looking into the plane's disappearance is (the three-initial) FAA investigator, Joe Daley. As noted previously, the FAA man's first name is the three-letter Joe.

*Fowler describes the three-word Desert Sands Motel as a "third-rate motel."

*Fowler tells Banacek that when he and Lou Wayne were operating their business in South Vietnam in the late 1950s, in their C-124, they would drop supplies for the people every three months.

*After Jay gives Banacek his theory as to how the plane disappeared (using hacksaws to cut the plane into small pieces, then hauling the pieces away in a truck), Banacek agrees that the theft could have been accomplished in this manner, if the thieves started sawing three days before the plane disappeared, then hauled the pieces away ... in thirty-two trucks.

*Tony Fowler repeats a number of words three times. Among these: "this," "somebody," "ten years," and the three-letter "how."

FIVES:

*During the conversation between Banacek and Brooke Collins, as they are driven to the home of Tony Fowler, the two-word, five-letter sentence fragment, "I'd say," is spoken a total of five times.

SEVENS:

*In the seventh-aired episode of the second season, Banacek is looking for a $7 million airplane.

*Towards the end of the story, Banacek, Fowler, and Wayne recreate the night flight which resulted in the disappearance of the airplane. Upon noticing the full moon in the sky, Banacek asks the two pilots, "Isn't that what they call a Bomber's Moon?" In Banacek's question, the seven-letter word "Bomber's" is the seventh word in the question. By referencing a Bomber's Moon (a full moon so bright it's almost like daylight; such moons made it easier for WWII bomber pilots to pinpoint their targets), the writers also drop another seven. A full moon is one of the four principal lunar phases the moon undergoes during its regular cycle. The other lunar phases are: new moon, first quarter moon, and third quarter moon. Each lunar phase lasts approximately seven days.

THIRTEENS:
*When discussing his time spent in Vietnam, the thirteen-letter Anthony Fowler reveals that he flew over Village 13.

Alliteration:
A: about anti-aircraft; anti-aircraft; Anything about Anthony; ask anybody, ask anybody
B: bankbook; been breaking; better because
C: crippled. Crippled!
D: Dave! Dave!; don't deny; Double D; duck down
E: everything except
F: five feet; finally figured; four forty-five
G: Gilbert. Get; gonna get; got grounded; gotta get
H: he had himself; Hi. Hi; How, How, How
I: insurance investigator
L: landing lights; little load; lousy. Lousy!
M: many men; meet me; motel management
N: No need, no need
O: only one
P: Pain. Pain; passport; Polish proverb
R: ready room
S: Saigon suspected; sandstorm; say surrendered; seen since; Sheriff! Somebody stole; shoot. She's; sightseer; Somebody, Somebody,

Somebody; Somebody shot; somebody stole; sound sleeper; started sawing; still see; Sunday schoolteacher; supplies, supplies

T: Ta ta; that third-rate; they took these; thirty-two trucks; This, this, this; tried twice. Tyson; trying to tow; two trucks

W: Well, we'll; Well, what was; Why? What's wrong; without warning

Double alliteration:
A&T: any attention to them
W&I: Well, where is it?

Matches to previous episodes:

*In the pilot, Carlie Kirkland catches a pajama-wearing Jay by surprise in his hotel room. In this episode, stewardess Brooke Collins catches a pajama-wearing Jay by surprise in his hotel room.

*In the premiere episode, "Let's Hear it For a Living Legend," Holly Allencamp is wearing a large letter "A" on her scarlet dress. In this episode, Banacek tells the motel manager that stewardess Brooke Collins reminds him of his former Sunday schoolteacher Hester Prynne. (In Nathaniel Hawthorne's *The Scarlet Letter*, the character Hester Prynne is forced to wear a large scarlet "A" (for adultery) on her dress.)

*In the fourth-aired episode of the first season, "A Million the Hard Way," Jay is waiting for Banacek at the Las Vegas airport. In this episode, Jay is waiting for Banacek at an airport near Las Vegas.

*In the aforementioned "A Million the Hard Way," while waiting for his boss to arrive, Jay has been gambling at the tables and losing. In this episode, while waiting for Banacek to arrive, Jay has been gambling at the tables and losing.

*In the first season's last episode, "The Two Million Clams of Cap'n Jack," Jack and Leo Osburn started their seafood business ten years ago. In the second season premiere, "No Stone Unturned," Davy Collier has a ten-year option on Owen Russell's work. In the next episode, "If Max Is So Smart, Why Doesn't He Tell Us Where He Is?" Lesley Lyle wonders what might

have happened had she met Banacek ten years ago. In this episode, Tony Fowler took Lou Wayne's man, Roy Gilbert, away from Wayne ten years earlier. In addition, the motel manager tells Banacek that the Desert Sands motel hasn't been this busy since they stopped work on the missile pad, some ten years ago.

*In the second-season's fifth-aired episode, "Horse of a Slightly Different Color," TV cowboy Chuck Smith talks to Banacek about the old TV series, *Frontier Circus*. In this episode, stewardess Brooke Collins tells Banacek that the best thing she's seen on the local television stations is a farm report and a rerun of the old TV series, *Circus Boy*.

*In the previous episode, Banacek is looking for a missing rocket engine. In this episode, the terms, "missile pad" and "ready room" are spoken to the sleuth. Both "missile pad" and "ready room" are terms which apply to rockets.

SECTION TWO

Behind the scenes: Executive producer George Eckstein: "Harold Livingston (who wrote the story) ... we had a funny situation there as I remember. Something about ... the airplane going missing ... he used that same story on another series, much to our dismay."[26]

(Eckstein may be referring to the October 17, 1970 fifth-season *Mission: Impossible* "Flight." The story had the IMF spiriting the villain away from the airplane where he and his fellow passengers were awaiting take-off, and putting him in their mock-up of an airplane in a warehouse. Livingston wrote the teleplay of the episode; Leigh Vance wrote the actual story.)

The Polish Connection:

*During Banacek's first visit to Tony Fowler's home, Fowler treats the sleuth to a beer he says is a Dortmunder. Dortmunder and Dortmunder Strong were mass-produced Polish beers which were introduced between 1972 and 1977 in an attempt to boost Poland's beer production.

Notes:

Setting this episode apart from the previous second season episodes is the lack of a competitor to Banacek such as Henry DeWitt, or Carlie Kirkland. Also missing is the sleuth's frequent employer, Cavanaugh. Other drawbacks: the episode offers very few Boston locales, and, as can best be determined, there's only one Polish connection. That being said, this episode still has a lot going for it. The theft of the airplane is one of the most outrageous presented on the series; Jack Kelly is likable in his characterization of Lou Wayne; Sterling Hayden's rapid-fire repetition of certain words and phrases definitely grabs the viewer's attention, and the Felix Mulholland/house of cards sequence has to be one of the funniest Felix bits in the entire series. Adding further interest to the show are George's scenes with one-time girl-friend Victoria Principal.

BANACEK Challenges: "Fly Me If You Can Find Me"

#1: In the teaser, the first shot and the last shot have the same thing in common. What is it?

#2: The last scene in the teaser produces another match. Can you identify it?

#3: After Banacek and Jay enter one of the gates to Fowler's property, a Fowler helicopter arrives to drive them off the grounds. The warning from the men in the helicopter creates a match. Can you identify it?

#4: Besides his being hired to retrieve it, how else does Banacek connect to the missing DC-8?

#5: At Banacek and Jay's motel, there is a sign saying, "Desert Sands Motel 'Where the Sun Always Shines,'" As we can see, there are three words in the sign: "Sands," "Sun," and "Shines," which begin with the same letter: "S." What else do these three words have in common?

#6 and #7: When Banacek calls Felix in Boston, his friend is building a house of cards with the help of his current girlfriend. Unfortunately for Felix, the phone is underneath his house of cards, and to answer it, he must destroy the house of cards. Besides the information just given, in what two other ways is Felix's "house of cards" connected to Banacek and George?

Reviews and Publicity:

February 23, 1974: *TV Guide* – Vol. 22, No. 8 – Issue#1091 – TV Crossword – 18 across – Belonging to Banacek star (abbr. 2 words)

Episode #16: "Now You See Me, Now You Don't," March 12, 1974

W: Stanley Roberts
D: Bernard McEveety

Guest Stars
Nancy Olson   Louise Merrick
Gretchen Corbett   Vicki Merrick
Jay Robinson   Bradley Merrick/Kurt Steiner
Also starring
Pat Harrington   Phil Ross
Peter Marshall   Hal Parker
Co-starring
Lynnette Mettey   Emily Parker
Bruce Gordon   Maxwell Barker

Philip Pine	Ed Harvey
Katherine Baumann	Gloria
Frank Maxwell	Higgins
Walter Burke	Walter Peterson
And	
Kathie Browne as	Shirley Cole
With	
Gene Dynarski	Leo
Lew Brown	Wilson
Kai Hernandez	Sandra
Gerald S. Peters	Davis
Sharyn Wynters	Lorraine

SECTION ONE: MATCHES

Matches in series credits:

*There are five guest stars billed in the opening credits. The first of these five is the five-letter by five-letter Nancy Olson.

*Third-billed in the opening credits is the three-letter first name, three-syllable last name, Jay Robinson

*The fourth-billed Pat Harrington plays the four-letter by four-letter Phil Ross.

*Twelfth billed in the full cast is Kathie Browne. There are a total of twelve letters in the actress' full name.

*In the guest cast closing credits, the last name Parker (as in Emily Parker) is followed by the (rhyming) last name Barker (as in Maxwell Barker).

Matches through physical production and editing:

*Two Los Angeles Amateur Magician shows; two seven-letter last name magicians (Merrick and Banacek) who perform the same trick.

*Three Merricks: Bradley, Louise, and Vicki; three swords stuck in the basket by the magician who precedes Merrick.

*Three stagehands who move the trunk Merrick uses on stage; three people from the audience whom Merrick selects to help with the trick; after locking and securing the trunk which holds his daughter Vicki, Merrick taps on the trunk three times; three plainclothes detectives who enter the theater/playhouse as Merrick is performing the trick.

*Three people in Felix's bookshop: Felix, Banacek, and Felix's female assistant.

*Three signs showing the company name for the three-named Trans Global Airlines (two refer to the company by the three-letter abbreviation: TGA.

*Three daughters from the three-named J. Maxwell Barker's first marriage in photograph on his desk.

*Three Las Vegas showgirls who talk to Banacek.

*Three men in the theater seats watch Banacek recreate Merrick's vanishing act; three women in the theater seats watch Banacek recreate Merrick's vanishing act.

*The magic show is presented at the Sixth Street Playhouse. The six-letter word Street follows the word, Sixth.

*Six people in the theater seats when Banacek presents the solution-on stage.

*Seven reporters who talk to Banacek when he leaves the Merrick home.

Matching through numbers:
THREES:

*The two words "coming apart" are spoken a total of three times. When Kurt Steiner responds to his partner Phil Ross, his first sentence is the three-word "She's coming apart!" After he speaks the third "coming apart," Steiner then tells Ross, "The drunken oaf on the spotlight has missed **three** cues already."

*One of the people Merrick selects for his magic trick is a girl sitting in the third row.

*Merrick tells the audience that if they give him three seconds, he'll exchange places with his daughter Vicki who is tied up in the bag and locked in the trunk.

*Banacek is told he'll have to recover the securities in thirty days.

*The three-named J. Maxwell Barker has a three-word nickname, "Butcher Boy Barker."

*Barker's chief hood is the three-letter Leo.

*At one point, Banacek calls Barker, "Max" (three letters).

SIXES AND SEVENS:

*Vicki tells Banacek she has spent the last six or seven years avoiding her less than ideal family.

THIRTEENS:

*Banacek tells Vicki he hasn't been worried about his reputation since he was thirteen and a half.

Alliteration:

A: Annual Amateur; audience applauded

B: bank business; bellboy; bonded Bradley; bonding business; Brad's bills; brokerage business; Butcher Boy Barker

C: campus chapel

E: every exit

F: father founded

G: gonna get; good girl, go

I: insurance investigator

L: little late; little later; love L.A.

M: many more; maybe maybe; met Mr. Merrick

O: Okay, okay; out one of

P: probably practiced

S: Sixth Street; social secretary; South Side; Southern Senator; split second; St. Swithins; standard situation; still stuck; straight sweet; success story; sweet suffering
T: this trunk thoroughly; through the trapdoor; to this trip
W: whole world

Double Alliteration:
N&T: not necessarily trying to
S&M: Sorry, Sir, Mrs. Merrick

Matches to previous episodes:
*In the pilot, Carlie describes the truck which Banacek is driving as a "Ralph Nader nightmare." In this episode, game show host Hal Parker speaks of two ad agency men who looked at him as if he were Ralph Nader trying out one of their products.

*In the first-season premiere, "Let's Hear it For a Living Legend," Banacek is looking for a missing man whose preferred first name (Hank) has the same number of letters as his last name (Ives). In this episode, Banacek is looking for a missing man whose first name (Bradley) has the same number of letters as his last name (Merrick).

*In "Living Legend," witnessing the disappearance of star football player Hank Ives, Banacek makes a reference to the famous magician Harry Houdini. In this episode, recreating the disappearance of Bradley Merrick, Banacek makes a reference to Harry Houdini.

*In the first season's second episode, "Project Phoenix" and the second season's "Horse of a Slightly Different Color," game show hosts Bert Convy (*Tattletales*) and Allen Ludden (*Password*) were guest stars on *Banacek*. In this episode, *Hollywood Squares* (game-show) host Peter Marshall is a guest star.

*In the series' third-aired episode, "No Sign of the Cross," two former Chicago gangsters are key figures in Banacek's investigation. In this episode, a former Chicago gangster is a key figure in Banacek's investigation.

*In "No Sign of the Cross," Banacek makes a reference to the 1959-1963 series, *The Untouchables*. In this episode, *Untouchables* semi-regular Bruce Gordon (who played gangster Frank Nitti on the series) is a guest star.

*In "No Sign of the Cross," art collector Robert Morgan speaks to Banacek of "Inquisitional Tortures." In the series' fourth episode, "A Million the Hard Way," after some probing questions from Banacek, Linda Carsini asks him if the "Inquisition" is over, and calls him Mr. Torquemada. In this episode, when Banacek returns to the Merrick home to ask Louise Merrick some more questions, she smart-cracks "More questions from the Grand Inquisitor?"

*In the series' first episode, "Let's Hear it For a Living Legend," Banacek receives a key piece of information connected to his current case from a woman named Hollis Barker Allencamp. In the fifth-aired episode, "To Steal a King," Banacek tells current girlfriend Sharon Clark that the notorious female gangster Ma Barker was his "first crush." In this episode, Banacek discovers he is working for former big-time Chicago gangster Maxie "Butcher Boy" Barker.

*In the series' seventh episode, "The Greatest Collection of Them All," we learn that the first name of Banacek's father is Leo. In the next episode, "The Two Million Clams of Cap'n Jack," one of the suspects in the theft is Leo Osborn. In the series' thirteenth episode, "Horse of a Slightly Different Color," Leo is the name of the company that manufactures the stopwatch used by horse-racing trainer Howard James. In this episode, Leo is the name of the chief goon employed by former Chicago gangster Maxwell Barker.

*In "The Two Million Clams of Cap'n Jack," the eighth and last episode of the first season, after Felix gives Banacek a brief biography of businessman Roger Sloan, Banacek describes the man as "a typical American success story." In this episode, the eighth and last episode of the second season, after Felix gives Banacek a brief biography of his quarry: magician Bradley Merrick, Felix describes the man as "a true American success story."

George Peppard and Anne Francis in the thirteenth-aired NBC/Universal *Banacek* "Horse of a Slightly Different Color."

*In the second-aired episode of the second season, "If Max is So Smart, Why Doesn't He Tell Us Where He Is?," Banacek seeks to recover the missing computer Max. In this episode, Banacek calls J. Maxwell Barker "Max."

*In "The Three-Million Dollar Piracy," the third episode of the second season, Henry DeWitt kisses his fiancee Carlie Kirkland on the forehead. In this episode, Banacek kisses the young Vicki Merrick on the forehead.

*In "Piracy," former actress Diana Maitland tells Banacek she's going to miss a lot of things about the U.S. once she marries the Shah of Baraga, and moves to his country. Banacek asks if she means TV shows like *Edge of Night* and *Hollywood Squares*. In this episode, as noted above, *Hollywood Squares* host Peter Marshall is a guest star.

SECTION TWO

Behind the scenes: George Eckstein: "George didn't socialize a lot with the actors (but) everybody had a good time doing the show. All the women were either people he knew or had worked with before; he just had a good time with it; good time working with those ladies, I mean Brenda (Vaccaro) and Annie (Francis) and all those people that he knew. He would turn down a director or two. We had a couple of, sort of, not happy circumstances with directors."[27]

The Polish Connection:

#1: While playing chess with Felix, Banacek asks him if he's been secretly meeting with Bobby Fischer. At that time, Fischer was considered to be the Greatest Chess Master of All. Fischer's mother Regina was a Jew of Polish ancestry.

#2: During Banacek's questioning of showmen Phil Ross and Kurt Steiner, Steiner frets that he and Ross will go down in history as producers of the biggest flop magic show of all time. Not necessarily, Banacek points out, asking Steiner if he's familiar with the name, Edward J. Smith. When Steiner says no, the sleuth tells him that Smith was the captain of the famously doomed ship, *Titanic*. In 1943, the German-made movie, *Titanic*, was released. Part of the location shooting was done in Poland.

Inside jokes and references:

*The special showing of the Amateur Magician's Show is at 8:30 p.m. Throughout its original prime-time run, *Banacek* aired at 8:30 p.m. (EST).

*Jay (whose first name is pronounced the same way as the letter J) is the first to speak the full name J. Maxwell Barker.

Notes:

Of all the *Banacek* episodes, this one's disappearance/mystery is the easiest to solve. In fact, the solution is obvious in the episode teaser. But the

Katherine Baumann's portrayal of the ditzy Gloria Barker was one of the high points in the series finale, "Now You See Me, Now You Don't."

episode holds the audience's attention thanks to the humorous situations and witty dialogue, not to mention the amusing performances of Bruce Gordon as former gangster Maxie "Butcher Boy" Barker and Katherine Baumann as his not-so-smart, second wife Gloria. The casting of Gordon as a one-time gangster is another *Banacek* inside joke. As noted earlier, George Eckstein wrote for *The Untouchables*; some of the best episodes of that series were those featuring Gordon in the semi-regular role of real-life gangster Frank "The Enforcer" Nitti. Adding further interest is the casting of another daily gameshow host: *Hollywood Squares*' Peter Marshall, in a dramatic role.

Marshall is the brother of 1940s and 1950s big-screen leading lady Joanne Dru. Unfortunately, for this series finale, no Polish proverb was written.

BANACEK Challenges:
"Now You See Me, Now You Don't"

#1: In the teaser, Ross tells Steiner: "Brad Merrick hasn't shown up yet, and his daughter is coming apart." Besides the obvious connection of father and daughter, how does Ross' reference to Merrick and his daughter Vicki, create another match?

#2: Can you identify the three matches in the Bradley Merrick line, "We've only had one fifteen-minute rehearsal?"

#3: This episode presents a match between Ralph Manza, and guest stars Jay Robinson, and Bruce Gordon. Can you identify it?

#4: With this episode, recurring guest Gene Dynarski accomplishes three *Banacek* "threes." Can you name any or all?

#5: When Simms tries to hire Banacek to work on the Bradley Merrick disappearance, the sleuth tells him he's planning to take off the entire month of March. Give the three reasons why this month is specifically mentioned by Banacek.

#6: In what two ways does guest star Philip Pine match series star George Peppard?

#7: This episode concludes with a match performed by Banacek which involves Jay. Can you identify it?

Episode#1: "Let's Hear It For a Living Legend"
[1] Eckstein-interview, 2009

Episode#2: "Project Phoenix"
[2] Ibid
[3] "Banacek a Fantasy to Real Life Investigators," *The Los Angeles Times*, November 30, 1972, pg. E17

Episode#3: "No Sign of the Cross"
[4] Eckstein-interview, 2009
[5] Michael Forest-telephone interview, 2007
[6] Andrew J. Fenady-telephone interview, 2004

Episode#4: "A Million the Hard Way"
[7] Eckstein-interview, 2009

Episode#5: "To Steal a King"
[8] Lou Antonio-telephone interview, 2007
[9] Don Pedro Colley-telephone interview, 2007

Episode#6: "Ten Thousand Dollars a Page"
[10] Eckstein-interview, 2009

Episode#7: "The Greatest Collection of Them All"
[11] Eckstein-interview, 2009
[12] Polier, Bulletin – *TV Time*, pg. 3

Episode#8. "The Two Million Clams of Cap'n Jack"
[13] Eckstein-interview, 2009

Episode#9: "No Stone Unturned"
[14] Ibid

Episode#10: "If Max Is So Smart, Why Doesn't He Tell Us Where He Is"
[15] Ibid

Episode#11: "The Three Million Dollar Piracy"
[16] Eckstein-interview, 2009

[17] Dick Gautier-e-mail-2011
[18] Harry Carey-telephone interview, 2010
[19] Eckstein-interview, 2009

Episode#12: "The Vanishing Chalice"
[20] Ibid
[21] Carey-interview, 2010

Episode#13: "Horse of a Slightly Different Color"
[22] Eckstein-interview, 2009
[23] Carey-interview, 2010

Episode#14: "Rocket to Oblivion"
[24] Eckstein-interview, 2009
[25] Carey-interview, 2010

Episode#15: "Fly Me If You Can Find Me"
[26] Eckstein-interview, 2009

Episode#16: "Now You See Me, Now You Don't"
[27] Ibid

BANACEK Challenges: Answers

"Tis nothing when you are used to it." –Polish proverb

"Let's Hear It For a Living Legend"

#1. Like Thomas Banacek, Jerry Brinkman has a total of thirteen letters in his full name.

#2. One: The fourth word in the line is the three-letter word, "for," which is pronounced the same as the number four. Two: Counting four words from four, we arrive at the four-letter first name, Hank. Three: Hank is the first of four four-letter words/names in the fragment: "Hank Ives more than." Four: Four words: "more than I do" follow the four-letter by-four-letter name, Hank Ives.

#3. One: The station is Channel 6. Two: The call letters of the station are the six-letter KMPK-TV. (This is nothing unusual. Most TV and radio stations had call numbers of six letters.) Three: Hank speaks a total of just six words during the interview.

#4. One: As we know, there are four letters apiece in the first name, Hank, and the last name, Ives. Following the four-letter name, Hank, we have four four-letter words: "this," "let's," "play," and "okay." Two: Hank Ives, whose first name begins with H: the eighth letter of the alphabet, plays football for a living. In the line talk-show host Ingels addresses to Hank, the eight-letter word "football" is the eighth word in the line. Three: Both the eight-letter words "football" and "chitchat" are combinations of two four-letter words: "foot," and "ball"; "chit" (meaning a voucher), and "chat" (meaning an informal conversation.) If we look at the Ingels line using this four-letter criteria we find that beginning with the fourth word "this," we have a total of eight four-letter words in a row: "this" "chit," "chat," "Let's," "play," "foot," "ball," and "okay."

#5. One: The third spoken "Henry" is the third word in the reply. Two: Following the three "Henrys" is the three-letter pronoun, "who." Three: Like the name "Henry," the pronoun "who" is pronounced with the same "H" sound.

#6. One: The postmark shows the four-letter abbreviation, "U.S.S.R." Two: Felix's address is (the four-digit) 8920 Beacon Street. Three: Felix lives in Massachusetts. Dmitri has abbreviated the state as "Mass." Four: There are four handwritten lines on the envelope.

#7. It's in the very first shot. The shot is a close-up of a football, which in a moment will be in play. The name on the football is Wilson. This of course is the name of the company that manufactures footballs and other sports equipment, but it is also the last name of the show's creator.

"Project Phoenix"

#1. It's in the episode title, "Project Phoenix." The same three letters: P, O, and E can be found in both words. POE is of course the last name of Edgar Allan Poe, who is considered the father of the detective mystery.

#2. **Match One**: there are six letters in the first name Joanna, six letters in the last name Pettet. **Match Two**: In the first name, Joanna, there are two of the same consonants (n) between the same vowel (a); in the last name Pettet, there are two of the same consonants (t) between the same vowel (e). **Match Three**: In the opening credit guest cast, six performers are listed; the top-billed performer's first name begins with Jo (as in Joanna

Pettet). In the closing credit guest cast, six performers are listed; the top-billed performer's first name begins with Jo (as in John Fiedler). **Match Four**: There are two performers who have the same number of letters in their first and last names: Joanna Pettet (six letters) and Bruce Kirby (five letters). **Match Five**: There are three performers who have double consonants in both their first and last names: Joanna Pettet (consonants n and t), Stafford Repp (consonants f and p), Warren Finnerty (consonants r and n). **Match Six**: There are six six-letter names which can be found in the complete guest cast: Joanna, Pettet, Windom, Warren, Fields, Seamon

#3. **Twos**: To begin with, the first two sentences, "Hey, Lieutenant," and "Lieutenant Keenan" both contain two words apiece. Next, the first "Lieutenant" is the second word in the first sentence, while the second use of the word, "Lieutenant" begins the second sentence. Finally, there are two "Lieutenant"s in a row. **Threes**: First, in the entire line, the three-syllable word "Lieutenant" is spoken three times. Second, the first use of the word, "Lieutenant" is preceded by the three-letter exclamation, "Hey." Third, the second time the word "Lieutenant" is spoken the word is the third word in the entire line. Fourth, the third and last time the word "Lieutenant" is spoken the word is the third word in the third sentence. Fifth, beginning with the second sentence, "Lieutenant Keenan," there is the numerical progression of a two-word sentence followed by a three-word sentence which is followed by a four-word sentence. **Fours**: First, there are four sentences in the entire line. Second, there are four words in the fourth sentence, "The whole damn flatcar." Third, if we count four from the four-letter word "gone" we arrive at the four-letter expletive, "damn." Fourth, the four-letter expletive "damn" begins with "D," the fourth letter of the alphabet.

#4. **Fours**: First, the first sentence is the four-letter word, "Easy." Second, the four-letter word, "Easy" is followed by four sentences. Third, The first use of the four-letter word, Easy" is followed by the four-word sentence,

"Easy on that fender." Fourth, the four-letter word "that" is the fourth word in the entire line. Fifth, the third sentence, "Take your time, Fred" contains a total of four four-letter words. Sixth, the three-letter word, "for," which is pronounced the same as the number four is the fourth word in the fourth sentence. Seventh, the fourth sentence, "They're gonna wait for you" contains a reverse numerical progression of four: the six-letter "They're" is followed by the five-letter "gonna" which is followed by the four-letter "wait" which is followed by the three-letter "for." Eighth, following the first four sentences is the four-word sentence, "Don't worry about it." Ninth, this fifth (four-word) sentence begins with the four-letter "Don't." **Fives:** First, there are five sentences. Second, there are three five-letter words: "gonna" "worry" and "about" in the entire line. Third, if we count five words from the five-letter "gonna," we arrive at the five-letter "worry." Fourth, there are five words (wait, for, you, Don't, worry) between the five-letter "gonna" and the five-letter "about." Five, "E," the fifth letter of the alphabet, begins this five-sentence line.

#5. The number two. There are two words in the first sentence, "Of course," four words in the next sentence, (2 x 2 = 4), eight words in the last (2 x 2 x 2 =8). In other words, this line is a case of George Eckstein and his associates writing a line in multiples of two.

#6. "The Two Million Clams of Cap'n Jack." The character is Erica Osburn, who is played by Jessica Walter.

#7. One: Like the six-letter first name Joanna, the seven-letter first name Jessica begins with a J. Two: Like the name Joanna, the name Jessica ends in an A. Three: Like Joanna, which has the same consonant (N) side by side, the name Jessica has the same consonant (S) side by side.

"No Sign of the Cross"

#1. If one reads the names vertically, with all three names, the second (and in the case of MacGowran, also the third) letter in the first name appears in the same position in the last, or second, name. With Broderick Crawford, this is the letter R, with Louise Sorel, the letter O, with Jack MacGowran, the letters A and C.

#2. ONE: a crosswalk, TWO: Banacek's car crossing the crosswalk, THREE: a couple across the street, FOUR: another couple crossing the street, FIVE: a train crossing overhead.

#3. The three, which is a numerical progression of three, is found in the character's alias, "Paulie 'The Nail' Anderson." There are six letters in the first name, Paulie, seven in his nickname, "The Nail," eight in his last name Anderson.

#4. He is named Enrique Rojas because he's the fifth Mexican Banacek encounters. There are five letters in the last name Rojas; the first name Enrique begins with E (the fifth letter of the alphabet.)

#5. Because of his one-word, seven-letter answer, "Digging" to Jay's two-word, seven-letter question, "Try what?"

#6. The two characters match through the number five. When Banacek speaks the word "hate," it is the fifth word in his sentence. The same holds true for DeRetzo when he twice speaks the word: the first time in sentence three, the second time in sentence five. Moreover the variations DeRetzo speaks of the word: the present tense "hates," and the past tense "hated" are both five letters long. Note that DeRetzo speaks a total of five "hate" sentences.

#7. The nail was eight inches long because Andros' former last name Anderson is a total of eight letters.

"A Million the Hard Way"

#1. First, she's the third performer whose first name begins with an M. (The other two are Margot Kidder, and Mark Harris.) Second, she's the third thirteen-letter performer. (The others are Claire Brennen and William Bryant.) Third, she's the third three-name performer. (The other two: J. Duke Russo and Stanley Ralph Ross.)

#2. The number twenty-one. In Blackjack, the player wins against the dealer if his cards amount to twenty-one. On the slot machine Big Betty, the player hits a jackpot if each one of the three spinning wheels in the machine stops at the number 7. Three times seven is twenty-one.

#3. The title, "A Million the Hard Way" is a total of five words; Banacek's first scene has him coming down the steps of the plane; he is the fifth person to come down the steps, preceding him are two passengers, who are preceded by two stewardesses. As for the first original shot in the show, the shot in the casino, this is the third scene. Banacek is the third passenger off the plane. (Note the distinction between "person" and "passenger!")

#4. One: The third word: seven is preceded by the two words, "A little." There are a total of seven letters in "A little." Two: Beginning with the third word, "seven," there are a total of seven words that follow the seven-letter "A little."

#5. Match one: in both cases, the word that will be rhymed: "seven" and "queen" is a total of five letters. Match two: in between the word "seven" and its rhyming word, "heaven" are a total of five words: "will," "take" "me" "right" and "to." The same holds true for "queen" and its rhyming word, "seen."

#6. First, there are thirteen days on the calendar where activities and events are scheduled; as we know, there are thirteen letters in the name George Peppard. Second, as already noted, there are a total of twenty-eight days on the calendar and thirteen days have been marked down for events and activities. This leaves a total of fifteen blank days. Fifteen is the number of letters in the name by which George Peppard sometimes went: George Peppard, Jr.

#7. Just one thing, a letter. The letter makes the thirteenth item lying on Leland's desk. This includes the pad on which the letter and other items are placed.

"To Steal a King"

#1. First, each character has five letters in their first name, seven letters in their last. Second, each character speaks of a "two-and-a-half." In the case of Linda Carsini, this is her two-and-a-half room apartment; as for Allen Markham, he expects to collect at least two-and-a-half million from the auction of his rare coins. Third, each character is physically connected to a "ten." Linda Carsini photographs the winner of the slot machine Big Betty's $10,000 jackpot; Allen Markham is the owner of the "Ten Kings."

#2. The number nine. Along with the hotel manager, the ninth-billed Traylor's nine-letter character Ballinger conducts the Markhams to the ninth floor, where Allen Markham has Lt. Hallohan set the time-lock of the safe to nine a.m. the next morning.

#3. Match one: Immediately upon discovering the theft, Markham shouts: "No! No! No!" He is the only one present. Match two: Alarmed by her husband's shouts, Lydia Markham enters the front room, asking him what the trouble is. "My kings!" he tells her. "My kings are gone." When Markham speaks then repeats the two words, "My kings," there are two people in the scene: Markham and his wife. Match three: Rushing out of his hotel room, and into the elevator going down to the lobby, Markham startles the two women in the elevator: Mrs. Liddell, and Dr. Dora Bancroft. "Sorry. Sorry," he apologizes. "There's been a . . . there's been a robbery." The three-word repeated "There's been a" matches the three people in the elevator: Markham, Mrs. Liddell, and Dr. Bancroft.

#4. The number thirteen. There are thirteen letters in the name Abraham Morris, and thirteen words precede the thirteen-letter state name Massachusetts on this same tombstone. As for the tombstone of Josephus Donniger, there are a total of thirteen words on the monument. Moreover, his date of death in 1776 yields another thirteen: 1776 was the year he died; 7+6=13.

#5. The progression comes through the tombstones where only the last name is shown. The first such tombstone shows the eight-letter name THOMPSON, the next last name tombstone is the seven-letter LIGGETT; the third such tombstone is the one at which Banacek and Donniger stop: the last name on this monument is the six-letter GERARD.

#6. They're all connected to the ten-zloty Wladyslaw IV of Poland coin. First, the king on the coin is the "IV" (the Roman numeral for four.) Second, the coin is the four-word, "Wladyslaw IV of Poland." Third, the coin was minted in 1640. Fourth, the coin is the fourth "king" shown in Felix's slide presentation.

#7. The fifth, sixth, and seventh sevens are as follows: Five: Grayson tells Banacek he saw him parking his (seven-letter) Packard. Six: Grayson was fired from his job at the Stafford seven months ago. Seven: Grayson is the seventh, one-time only character with whom Banacek talks. Lt. Hallohan appeared in a previous episode; Banacek's rival Church will return. The six one-time only characters preceding Grayson are, in order of Banacek's talking to them: one: Sharon Clark, two and three: Allen and Lydia Markham; four and five: Oliver and Roland Garson, six: Matthew Donniger.

"Ten Thousand Dollars a Page"

#1. One: The full name of each performer is a total of thirteen letters. Two: The STE in the first name STELLA is aligned with the STE in the last name STEVENS; the CHA in the first name RICHARD is aligned with the CHA in the last name SCHAAL.

#2. It's the sentence, "You think someone stole the book because of a grudge." The sentence is spoken during the sequence where Banacek and Jill Hammond are walking through the grounds of the Tyson mansion and towards the exit. There are ten words in the sentence; the title of this episode is "Ten Thousand Dollars a Page." The third and fourth words in the sentence: "someone stole" provide the match to the actress playing Jill: Stella Stevens. As for the clue: someone stealing the Book of Hours because of a grudge, as we learn, this is indeed the motivation for the crime, and the brains behind the theft is none other than the speaker of the sentence: Jill Hammond.

#3: The other five elevens are: One: Book of Hours (the object stolen); Two: Tyson Museum (the scene of the theft); Three: Walter Tyson (the owner of the Book, and the man for whom Banacek is working); Four: Art Woodward (the man who convinced Tyson to put the Book of Hours on display); Five: Jill Hammond (the brains behind the theft)

#4: One: both actors play characters who are fives. Doyle's character, Elliott begins with E, the fifth letter of the alphabet; Jerry, the first name of Cassidy's character, is a total of five letters. Two: Both characters speak in "fives" in their first on-screen appearances. Elliott delivers a total of five straight lines in the teaser; his fifth line: "Take that as a compliment" contains a total of five words. In the case of Cassidy's Jerry Crawford, his conversation with Banacek has him speaking the number "five" then following that with another kind of five: Example One: "Eight-o-five sharp"; Example Two: " . . . five minutes. Seemed like hours you know." In the first example, the number 5 is followed by the five-letter word, "sharp." In the second example, the time: "five minutes" is followed by the five-word sentence, "Seemed like hours you know."

#5: The numerical progression of three-four-five-six-seven comes from the first names of Tyson and his employees, as shown below: Three is ART Woodward; Four, JILL Hammond; Five, STEVE Crawford; Six, WALTER Tyson; Seven, WILLIAM (the chauffeur)

#6. One: There are twelve words in the entire line. Two: There are four three-letter words: "you," "can," "see," and "the" in a row. This produces a total of twelve letters. Three: There are three four-letter words: "time," "have," and "done" in a row. This produces a total of twelve letters.

#7. One, Two, and Three: Three of the six sixes appear in the repeated two-word, six-letter sentence fragment, "be done." Four: Preceding the first "be done" is the two-word, six-letter sentence beginning, "It can't." Five: In the second six-letter "be done," "be" is the sixth word in the sentence.

Six: The third and last "be done" is followed by the six word ending, "if I have to do it."

"The Greatest Collection of them All"

1: The match number is the number Six. Gloria speaks the names of six French Impressionist painters; the policeman in the back seat jokes that the insured value of $23 million for the pictures in the traveling exhibit is more than he and his partner make in six months.

#2: Answer: The something is the movie theatre marquee. It connects to *Banacek* story editor Paul Playdon in three separate ways: First: It contains eleven words: "Don't Shoot Me, I'm Only the Piano Player, Starring Elton John"; there are eleven letters in the name Paul Playdon. Second: The marquee contains the alliterative words, and Elton John's job description, "Piano Player." There are a total of eleven letters in the two words, Piano Player. As we have just noted, the same holds true for the alliterative name, Paul Playdon. Third: like the second name Playdon, the second word Player contains the word, Play.

#3: Banacek echoes a total of five words: "the last man on earth." It's five words because the last word, earth, is five letters and begins with the fifth letter of the alphabet.

#4: The astrological sign Leo begins in July: the seventh month of the year; this is the seventh-aired episode of the first season.

#5: After telling Banacek her favorite color is teal blue, and her favorite composer is DeBussy, Gloria reveals her astrological sign: Aquarius. As noted in answer #4, Leo: the first name of Banacek's father, is an astrological sign.

#6: It's a match of threes. At the bus ticket counter, Banacek and Gloria are standing underneath three signs showing three numbers: 17, 18 and 19, and three word groupings: "OUT TICKETS," "BAGGAGE," and "WILL CALL." In all three signs, the third and fourth letters in each sign: (in order, TT, GG, and LL) are the same. In the subsequent walk-and-talk sequence, Gloria repeats three words: "Well," "Say," and "That."

#7: The missing paintings are found in the nearby five-word "Back Bay Public Warehouse Storage" building.

"The Two Million Clams of Cap'n Jack"

#1: In the closing credits, Michael DeLano is third-billed in the "With" section. In his first name, Michael, c: the third letter of the alphabet, is the third letter in his name. As for the last name, DeLano, the name is three syllables.

#2: One: Each actress' full name is a total of three syllables. Two: Each actress' full name is a total of eleven letters. Three: Each actress' full name is the reverse match of the other's.

#3: Football and a long-time friendship with Banacek. In the premiere episode, "Let's Hear it For a Living Legend," Webber plays Jerry Brinkman, the owner of a football team who asks his friend Thomas Banacek to find his missing star player Hank Ives. In this episode, White's insurance company executive W. Crawford Morgan asks Banacek to recover the stolen plates his company has insured for $2 million; when Morgan visits Banacek, the sleuth is playing football with his friends.

#4: One: The amount stolen is $2 million. Two: Banacek is given just two days to recover this $2 million.

#5: In "A Million the Hard Way," Brennen played a character named Betty Janus. The last name Janus (the name of the Roman god) means "two-faced." The "Gemini" poster in the stairway of the *Open Secret* office shows the Gemini twins as "two-faced." One twin is facing left, the other facing right.

#6: There are eight floors under discussion. If one boarded the elevator on the first floor, he would be on floor eight after eighteen seconds.

#7: First: There are a total of ten words in the ad. Second: The ad gives ten p.m. as the time to contact the person who has the stolen plates. The only character in "The Two Million Clams of Cap'n Jack" who matches these two tens is the title character: Captain Jack Osburn. Not only does the name Jack Osburn contain a total of ten letters, the first letter in the name is J: the tenth letter of the alphabet.

"No Stone Unturned"

#1: The number thirteen. If we add each of the three numbers on the side of his crane: 4, 5, and 4, we arrive at 13. Thirteen is the number of letters in the name Pete Biesecker.

#2: A ton is 2,000 pounds. If we measure the weight of "Man in Harmony" in tons, we have a three-word statue that weighs 3 tons.

#3: Jay's mention of the Book of Hours is the clue. As noted in the discussion of "Ten Thousand Dollars a Page," there are eleven letters in the title, "Book of Hours." There are also eleven letters in the name, Paul Playdon.

Eleven feet is the height of "Man in Harmony," the statue which Banacek is seeking to recover in this episode. Creator of "Man in Harmony" is the eleven-letter Owen Russell. Asking Banacek to recover the statue is the eleven-letter Henry DeWitt.

#4: "Man in Harmony" is the three-word title of the statue. In the ransom note, Carlie and Jay are directed to do three things when they see the stolen object. These are, in order: One: Stop car. Two: Toss out money. Three: Count to three, slow.

#5: In the first season premiere, "Let's Hear It For a Living Legend," Walton plays a character whose first name: Judy, begins with J. In the second season premiere, "No Stone Unturned," Walton plays a character whose first name: Jennifer, begins with J.

#6: In the biography he gives Angie Ives in "Living Legend," Banacek references three U.S. presidents: George Washington, Thomas Jefferson, and Abraham Lincoln. On October 3, 1863, President Lincoln issued a presidential proclamation in which he declared the fourth Thursday in November as a National Day of Thanksgiving. October 3, 1973 was the premiere date of this episode, "No Stone Unturned." Displaying further examples of Eckstein and company's brilliance in coming up with the Thanksgiving Day reference, the month of November is the eleventh month in the year. As we have already noted, the eleven-foot Man in Harmony (which is the object of Banacek's search) was created by the eleven-letter Owen Russell. Beginning with November 26, 1863, there had been a total of 110 Thanksgiving Days celebrated on the fourth Thursday in November by the time this episode aired. More than a month later, November 22, 1973 became the 111th Thanksgiving Day to be celebrated on the fourth Thursday in November. 111 divided by 11 is 11.

#7: It's the deadline Banacek's employer gives him to recover the stolen item: two days. In "Cap'n Jack," Chiles' Penniman is present when his boss: W. Crawford Morgan gives Banacek this deadline. In this episode, it's Chiles' Henry DeWitt who gives Banacek the two-day deadline.

"If Max Is So Smart, Why Doesn't He Tell Us Where He Is?"

#1: First: The first line of dialogue in the show is Lesley Lyle's "I am fed to the teeth with your insipid diets and your exhausting experiments." There are a total of fourteen words in this line; there are a total of fourteen letters in the full name Robert Van Scoyk. Second: In the teaser, when Lesley Lyle tells Logan Howard she wants him to demonstrate MAX's capabilities right then, he tells her, "the official demonstration's only fourteen hours away." The number of hours mentioned matches the number of letters in the name Robert Van Scoyk.

#2. It rings nine times because the nine-letter Cavanaugh is on the phone.

#3: In the park where Banacek and Carlie are enjoying a picnic, the Boston St. Williams CYO Band is seen and heard rehearsing a medley of three tunes. One of these tunes is "Yankee Doodle." When Banacek first enters Lesley Lyle's room, he is whistling the George M. Cohan tune, "Yankee Doodle Dandy."

#4: Dr. Kanter describes Dr. Stahl to Lesley as a "pill pushing parasite." Each of these three words begins with a P. There are three Ps in the last name Peppard.

#5: Banacek's very first sentence is the three-word, "Cream and sugar." There are a total of thirteen letters in this sentence.

#6: A wink is done with the (three-letter) eye.

#7: The author of each book is a seven or thirteen when it comes to his/ her full, or last, name. Author of *The Wind in the Willows* is the (seven letters in his first name/ seven letters in his last name) Kenneth Grahame. Note that the seven-letter last name Grahame begins with G: the seventh letter of the alphabet. Author of *Winnie the Pooh* is the seven-letter A.A. Milne. Author of *Peter Rabbit* is the thirteen-letter Beatrix Potter.

"The Three Million Dollar Piracy"

#1: The episode aired in November: the third month in the traditional television season. The traditional television season begins in September of the current calendar year, and ends in early September of the next calendar year. For example, when Banacek premiered the previous year, its first episode, "Let's Hear It For a Living Legend," aired on September 13, 1972. The series last broadcast was on September 3, 1974.

#2: After Henry chalks a number on the crate carrying the Golden Wedding Coach, Carlie takes the chalk from him, and, below the number, draws a heart, then an arrow through the heart. In other words, she follows her drawing of a (five-letter) heart with her drawing of a (five-letter) arrow. As an arrow through the heart is the symbol of love and Carlie is drawing that symbol on a crate containing a Golden Wedding Coach in front of her fiancee, the fact that she is also performing a match is hidden from the audience, even though the match is right before their eyes.

#3: Like Thomas Banacek, Diana Maitland and Mario Fratelli are thirteen-letter characters.

#4: The last names Hitchcock, Truffaut, and Fellini create a reverse numerical progression of three: there are a total of nine letters in Hitchcock, eight in Truffaut, seven in Fellini.

#5: The three is in the syllables of each word Banacek uses to describe DeWitt. His first description, "solid" contains two syllables, his next, "upstanding" three, his last, "predictable" is a total of four syllables.

#6: The name Lila is four letters, the direction "left" is four letters. The name Wilda is five letters, the direction "right" is five letters.

#7: Because of the "three" that can be found in both episode titles. There are a total of three words in the episode title, "No Stone Unturned." The title of this episode is "The Three Million Dollar Piracy."

"The Vanishing Chalice"

#1: First, this is Kowalski's third *Banacek*. His two previous episodes were "A Million the Hard Way," and "If Max Is So Smart, Why Doesn't He Tell Us Where He Is?" This third episode has the three-word title: "The Vanishing Chalice." Second, each word in "The Vanishing Chalice" is a three of some sort. The first word, "The" is three letters. The second word, "Vanishing" contains three syllables. The third word, "Chalice" begins with the third letter of the alphabet. Third, there are a total of three syllables in the last name Kowalski; when the director's name is shown on the screen, there are a total of three people in the shot: Banacek, Jay, and Banacek's date.

#2: There are a total of fourteen letters in the name Carlie Kirkland. Total number of words from the two lines Carlie uses to describe herself is fourteen.

#3: Like the full name Thomas Banacek, the full name John Paul Jones contains a total of thirteen letters.

#4: First, in "A Million the Hard Way," Banacek is working for casino owner Jonathan Jackson. The name Jonathan is a variation of the name John. Second, Jonathan Jackson is often referred to by his initials: JJ. Were one to refer to John Paul Jones by his first and last name initials, they would also be JJ.

#5: Harlan names four sports: basketball, football, hockey, and boxing. Together these four sports create three pairs. In the first pair, there are two sports where the last syllable is "ball": basketball, and football. In the second pair, there are two six-letter sports: hockey and boxing. In the third pair, there are two sports that begin with the letter B: basketball and boxing.

#6: Each proverb uses a number of alliterative words as its beginning, or ending. The first proverb uses four such words: "Though the hippopotamus has . . . ." The second concludes with three alliterative words: "to the turkey."

#7: Like his portrayer George Peppard, the fictional Thomas Banacek served in the military. In military time, 1:00 p.m. is 13:00.

"Horse of a Slightly Different Color."

#1: First, in both the names John Crawford and Harry Carey, Jr., the total number of letters in each full name is twelve. Second, in both the character names "Owen Summers" (Crawford) and Dean Barrett (Carey), the total number of letters in each full name is eleven.

#2: One: her last name "Wells" is five letters. Two: she has two people by the five-letter last name of "James" working for her. Three: she has a woman by the five-letter first name of "Sally" working for her. Four: Katherine usually bets $5 on a horse. Five: she sold Oxford Don to John Hargroves for $5 million.

#3: As Banacek notes, the theft succeeded because of the dye job on Oxford Don by Owen Summers and his men: the dye job made Oxford Don look like Appian Way. The clue the writers provide is through the number match in the names of both horses; in both cases, the full name of each horse yields a total of nine letters. In both cases the first name of each horse is six letters, the second name three.

#4: One: The Belmont Stakes is one of the three races in the Triple Crown. (The other two are the Kentucky Derby and the Preakness.) Two: The Belmont Stakes is the third race in the Triple Crown. Three: The Belmont Stakes is open to three-year-old thoroughbreds.

#5: One: the number three. (Why has already been noted in the above answer to "Horse of a Slightly Different Color" Challenge#4.) Two: the number five. The Belmont Stakes is always held on the first Saturday that falls on, or after, June 5. Three: the number thirteen. There are a total of thirteen letters in the words, "Belmont Stakes."

#6: One: the first name of Wilson's character is the five-letter Chuck. Two: the last name of the character is the five-letter Smith. Three: Chuck Smith works at (the five letters in the first name) Globe Studios. Four: Chuck Smith is asked a question concerning the $5 million horse Oxford Don. Five: Chuck Smith tells Banacek the dye job on Oxford Don would have taken only five minutes.

#7: One: in both episodes, one of Banacek's proverbs concerns a certain fowl: in "The Vanishing Chalice," a duck and a turkey; in this episode, a chicken. Two: in both episodes, Banacek's other proverb concerns a huge mammal found in Africa; in "Chalice," this is a hippopotamus; in this episode, an elephant.

"Rocket to Oblivion"

#1: The match is the number twelve. In her first meeting with Banacek, Cherry tells him she's been working on the Science and Industry Exposition for twelve months. At the end of the story, Banacek remembers that Cherry started lying to him when she was twelve years old.

#2: There are a total of twelve letters in the words, "twelve months."

#3: The name Donald Morgan is a total of twelve letters. The word "laser" begins with "L," the twelfth letter of the alphabet.

#4: Gallagher's last name starts with the seventh letter of the alphabet; Carlie is the seventh person in line.

#5: The progression is a reverse division by two in number of syllables. There are eight syllables in the first line, "Turn on the emergency lights," four in the next, "Get those lights on," and two in the last, "Lights, please."

#6: In the opening credits, there are five five-letter actor names, in order: Linda Evans, Prine, Drake, Carey. In the closing credits, there are five five-letter actor names, in order: Poole, Polly, Jayne, Jimmy Joyce.

#7: The two crooks are a man and a woman; in both cases, the woman is an attractive blonde.

"Fly Me If You Can Find Me"

#1: There are a total of three men in both shots. There are three men sitting in the airplane in the first shot; there are three men standing at the Hangston airfield in the last shot.

#2: The match comes from the last line spoken: "Sheriff, somebody stole our airplane." The first three words each begin with the letter "S."

#3: After firing a total of five shots close to Banacek and Jay, the man in the chopper then says, via bullhorn, "That was only a warning." There are a total of five words in the line.

#4: As we know, there are a total of three syllables in the last name Banacek, and the third syllable "cek" begins with the third letter of the alphabet. In addition, the "c" in "cek" is preceded by four letters: B, a, n, a. The missing object: the DC-8 is a total of three letters/characters. Preceding the C is the letter D: the fourth letter in the alphabet.

#5: Each of the three words is connected to a six. The first word, "Sands" is preceded by the six-letter word, "Desert." The second word, "Sun" is the sixth word in the sign; note that the six-letter word, "Always" follows this word. As for the last word, "Shines," it is a total of six letters.

#6 and #7: One: in 1968, George Peppard starred in the Universal Studios picture, *House of Cards*. Two: a deck of playing cards contains fifty-two cards. There are four suits: clubs, diamonds, hearts, and spades, in each deck. Each suit contains a total of thirteen cards: ace, two, three, four, five, six, seven, eight, nine, ten, jack, queen, king. As we know, there are a total of thirteen letters in the names George Peppard, and Thomas Banacek.

"Now You See Me, Now You Don't"

#1: Ross calls the soon-to-be-missing magician, Brad Merrick, not Bradley Merrick. The name Brad Merrick is a total of eleven letters. As for Vicki, Ross refers to her as "his daughter." The two words, "his daughter" produce a total of eleven letters.

#2: One: The first two words, "We've" and "only" are four letters apiece. Two: The next two words, "had" and "one" are three letters apiece. Three: "f," the fifteenth letter in the line, is the first letter in the word, "fifteen."

#3: All three performers are a "Jay." Either in real life: Jay Robinson, or in the episode: Manza as Jay Drury, Gordon as J. Maxwell Barker.

#4: One: Dynarski is the third "Leo" with whom Banacek has direct contact. The other "Leos" are: Banacek's father (never seen on the series, but obviously someone with whom the sleuth would have direct contact), and "Leo Osburn" (from the first season finale, "The Two Million Clams of Cap'n Jack.") Two: Dynarski appears in a total of three *Banacek*s: one: the pilot film, "Detour to Nowhere," two: "The Greatest Collection of Them All," and three: this episode, "Now You See Me, Now You Don't." Three: Each Dynarski *Banacek* has a "three" of some kind in its episode title. The pilot film, "Detour to Nowhere" is three words; "Collection," the third word in the actor's next episode, "The Greatest Collection of Them All," is three syllables and begins with the third letter of the alphabet; as for Dynarski's last guest appearance, "Now You See Me, Now You Don't," the first three words in the episode title: "Now," "You," and "See" are a total of three letters apiece.

#5: One: as we have learned, three was very important in the *Banacek* series; March is the third month of the year. Two: *Banacek* premiered in March 1972. Three: this episode (the series' last) first aired in March 1974.

#6: One: there are a total of three Ps in the name George Peppard; there are a total of three Ps in the name Philip Pine. Two: in the name George Peppard, the second and third Ps are side by side; in the name Philip Pine, the second and third Ps are side by side; in Pine's case, the second P is the last letter in the first name, and the third P is the first letter in the last name.

#7: After telling Jay, his chauffeur, that he's going to change him into "a beautiful Las Vegas showgirl," that showgirl, whose body was being blocked from Jay's view by Banacek, sits up in the driver's seat of the car Jay has rented for this Banacek investigation. Banacek then gives Jay a $5 bill to pay for a taxi ride back to the two men's hotel. The $5 bill matches Banacek's five-word description of his new chauffeur: "a beautiful Las Vegas showgirl."

Epilogue:
George Eckstein Says Goodbye to **BANACEK**

"Everything has its day." –Polish proverb

For a series that placed so much emphasis on the number three, it was somehow appropriate that a third season of *Banacek* was in the works. "We actually came up with more," says George Eckstein. "They eventually had an order for six hour-long *Banaceks*, which I worked on and developed with a bunch of writers. They were never made . . . somewhere . . . they're somewhere in Universal's files. I don't know whether anybody there still remembers that they have them."

Despite that shorter running-time for each episode, despite that smaller package of episodes Eckstein and company were asked to deliver, and despite his working with "a bunch of writers," after two seasons of impossible disappearances, and two seasons of match scripts, Eckstein had had enough of *Banacek*. "I quit because I just got burned out trying to come up with these locked door mystery kind of things," stated the producer. "And when I left, George left. He was very . . . I don't know what the word is . . . 'supportive' of my decision to leave. I liked the locked room mysteries, but it was just too hard to come up with these projects for me. I just wanted to go on. My greatest satisfaction in my producing career, as opposed to my writing career, was doing movies of the week in long form. I'm more proud of the TV movies, and particularly on the producing side of it. There are very few series episodes that I am totally enamored with." Including those presented on *Banacek*.

"*Banacek* was formulaic," stated Eckstein. "You'd have a locked room mystery, and at the end of it, George would explain how everything happened, and that was the series. They used to call it 'Morris the Explainer.'* It was a limited series. You didn't have the luxury of what you were dealing with in real long form. They (the TV series Eckstein did) were all gimmicky premises. It wasn't anything you want on your obituary particularly."[1]

Maybe so. And while Eckstein's "low threshold of boredom" was a factor in his decision to quit *Banacek*, the unusual approach he and his associates took when writing the series made it anything but boring. Even when the plots seemed farfetched, or the mysteries much too easy to solve, the many match games that were worked into each episode, made even the weakest episode a treat. Whether this matching put *Banacek* among the most cleverly written series in the history of television is a point others can debate. One thing for sure: like so many other series from the real Golden Age of Television, the 1960s and 1970s, it was a one-of-a-kind show.

---

* "Morris the Explainer" is an old Hollywood term for a police or detective character who, after all of the suspects are gathered together, then explains to one and all how the crime was committed, and who did it.

[1] Eckstein-interview, 2009

George in a publicity shot for *Banacek*

About the Author

Graduating from Wright State University in 1983 with a B.A. in History, Jonathan Etter began his writing career as film historian for the Dayton Victory Theatre's Summer Film Festival from 1985-1987. He then began publishing articles in such periodicals as *Filmfax, The Big Reel, The TV Collector,* and *Movie Collector's World*. In 2003, Jon published *Quinn Martin, Producer* (the behind-the-scenes story of QM Productions) with McFarland Publishers, Inc. That book (now in its second printing) resulted in Jon becoming a contributor to the TV Land network special, *TV Land Moguls: the '60s*. Lightning struck twice a few years later, when Jon's first book for BearManor Media: *Gangway, Lord! (The) Here Come the Brides Book* led to his becoming an on-screen commentator for the Shout Factory DVD releases, *Mystery Science Theater 3000: Volume XIII* and *Here Come the Brides: The Complete Second Season*.

Now at work on a history of the 1966-1968 ABC-TV hit series, *The Rat Patrol*, Jonathan Etter makes his home in Oakwood, Ohio.

www.ingramcontent.com/pod-product-compliance
Lightning Source LLC
Chambersburg PA
CBHW050335230426
43663CB00010B/1864